MW00581220

CODE AND CLAY, DATA AND DIRT

CODE + CLAY... DATA + DIRT

Five Thousand Years of Urban Media

Shannon Mattern

University of Minnesota Press
Minneapolis | London

A portion of the Introduction appeared in a different version as *Deep Mapping the Media City* (Minneapolis: University of Minnesota Press, 2015). Portions of the Introduction and chapters 1, 3, and 4 appeared in "Deep Time of Media Infrastructure," in *Signal Traffic: Critical Studies of Media Infrastructures*, ed. Lisa Parks and Nicole Starosielski (Urbana-Champaign: University of Illinois Press, 2015), 94–112. Portions of the Introduction first appeared in "Instrumental City: The View from Hudson Yards, circa 2019," in *Places* (April 2016). Portions of chapter 2 appeared in "Edge Blending: Light, Crystalline Fluidity, and the Materiality of New Media at Gehry's IAC Headquarters," in *Media Houses: Architecture, Media, and the Production of Centrality*, ed. Kristina Riegert and Staffan Ericson, 137–61 (New York: Peter Lang, 2010). Portions of chapter 2 appeared in *Places*: "Marginalia: Little Libraries on the Urban Margins" (May 2012) and "Paju Bookcity: The Next Chapter" (January 2013). Chapter 3 appeared as "Of Mud, Media, and the Metropolis: Aggregating Histories of Writing and Urbanization," in *Cultural Politics* 12, no. 3; copyright 2016, Duke University Press. All rights reserved. Republished by permission. The introduction to chapter 4 was written during the author's residency at the Canadian Centre for Architecture as a visiting scholar in the summer of 2012. It was originally published as "Sounding Towers" on the CCA website: http://www.cca.qc.ca/en/issues/16/the-rest-of-your-senses/1495/sounding-towers.

Copyright 2017 by the Regents of the University of Minnesota

All rights reserved. No part of this publication may be reproduced, stored in a retrieval system, or transmitted, in any form or by any means, electronic, mechanical, photocopying, recording, or otherwise, without the prior written permission of the publisher.

Published by the University of Minnesota Press
111 Third Avenue South, Suite 290
Minneapolis, MN 55401-2520
http://www.upress.umn.edu

Printed in the United States of America on acid-free paper

The University of Minnesota is an equal-opportunity educator and employer.

24 23 22 21 20 19 18 17   10 9 8 7 6 5 4 3 2 1

Library of Congress Cataloging-in-Publication Data
Names: Mattern, Shannon Christine, author.
Title: Code and clay, data and dirt : five thousand years of urban media / Shannon Mattern.
Description: Minneapolis : University of Minnesota Press, 2017. | Includes bibliographical references and index. |
Identifiers: LCCN 2017001740 (print) | ISBN 978-1-5179-0243-8 (hc) | ISBN 978-1-5179-0244-5 (pb)
Subjects: LCSH: City planning—Data processing. | Cities and towns—Information services. | Cities and towns—Social aspects. | Urban ecology (Sociology) | Municipal engineering—Data processing. | Internet of things. | BISAC: SOCIAL SCIENCE / Media Studies. | SOCIAL SCIENCE / Sociology / Urban. | ARCHITECTURE / Criticism.
Classification: LCC HT166 .M293 2017 (print) | DDC 307.1/2160285—dc23
LC record available at https://lccn.loc.gov/2017001740

Contents

Introduction

ETHER/ORE

There aren't too many places on this congested island where a developer can build a single high-rise, let alone a cluster of them, tabula rasa. But over on the West Side, where a wide gully of railroad tracks had long undergirded a veritable barrens, we now find perched a herd of cranes hoisting I-beams into the sky. Engineers have plunged hundreds of caissons into Manhattan schist to construct two gargantuan platforms that straddle thirty active rail lines and several transit tunnels. The city's old railways have served as conduits to some of its most lucrative developments in recent years. The nearby High Line Park, for instance, which germinated atop an abandoned elevated railway, transformed far west Chelsea—already the city's prime gallery district—into a residential and commercial hot-spot, despite its distance from the subway. Over the next decade or so, the 28-acre Hudson Yards development is expected to bring to New York 17 million square feet of new commercial, retail, and residential space, a cultural venue, parks, a new school, and a hotel—all in signature architecture by high-profile firms.[1] The impending influx incited an extension of the 7 train line, which now connects wildly diverse, solidly middle-class Flushing, Queens, about ten miles away, to this new floating island of oligarchs. A partnership between Related Companies and Oxford Properties Group, the project rivals Rockefeller Center as one of the largest private real estate projects *ever* in New York, and in the United States at large.[2]

Building Hudson Yards

Here, as elsewhere, infrastructure begets infrastructure. Track beds carve a foundation for further development. All those new steel and concrete

FIGURE 1. View east of 10 Hudson Yards from the High Line, across the West Side Yard, 2016, Manhattan. Photograph by the author.

structures serve as scaffolding for the installation of wired, wireless, and satellite technologies, providing commercial tenants with super-fast, dead-zone-free connectivity. And those massive platforms and building facades provide seemingly boundless surface area for all the embedded technology needed to transform this entire development into the country's first-ever "Quantified Community." New York University's Center for Urban Science and Progress (CUSP) is partnering with the developers to install sensors, implement tracking apps, embed Internet-of-Things linked devices, and apply modeling software to capture data on pedestrian flow and traffic, air quality, energy production and consumption, waste flows, and residents' health and activity levels. This datafication of the city is also, simultaneously, the mediation of the city: those data are harvested, cleaned, filtered, analyzed, rendered visible and intelligible and *actionable* via an assemblage of media, from sensors to screens, smartphone apps to building management systems.

All that data will then inform the operation of other infrastructural systems—pneumatic tubes for waste-removal, an on-site power-generating plant, transit systems, and perhaps even social infrastructures focusing on public health—thus generating a "more productive, livable, equitable, . . . resilient . . . [and] efficient" city.[3] Data drive the placement and operation of pipes and cables; ether tempers ore, figuratively speaking. According to Constantine Kontokosta, director of the initiative at CUSP, "The 'Quantified Community' will create a unique experimental environment," a "testing ground for new physical and informatics technologies and analytics capabilities." Such "test-bed urbanism" promises to advance the fields of urban engineering and urban systems operation and planning, as well as the social sciences.[4]

Related Companies' project head Jay Cross boasts that Hudson Yards will be the "most connected, measured, and technologically advanced digital district in the nation." There are lots of other U.S. cities—Austin, San Francisco, and Chicago among them—that are integrating "smart" technologies into their existing architectures in order to improve efficiency and sustainability. And there are myriad sites around the world—from Songdo in South Korea to Masdar in the United Arab Emirates to Lavasa in India—that, like Hudson Yards, are building "intelligently" from scratch. Cities the world over, old and new, are clamoring to "get smart." There are lucrative corporate contracts to be brokered and much federal money to be made in such efforts. Yet this global urban "enlightenment" has a wide variety of potential applications: its open-data initiatives and urban informatics projects might aim to improve residents' quality of life—by aiding in wayfinding and tracking the location of hazardous cracks in the sidewalk—or perhaps even to empower citizens to effect changes in their cities. At the political extreme, those same technologies might be employed to monitor citizens' behavior and impose sanctions or restrict movement, and even to transform entire cities into proprietary operating systems. Or, they could do both simultaneously: "empower" and surveil, optimize and oppress. Given the services and conveniences that "residents in cities are demanding," Kontokosta told *Fast Company*, they should expect greater surveillance and instrumentalization.[5] Such initiatives of course raise a host of questions and concerns—perhaps most obviously about the politics of data and the methodologies and ideologies of data-collection: how data are harvested, who owns them, and how they are applied. Some critics, including me, also wonder about the epistemologies of data-driven urban "intelligence," and the ontological significance of that intel—that is, how the quantifiable, measureable aspects of urbanity come to delimit our conception of what an "ideal" (productive? livable? resilient?) city can be.

There are indeed countless developers, engineers, designers, financiers, and city officials around the globe who are fervently pursuing these data-driven urban efficiencies, and all the profit that is to be made from them, at the possible expense of other civic values. But we also have lots of healthily skeptical designers, scholars, and critics posing questions about the wisdom of such "smart" initiatives.[6] I've been exploring these concerns in a series of long-form articles I've written for *Places* journal since 2013, and in a number of other events and discussions.[7] There's a rich, if restricted, contemporary debate about the mediated cities we're building for today and tomorrow.

Our focus here, however, will be on the foundations—not only the concrete caissons and steel tracks, but also the historical, intellectual, material, and political contexts—for our current-day obsession with urban intelligence. Were our cities dumb before we had building information modeling (BIM) software, before machines could count the number of cars passing through their intersections? Are we dependent on the proprietary knowledges of IBM, Cisco, Alphabet, and SAP—partners in many smart city projects around the world—to build responsive, resilient, equitable cities? Is New York unique in its efforts, as Kontokosta claims, to systematically measure "how the design of physical space influences activity, public health, and social interaction"?[8] Are we to believe that urban designers, administrators, and advocates were *not* attending to such communicative and quality-of-life concerns before they had the quantitative means to do so—and that such data-driven formalist or behaviorist approaches are better than old-fashioned formalism and behaviorism? Are we to presume that Big Data and the "science" of urbanism make everything better, that citizens are better served when their agency is tethered in part to their functions as data points?

As we head into a future offering ever more potential for mediated control of the urban landscape, and, at the same time, a pervasive sense of our *loss* of control over the proliferation and sometimes uncritical application of networked technologies and data-driven methodologies, we would do well to enlighten *ourselves* about what kind of "smartness" or "sentience" we want our cities to embody and to encourage in its leaders and inhabitants.[9] And doing so, I argue, requires that we also recognize that today's smart cities don't have a monopoly on urban intelligence. In fact, we can trace that "smart" genome all the way back to ancient Rome, Uruk, and Çatalhöyük. Cities, including many far afield from our contemporary data hubs and R and D labs, embodied networked smarts and forms of "ambient" intelligence well before we implanted sensors in the streets. Yesterday's cities—even our earliest settlements—were just as smart, although theirs was an intelligence less computational and more material and environmental. For millennia, our cities have been designed to foster "broadcast"; they've been "wired" for transmission; they've hosted architectures for the production and distribution of various forms of intelligence and served as hubs for records-management; they've rendered themselves "readable" to humans and machines; they've even written their "source code," their operating instructions, on their facades and into the urban form itself. They've coded themselves both for the administrative technologies, or proto-algorithms, that oversee their operation and for the people who have built and inhabit and maintain them.

FIGURE 2A. Amazon Web Services data center, 2016. Photograph by Ingrid Burrigton.

FIGURE 2B. Göbekli Tepe archaeological site, 2011, in Şanlıurfa, Turkey. Photograph by Teomancimit / CC-BY-SA-3.0.

Malcolm McCullough, who has written widely about urban computing, agrees that historians and managers of information need to reconceive the urban "environment" as more than a *site* of information access, but also as a medium itself.[10] Our physical landscapes inscribe, transmit, and even embody information—about their histories, their state of repair, their potential uses, and so forth. As McCullough advocates, we need to "expand the role of environment beyond the sites of reading, to reexamine the distributed application of information to the innate and built world." In other words, cities aren't just where we "read" information; they're made of information themselves. And as we expand our urban site of exploration, we need to expand our historical scope, too. Calculation, coding, and "embedded" technologies have long been integral to urban infrastructures.[11] As we'll see in the following pages, our cities have been smart and mediated, and they've been providing spaces *for* intelligent mediation, for millennia. That intelligence is simultaneously epistemological, technological, and physical; it's codified in our cities' laws and civic knowledges and institutions, hard-wired into their cables and protocols, framed in their streets and architectures and patterns of development. The city mediates between these various materialities of intelligence, between the ether and the iron ore. Clay and code, dirt and data intermingle here, and they always have.

Histories of the Mediated City

This project itself has quite a long and undisciplined history. It began almost two decades ago, when I was in graduate school, piecing together a curriculum that combined media and urban studies with architectural and urban history. I was studying in New York during the first dot-com boom, a period characterized by widespread conviction that our new mobile, geolocative technologies and e-commerce ventures would render material shops and schools, bodies and buildings—perhaps even cities themselves—obsolete. Sages predicted that we would collapse geographic distances, even-out spatial disparities, extend opportunity, build universities and workplaces and global communities in the ether.

But we'd heard it all before. History shows us that time and again, whenever a new "game-changing" technology—television, radio, the car, the steam engine, the printing press, even writing—emerges, latter-day "futurists" have offered up breathless predictions regarding its capacity to radically reshape our brains, families, homes, neighborhoods, cities, nations, and world; to offer new forms of convenience and enlightenment; to promote world peace and liberation. And we're hearing it again in the latest Silicon Valley boom, whose start-ups seem obligated to practice willful historical inattention in order to make their claims of innovation and "disruption."

Back amidst the hubris of the first boom, I sought to use my teaching as a small historical corrective. Inspired in part by Marshall McLuhan's recognition of roads, paper routes, and houses as media, and by his mentor Harold Innis's recognition of media as critical political-economic forces, I designed a course that examined the long-standing links between media and architecture.[12] In the class's inaugural run, in 2003, we looked at the histories of architectural rendering and spaces of writing, like the scriptoria where medieval monks copied manuscripts; at the public stage and public sphere as sites of public address; at the history of the architectural treatise and the metaphor of "legible" cities and building facades; at the telephone's arrival in the home and office, and telecom's impact on urban form; at the rise of nineteenth-century architectural plans books and contemporary shelter magazines; at architectural photography and the use of the photograph as a design tool; at cinematic cities and movie palaces; at television screens in mid-century homes and the architectural facade-as-screen; and, finally, at the fold, the "blob," and other digital morphologies. And we topped it all off with a field trip to the Diller + Scofidio exhibition at the Whitney Museum, where the designers put on display new data-driven architectural forms and tools of computational fabrication. Our survey progressed more or less chronologically. As the semester advanced, my freshman students found themselves on ever more solid footing. Each week brought them closer to the present—closer to the material technologies and material landscapes they lived with. It was only at the end, when we retraced our steps, that those early topics, which at first seemed like so much distant history, revealed themselves as foundations for, foreshadowings of, the built world of today and tomorrow. We wrapped the semester recognizing that our cities have *always* been mediated, and that the exceptional advances of our current age maybe aren't so exceptional after all. Perhaps a bummer of an epiphany, but also an empowering one for budding art historians and designers who would soon begin grappling with the anxiety of influence and the generative powers of precedent.

In subsequent iterations of the class, I flipped the script. We started with the present day—with what the students lived and knew intimately— then defamiliarized it, contextualized it, by digging farther and farther backward in time. We started with urban informatics, data centers, and digital architecture and ended with clay tablets and bricks in Çatalhöyük. And with each new-old layer unearthed, we heard preambles and observed prefigurations of contemporary tropes and promises: of distance collapsed and time saved, of technological solutions to persistent urban problems.

Research from my own field, media studies, sustained us for only the first few weeks of the semester. For our deeper-historical discussions, and for our cross-format studies of diverse media, I had to piece together resources from other fields: architectural and urban history, book history, musicology, archaeology, paleography, and classics. At the time (and, frankly, still today, to some degree), most existing scholarship within media and design studies suggested that the mediated city is a *modern* development. We enjoy a plethora of research on architecture and cities in relation to mechanically reproduced still and moving images—in other words, photography, film, animation, motion graphics, and the like. For instance, many photographic, architectural, and cultural historians (many greatly inspired by Walter Benjamin) have examined the city as a photographic subject; photography's early role in the documentation of urban transformation and as an instigator of social change; and photography's influence on particular modern architectural and urban designers.[13] There's also a tremendous amount of work on the city and film as contemporaneous developments; on the representation of the city *in* film; and on film's influence upon architects and planners, and vice versa.[14] In more recent decades, scholars like Lynn Spigel, Anna McCarthy, and Nanna Verhoeff have begun to address the synchronous rise of television and postwar suburbs and the politics of screens in public places. We've also observed an explosion of recent works—from media studies, urban studies, geography, architecture, and elsewhere—exploring the impact of networked digital media on urban design and urban experience.[15] And thanks to the rise of sound studies, we've enjoyed some excellent research on radio and modern sound technologies' impact on architecture, zoning, and city life.[16]

The sheer number of books and conferences and exhibitions on the city in photographs, the cinematic city, and the digital/networked/cyber/ smart/sentient city indicates that most of our attention—at least within the fields of media and design theory and practice—has focused on these modern media technologies' relationships to the city, and particularly on the *representation* of the city *in* these modern media. Furthermore, the emphasis on imaging technologies has historically reinforced an ocular-centric approach, to use historian Martin Jay's term. There has been in many cases an assumption that the mediation of the city began with these modern media. For instance, media scholar Eric Gordon, in *The Urban Spectator*, argues that, "from the hand-held camera at the end of the 19th century to the mobile phone at the end of the 20th, the city has *always* been a mediated construct."[17] Yet that "always," I'd say, begins well before the late nineteenth century. As Scott McQuire argues in his *Media City*, the mediation of urban experience "has been underway at least since the development of technological images in the context of urban 'modernization' in the mid-19th century."[18] At least. The "always" of urban mediation, which extends all the way back to the days of Eridu and Uruk, is a story that's been parceled out across the research agendas and literatures of multiple fields, many of which all-too-rarely talk to one another.

An Archaeology of Media

It wasn't until the late-aughts that I discovered the field of media archaeology (which has been around, particularly in film studies, for a few decades) and found a fitting retroactive justification for my surveying-and-excavating-across-multiple-sites pedagogical methodology. Work in this gallantly named field offered a set of conceptual and methodological tools—notably, its focus on the materiality of media, and its embrace of nonlinear histories and forking paths—that were pertinent to my interest the *longue durée* of urban mediation. Media archaeology's unofficial slogan—"challenging the newness of the 'new'"—was something I could totally get behind.

But we'd heard this before, too. Historians have long been engaged in the search for precedents and have challenged the notion of linear progress. Within media studies, Carolyn Marvin and Lisa Gitelman had already demonstrated that, at one time or another, all "old technologies were new," that media are "always already new," that emerging technologies typically follow the "scripts [and] grooves" carved out by their predecessors.[19] Marvin's and Gitelman's were among the few female voices that resonated within the predominantly male—and, according to video game historian Laine Nooney, often masculinist—media-archaeological terrain.[20]

As one who often bristles at the absurdities of the capital-T Theory economy, I tend to approach fashionable theoretical movements with a measure of skepticism.[21] Yet media archaeology's spokesmen present it as a humble "traveling discipline" characterized more by "mobile concepts and shifting institutional affiliations" than by a comprehensive, inclusive statement of purpose.[22] This lack of a defining method and unifying objective (what is the problem to which media archaeology is the solution?) has been both a prime target for the field's critics and a cause for celebration—an opportunity for topical and methodological diversity—among its proponents. Some of the field's most prominent actors have put forward their own intellectual histories and surveys of the field.[23] And in the wake of those synthesizing texts, Nooney and film historian Thomas Elsaesser have both offered analyses of media archaeology as a "symptom," a "socio-historical academic phenomenon" that is the product of its time and culture. Defining its context are the "disruptions" of the digital, expanding global circuits of e-waste, the rediscovery of old media artifacts and archival material, the widespread embrace of data-driven methodologies, as well as new varieties of the various "crises" that always seem to plague academia (crises of the archive, of the image, of the humanities, of higher education, of crisis itself, and so forth).[24] This is the world into which media archaeology emerged.

We now have some new crises and epistemic ruptures to add to the list: climate change and global conflict have incited concern about their potential impact on the world's vulnerable populations and our shared material cultural heritage; the spread of automated labor has pressed us to reconsider our collective investment in and obligations to our fellow human beings; and reorientations of global power have necessitated that we redraw our geopolitical maps. And alongside the real-time, fraction-of-a-second temporality of our data-driven technologies and markets, we've witnessed the rise of a "long-term" Anthropocenic scope of vision. That's a fraught terrain for a theory to traverse, yet it's within this context of seeming contradictions that I humbly situate my own intervention. Before I get to that, however, I'll offer an abstracted sketch of media archaeology, emphasizing what it does and doesn't offer to help us make sense of these new "disruptions." Rather than trying to pin down this traveling discipline (one whose road map doesn't always match my own), I'll focus instead on the media-archaeological themes that are especially pertinent to our interests in the material, the environmental, the temporal, and, relatedly, the archival.

To begin, media archaeology turns our attention away from traditional hermeneutics—i.e., textual interpretations of what's on the page or the screen—and toward the page and the screen themselves: toward the hardware of media. Some practitioners take that hardware-focus to the extreme of post- or even anti-humanism. Friedrich Kittler, among the forefathers of media archaeology, heeded the call of *his* forefather, Foucault, in seeking out a "method of historical analysis purged of all anthropologism."[25] Kittler's offering: a theory of technical media—gramophones, typewriters, film, other optical technologies—as prime historical actors and shapers of human perception and subjectivity. In Kittler's world, media are data processors, engendered and diffused largely by war. As John Durham Peters explains, Kittler "gives us a media studies without people. In a sense, Kittler is Mr. Anti-Cultural Studies."[26] Wolfgang Ernst, in turn building on Kittler's work, likewise prioritizes signal processing over semiotics, focusing on the "non-discursive," operative processes— the codes and software, the "techno-epistemological configurations"— powering our media.[27]

In focusing on machines and signals, media archaeologists often bracket out not only the people with which, but also the environments *within* which, those media interact. Yet Kittler offers one notable exception. In a 1996 essay, he examined the hardware of the city, portraying the urban environment as an information-processing, -storing, and -transmitting machine complete with support systems—like postal offices and addresses, logistical systems, currency, and so forth—that serve to format and address the information surging through it.[28] While such an approach does help us to appreciate computation and information management writ large, at the scale of the urban, and it calls out the role of the material landscape in that computational work, Kittler's analysis still leaves little room for affect, for meaningful experiences, for *humans*.[29] Kittler's city is a means of efficient information management, much like Hudson Yards. But Hudson Yards' developers, unlike Kittler, at least acknowledge the important roles that architecture and art and human experience play in urban design.

Erkki Huhtamo, meanwhile, does attend to human experience in mediated spaces. Through his work on alternative histories of cinema, Huhtamo examines panoramas and other early cinematic environments, drawing attention to media within their urban contexts.[30] Yet Huhtamo's work, like that of most media archaeologists, doesn't follow the historical trail back much farther than the late eighteenth century. As I noted earlier, most historians of the mediated city likewise present it as a *modern* spatial phenomenon: a product of photography and film and mass-produced periodicals. Siegfried Zielinski has dug a bit deeper than the rest, back into the "deep time" of media.[31] The term "deep time" references eighteenth-century geologist James Hutton's proposal that the earth has evolved through a cyclical process of accumulation and erosion—of oceans flooding lands and continents emerging from seas—that has unfolded, and continues to unfold, over a timespan that far exceeds the notions of "Biblical time" that dominated in Hutton's own lifetime.[32] Transforming Hutton's concept into a media-archaeological framework, Zielinski studies historical variations in the technics of seeing and hearing, highlighting several "qualitative turning points," "attractive foci, where possible directions for development were tried out and paradigm shifts took place."[33] His "variantology" focuses on a rowdy band of visionaries: among them, Greek philosopher Empedocles, Jesuit polymath Athanasius Kircher (who offers several reverberant examples of acoustic spaces that are tangentially pertinent to our study), and Russian avant-gardist Aleksej Kapitanovich Gastev.[34] Zielinski refers to his own work as *an*archaeology, because of its brazen disinterest in origins and "firsts." For all its self-professed radicalism, however, this is still a story of curious Great Men.

Nevertheless, Zielinski's project demonstrates that digging back into "deep time"—well past the nineteenth century, where many modern media histories begin—often yields evidence that "everything has always been around, only in a less elaborate form."[35] Jussi Parikka's work on the geology of media takes this statement literally, and simultaneously reinserts the geologic into the concept of "deep time." Parikka examines the elemental, earthly components of our media objects—the unelaborate natural materials that "have always been around," embedded in the earth, as well as the material traces they leave in the environment throughout their lifecycles, as they're mined, assembled, distributed, used, discarded, or recycled.[36]

Those impacts, those traces, represent another of media archaeology's traditional interests: the archive, which has served as both a research resource and a research topic, a subject for theorization. Media archaeologists typically rely on archival materials—the papers of defunct manufacturing companies or eccentric inventors, old technical manuals, personal collections of antique video game packages—or assemblages of preserved technologies: warehouses full of copy machines, drawers stuffed with old joysticks, or closets full of wax cylinders. The field's key theorist of the archive is Ernst. His interest in signal processing attuned him to the distinctive temporalities—the inscription and processing speeds, for instance—of different media. Those temporalities then impact how media record their own existence and operation: how they "archive" their own pasts, in their own codes, at their own speeds, on their own disks or membranes (or, in our urban case, on their own facades or in city form).[37]

FIGURE 3. Atari cases and cartridges unearthed during 2013 excavation of landfill in Alamogordo, New Mexico. Photograph by taylorhatmaker, via Wikimedia Commons / CC-BY-2.0.

Ernst's archive "refers to what is actually there: what has remained from the past in the present like archaeological layers, operatively embedded in technologies."[38] And "what is actually there," he claims, isn't always humanly empirical. Technical media's signals and operations often exceed human sensation and comprehension. Thus, one doesn't *read* that media archive; one reverse-engineers it. And one doesn't use it to "write history" with narrative coherence, a pursuit that Ernst regards as a distinctively human means of understanding media's pasts; one "processes" the data in the archive to find a temporal logic and to appreciate the poetics in "discrete, serial strings of information."[39]

Yet not all media archaeology brackets out human discourse. In his "topoi studies," which borrow from classical rhetoric, Huhtamo studies the archive to identify discursive patterns, conceptual "molds" that recur in slightly different forms in different contexts across time, to help us imagine media and their place in the world.[40] The figures of the cyborg, the cloud, the "hand of God," for example, have repeatedly appeared in fiction and film, advertising, and even religious and economic discourse.

The panorama is another formal and phenomenological topos that has been variously imagined and materialized across millennia. As we'll see in the following pages, our cities have hosted countless communicative topoi—modular material sites for mediation—and they've engendered countless commonplace, perhaps clichéd, ways of talking about those urban media: as portals, podiums, substrates, screens, as collapsers of distance and even as obsolescers of cities themselves. Evangelists of our always-already-new media have long promised that new technologies would alternatively allow cities to sprawl luxuriously into disparate wire-linked nodes, or concentrate intensively into clusters of crystalline towers or close-knit communities united by the audible voice. Those media technologies would either render cities obsolete or, alternatively, drive them to their utopian apotheoses. Such a variety of topoi—urban and mediated fantasies, recited across the ages and manifested in diverse forms across the globe—demonstrate that our urban media histories are cyclical, entangled, a messy mix of discourses and dirt, imaginaries and I-beams, sketches and sensors.

Trowel-wielding archaeologists—along with scholars and practitioners in allied fields concerned with the human-made material environment: architectural and urban historians, anthropologists, geographers, material culture scholars, and so forth—have long been gathering concrete evidence of urban and media evolution. And they, like Ernst, have also had to look beyond the historical record to reconstruct the past. Yet the "archaeology" in media archaeology has been mostly metaphorical, a figurative "digging back" into history. Or it has signaled a Foucauldian methodology: a search for historical ruptures and the underlying conditions and conventions that make particular knowledges or discourses, in particular historical contexts, possible. While Foucault's archaeological "artifacts" consist of statements, or enunciations, the media archaeologist focuses on media artifacts—"dead" media, forgotten ancestors to contemporary gadgets, legacy software, old memes, and so on—and "digs" all around the artifact in order to figure out what conditions made it possible. That digging, as we noted above, typically takes place in archives and collections of preserved technologies.

An Urban Media Archaeology

In the introduction to their 2011 anthology, Jussi Parikka and Erkki Huhtamo clarify that "media archaeology should not be confused with archaeology as a discipline. When media archaeologists claim that they are 'excavating' media-cultural phenomena, the word should be understood in a specific way."[41] But what if we took media archaeology literally, and borrowed a few tricks from archaeologists of the stones-and-bones variety?[42] What if we picked up their trowels and surveying tools? There's much to be gained in a study of media-networked sites, like any city, by considering how archaeologists-proper understand fieldwork and assessment—how they dig both metaphorically and literally into physical terrain—and by productively "confusing" media archaeology and archaeology-proper.[43]

In recent years we've witnessed the rise of more productively messy disciplinary "confusion," including Parikka's own work in the "geology" of media, Lisa Parks's and Janet Vertesi's "cosmology" or "astronomy" of extraterrestrial media, John Durham Peters's "meteorology," "cetology," and "cosmology" of "elemental" media, and Nicole Starosielski's "oceanography" of submarine Internet infrastructure.[44] The past two decades have also brought us books offering archaeologies of materiality, memory, colonialism, vision, trade, conflict, attachment, the future, and so on and so forth. "Real" archaeologists, occasionally perplexed by these other-archaeologists' seeming disregard for their own field, have wondered about possible exchanges between media archaeology and "archaeology-as-such."[45] *Code and Clay, Data and Dirt* is meant to offer one such exchange. In advocating for an urban media archaeology, I certainly don't intend to exacerbate the archaeological proliferation or to offer yet another theoretical neologism. Instead, I'm using "urban media archaeology" as shorthand for a generalizable approach: a *literal* archaeology of the mediated city, a materialist, multisensory survey and excavation of the deep material history—that is, a cultural materialist history that acknowledges the physicality, the "stuff," of history and culture—composing our mediated cities and urban intelligences.

Amidst these multiplying metaphorical archaeologies, even the "real" archaeologists would admit that their own field—the *ur*-archaeology, we might say—contains multiplicity. There is no essentialized, naturalized, neutralized "archaeology-as-such," no single archaeological lineage. The field has been consistently committed to studying the material record of the human past (even the relatively shallow past of *yesterday*). But over the last century, its conception of that "study," those "records," and that "past" (and whether it is exclusively "human") has evolved considerably.[46] Archaeologists have questioned their own agency, the agency of their human subjects, and the agency of nonhuman creatures and objects in the archaeological terrain. They've debated who owns the past, and who does, and should, have the right to shape cultural memory. They've deliberated over how that past is told: does the archaeologist *describe* artifacts, does she attempt to explain the cultural processes that give them context, or is her mission something else? Are archaeological practice and its prevailing epistemology gendered?[47] Many archaeologists have grappled with the field's own colonialist, imperialist, and patriarchal history (and present?) and with the ways in which their work can lend itself to commercialization by the "heritage industry," to romanticization in the creation of local identity, or to politicization in nationalist agendas.[48] They've wondered if their theoretical models have served them well: what is left out when one "reads" material culture as a "text," for example? Is archaeology a science, a social science, an art? Is it more closely allied with anthropology, which also studies humans past and present but not exclusively through their material remains; or with history, which studies humans primarily through their written records? Does the archaeological record exist "out there" to be excavated, or do archaeologists create those "records" by deciding where to sink the shovel, so to speak? Is archaeological practice inherently political?

While they might have particular leanings and allegiances, archaeologists themselves don't have definitive answers to these questions. These are not the kinds of questions that lend themselves to definitive answers. Yet the fact that archaeologists are *inquiring*, and that they've been engaged in lively debate over these issues for decades, demonstrates a degree of self-reflexivity and political consciousness that, some claim, media archaeology—with its occasional techno-fetishism, cabinet-of-curiosities historiography, and martial "masculinism"—is sometimes lacking. Granted, Kittler's work is rooted in the history of war, and Parikka's recent work speaks to ecological issues: two undoubtedly political concerns. And media archaeology (as well as archaeology-proper) has drawn inspiration from the various "new materialisms," from Bruno Latour's actor-network theory, and (for better or worse) from the multiplying object-oriented and "thing"-based philosophies—all of which propose a redistribution of agency and a model of nonanthropocentric politics.[49] Yet archaeology-proper's willingness to confront the ideologies and geopolitical imbalances underlying its entire enterprise, the cultural politics of its practice, and the exploitative ends toward which its work is sometimes put—nationalist land claims, heritage theme parks, global antiquities markets—could set an example for media archaeology. Archaeology's *self*-analysis, its Foucauldian "archaeologizing" of its own discipline, could potentially compel media archaeology to rethink its own prevailing Western orientation, its occasional "orientalist" treatment of curious devices from other cultures and times, its mostly male bibliographies, and its other biases and limitations. My hope is that our inquiry throughout the book will also prove useful to archaeologists and practitioners in allied material culture fields as they press forward in their ongoing, critical self-reflection.

We can even draw instructive, perhaps cautionary, parallels between archaeology's own disciplinary evolution and media archaeology's current fascinations. Consider the "scientism" of what were called the "processual" archaeological approaches that emerged in the 1960s, and the romanticism of some of the phenomenological approaches that emerged later, as an intended corrective.[50] Media archaeology has its own processualist "science"—particularly Ernst's techno-mechanical focus on signal processing and operating procedures, and the various critical practitioners inspired by his work. It's got its Romantic elements, too: its fetishizing of the old, the curious, the misfit (not to mention the wider cultural lionization of khaki-clad men in pith helmets, and their contemporary T-shirted hacker descendants).[51]

Equally significantly, archaeology promotes a more global view than has been customary within media archaeology and media studies at large. The "media city," for example, has frequently been conflated with the "global city," which is global primarily in that it is a privileged central hub in overlapping international networks.[52] Consequently, much work on the media city focuses on global capitals like New York, Paris, Berlin, London, and Tokyo. While there is still much insight about urban mediation to be surveyed and excavated at these sites, and while some scholars have explored areas of the Global South (aka the developing world) and other under-studied regions of the world, we can do more to look beyond the heavily networked cities that dominate the existing research.[53] By expanding the geographic focus of our study of urban mediation—in part by drawing on the work of archaeologists and anthropologists—we can show that nodes in our mediated networks exist in parts of the globe that are rarely on our radar, and that the network manifests itself differently in different cities. Highlighting this variation can help us to better appreciate the politics of the media city, too. We can be more attuned to the uneven spread of networks and access to infrastructurally distributed resources, uneven rates of technological development and commitment to maintenance, and diverse systems of ownership and control.

This focus on different cultural contexts also has the potential to expand media studies' understanding of what constitutes media, of what materials and systems serve communicative functions. Archaeologists have found communicative potential in brick walls, stone structural elements, dirt mounds, bone tools, and even cities writ large. By examining how cities themselves have served as media (and how they've *been* mediated) across time, we'll see how media materialize in and through urban practices and processes—how they're the products of their urban environments and their human creators and users—and how those urban processes themselves are agglomerations of various media: stones and bones, streets and circuits, plazas and people. Archaeologists know well that artifacts don't exist apart from their material environments and human agents; that "what is actually there" in the archaeological field is not so easily extracted from its context and then reduced to data through clinical analysis. While archaeologists-as-such might rely on scientific tools, like those Ernst employs in his study of technical media, to locate buried remains, date artifacts, or test the reverberance of an ancient room or instrument, those tools aren't meant to offer some form of "pure data navigation" unencumbered by "hermeneutic empathy" or historical narratives, as Ernst would prefer.[54] To the contrary, archaeologists' scanning, measuring, and modeling are almost always meant to help us better understand the connections between humans, their things, and their environments.

Those very same connections also determine "what is actually there" (or not there) to be discovered in the first place. Ernst seems to "naturalize" the media archive, the "*arché* of [media's] source codes," and assumes its presence to be an objective fact of engineering.[55] Yet archaeologists and archivists have long acknowledged that both the archaeological and historical records are political constructs, as much *human* creations as technical or environmental ones. As Nooney explains,

> Not all archives are created equal, not all media are valued and saved, not all information leaves an inscription, and sometimes the "things" that we search for can't be studied except in their ghostly residue— and there can be political, social, gendered, and racial dimensions to how these ex- and inclusions come to be.[56]

The same is true of the archaeological record. The gaps and exclusions in the record—what is *not* actually there, the artifacts weathered or demolished, the lives excluded—can also reveal, even through absence, their own operative logics: about natural and cultural processes of erosion, destruction, and erasure, and also, importantly, about cultural politics and epistemologies.

Integrating media archaeology and archaeology-proper has the potential to shape the epistemologies and politics of *other* fields, including urban and architectural history, as well as urban and architectural design practice. Recognizing the "deep time" of urban mediation, urban historians will ideally be incentivized to reevaluate their prevailing theories about the birth of cities, which tend to privilege economic explanations for urbanization, and to pay greater attention to the central role played by media and communication in urban history. Various anthropologists, archaeologists, and urban historians, like Clifford Geertz, Peter Hall, and Paul Wheatley, have posited that the birth of cities is rooted not (or not only) in economics, but in the need for ceremony and communication.[57] Lewis Mumford, author of two grand histories of urbanity, likewise suggests that "what transform[ed] the passive agricultural regimes of the village into the active institutions of the city" was not merely a growth in size or population density or economy, but an extension of "the area of local intercourse, that engenders the need for combination and co-operation, communication and communion."[58] That "area of local intercourse" is an infrastructure, a structure that undergirds communication and communion. One of our goals, then, will be to account for the critical roles that communication and mediation have played, since the early days of civilization, in giving rise to and sustaining our settlements and cities. Furthermore, we can reinforce the role of communication in giving *form* to our cities. Prevailing theories suggest that urban form is shaped mainly by topography, transportation, defense, or even cosmological or philosophical views. We can assert that the means of communication—whether the voice, the printed page, or cellular networks—have also shaped cities throughout history, and that those cities have in turn given form and vitality to their media. Cities and media have historically served as one another's "infrastructures."

Over the past several years the term *infrastructure*, like *archaeology*, has proliferated across scholarly, artistic, and design fields—almost to the point that the term has become infinitely elastic. Still, I believe that, if used in moderation, it can be a useful concept for us here. Thinking about media through infrastructures, as I've done in some of my own work on cities and knowledge institutions over the past decade or so, enables us to appreciate media as potentially embodied on an urban or even global scale, as a force whose modes, ideologies, and aesthetics of operation can be spatialized, and materialized, in the landscape.[59] Aspects of these infrastructural systems constitute a layered landscape that lends itself to digging; they leave asphalt, copper, and plastic residues that we can dig up. Historical communication infrastructures offer artifacts like pneumatic tubes, gutta-percha-coated telegraph cables, old postal roads, technologies for the production and dissemination of early print forms, palimpsests of writing on city walls, ruins of ancient amphitheaters and old libraries. For the archaeologists of tomorrow, today's wireless technologies will leave behind fiber-optic cables, massive data centers, and piles of e-waste. But it's when we're dealing with more "ethereal" media—those, like radio or public address, that seem to have limited material apparatus, little "actually there"—that the city-as-media-infrastructure model proves particularly useful. By studying these seemingly bodiless media's urban contexts, we can better understand how the material environment supports them: how the city provides broadcast sites and acoustic venues; how urban surfaces, volumes, and voids have functioned as sounding boards, resonance chambers, and transmission media. We'll listen to such sonic infrastructures in chapters 1 and 4. What we'll ultimately find, in examining the city as a media infrastructure, is that our media histories are deeply networked with our urban and architectural histories, and that, in most cases, these cultural and technological forms are mutually constructed.

This historical and critical sensibility about media infrastructures could then inform the practice of those who are designing and engineering our contemporary built environments. Both Zielinski and Parikka emphasize the generative possibilities of media archaeology: its potential to inform, and be informed by, creative practice. As they retrofit our existing cities and build our networked cities of tomorrow, urban and architectural designers and engineers of all stripes can consider how they might honor and integrate the "deep time" of urban mediation, the legacy networks and customary communicative practices that have shaped communities and local identities, into their work. One of their responsibilities, as they strive to create sustainable, responsive urban environments, is thus to make provisions for a layering of communicative infrastructures old and new, informal and formal, made of both ether and ore, data and dirt.

There is much more at stake here than methodology and historiography. The "productive confusion," or aggregation, of archaeologies should compel us to reassess the politics and purpose of both disciplines. A more global and more deeply historical framing for media archaeology, for instance, reveals that media history, particularly when conceived at the scale of the city, is in part about human cultural heritage: the very resource that Kittler's model of urban-scale computation brackets out. And that heritage encompasses human rights and freedoms and responsibilities. Media and urban history, entwined, have long given form—material, legal, technical—to these critical, timeless concerns. Scholars and practitioners in both fields thus have the capacity to advocate for protocols and practices that will promote more ethical and enriching future developments: urban neighborhoods and amenities, gadgets and platforms, infrastructures and institutions that reflect both critical progress and historical sensibility, that embody a "newness" that knows and learns from its own pasts, and makes room for those pasts to be present *in* the present and future.

Temporal Entanglements

Given the simultaneous *timelessness* and *timeliness* of archaeology's most profound concerns, we need to pay particular attention to questions of temporality. An archaeological sensibility prompts us to shift our focus from "real-time" data-streams and various speculative "futures"—the obsessions of so many contemporary tech developers, content managers, design consultants, urban planners, and administrators—toward the *longue durée* within which those presents and futures take shape. In order to promote this temporal shift, perhaps we need to reconcile the temporalities of our two archaeologies, or at least be aware of their consistencies and incongruities.

While media archaeology seeks to offer alternatives to canonized historical media narratives and the "idea of inexorable, quasi-natural, technical progress," the familiar notion of archaeological "stratification" seems to make manifest the very idea of layered epochs of "progress."[60] Yet many archaeologists have challenged the classical stratification model, arguing that it "wraps blocks of linear temporality up into periods placed into neatly stacked boxes," separated by "arbitrary divisions."[61] Archaeologist Christopher Witmore suggests that the metaphor of the palimpsest presents similar conceptual problems: historical layers aren't simply "written, erased, and rewritten"; instead, there are plenty of "points of connection, proximity, and action between various pasts."[62] Many archaeologists (some drawing inspiration from theorists like Henri Bergson, Gilles Deleuze, Michel Serres, and Karen Barad) have embraced the notion of temporal entanglement. If we reject the idea that there are stratified epochs of "revolution"-based history, with new developments eradicating old systems, we need to rethink how the archaeological object—whether an ancient urn, a cuneiform tablet, or a network of fiber-optic cable—is conceived. Seemingly "modern" things, Witmore says, are "really [just] gatherings of achievements from various times and numerous places."[63]

These theoretical models of entanglement and assemblage actually take shape and become physical in our urban infrastructural landscapes. In many cases our older media networks have laid the foundation for our modern-day systems (as per the technological and economic principle of "path dependence"), but the "old" systems—those we might regard as buried on the "lower strata"—are also very much alive in, and continuing to shape, the contemporary city. These historical media are, like Raymond Williams' category of the "residual," "formed in the past, but . . . still active in the cultural process, not only and *often* not at *all* as an element of the past, but as an effective element of the present."[64] This is why our cities today are not solely virtual, but are simultaneously aural, graphic, textual, sonic, visual, and digital. "Old" media are still very much alive in them. We tend in media studies to write format-specific histories, and to suggest that new technologies supplant the old. But when we look at our media histories through our cities, we observe a layering or resounding, a productive "confusion," of media epochs. Such realizations open up new methodological opportunities for studying media, and, for me, they necessitate an alternative means of writing history—one that looks beyond revolutions, Great Men's accomplishments, origin stories, and reductive distinctions between "old" and "new."

What's more, these entangled systems have distinctive temporalities and evolutionary paths; they don't all "progress" at a standard rate. Local variations in media and urban history have implications for how archaeology demarcates its terrain: the abstract line between prehistory and history, which ostensibly marks the disciplinary territories of archaeology and history, varies in different cultures depending upon when people began creating written historical records. The presumption here is that most societies "progress" toward ever more complex literacies. Yet archaeology offers us plenty of evidence of nonlinear, non-"successive" evolution. Through archaeological investigation we can assess the lifespans of media objects and networks, and ascertain when "old" infrastructures leak into new-media landscapes, when some areas "leapfrog" particular stages in normative patterns of progress (as much of Africa has done with landline phones, for example), when media of different epochs are layered palimpsestically, or when new urban media remediate their predecessors.[65] Richard John, who's written histories of American telecommunications and the postal system, has found that the infrastructures he's studied were "complementary rather than mutually exclusive. Telegraphy supplemented mail delivery, and telephony supplemented telegraphy, without rendering either mail delivery or telegraphy obsolete."[66] While the electronic and digital ages have dealt serious blows to both the post and telegraphy, new media need not necessarily obsolesce the old; we'll likely still listen to the radio and scratch out handwritten notes (on paper or screens) in our "sentient cities" of tomorrow, for instance. Various networks also provide material support for one another. Geographers Stephen Graham and Simon Marvin write, "Because of the costs of developing new telecommunications networks," for instance, "all efforts are made to string optic fibers through water, gas, and sewage ducts; [and] *between* cities, existing railway, road, and waterway routes are often used."[67]

The notion of temporal entanglement has gained purchase within both media studies and archaeology. And media and network archaeologists have managed to question the notion of "inexorable progress" by excavating our new media technologies' diverse roots in the nineteenth, and occasionally the eighteenth, century. Yet, as I noted earlier, most existing media history and media archaeology work doesn't dig much deeper than the 1700s; it doesn't offer a terribly deep historical perspective. Among the few exceptions are Zielinski's choice of a Greek philosopher among his "variants"; Parikka's work with geologic time; and Grant Wythoff's investigation of mobile media "gadgets" through paleoanthropological tool studies.[68] Thus, another benefit of infusing media archaeology with archaeology-proper is that, once equipped with theoretical trowels, we can dig much deeper.

My hope is that *Code and Clay, Data and Dirt* models a different kind of temporal orientation for media studies: one rooted in the recognition that, in cities across time and across the globe, both "ethereal" and resolutely material media have always coexisted; that the "old" and "new" have always overlapped. What I offer here is something messier—productively muddier and more discordant, I hope—than conventional approaches to genealogy, archaeology, and geology.[69] What I'm proposing is a historiographical and methodological alteration to the way we do media and urban history. I want us to reassess archaeology's and history's implications for contemporary practice in a whole host of fields: urban and architectural

FIGURE 4. "Marten," by Morehshin Allahyari, from *Material Speculation: ISIS,* a series of 3D-printed reconstructions of ancient artifacts destroyed by ISIS in 2015. Courtesy Morehshin Allahyari.

design, media design and tech development, administration and policy (even among the archives, libraries, and museums who preserve and present cultural heritage for contemporary publics). We in media and design studies need to recognize our objects of study as situated, embedded in particular material contexts, and activated by their interactions with people and nonhuman actants—other media, other infrastructures, other creatures and things—in those environments. We need to appreciate the temporalities of those objects as entangled and overlapping, following various paths of development and knotted up with both their "pasts" and "futures." There is no universal, normative evolutionary trail. To misquote L. P. Hartley, our urban and media pasts are *not* foreign countries; they're here, now, and tomorrow.

These seemingly abstruse theoretical propositions actually become "facts on the ground" in our built environments. We could easily find evidence of temporal and spatial entanglements at myriad scales: in particular neighborhoods, within larger geographic regions, even at the planetary scale. While our focus here in *Code and Clay, Data and Dirt* is on the urban scale, it is important to note that the urban is a constellation of blocks and neighborhoods, and that it's a product of regional flows and planetary dynamics. Our scales of investigation and operation are entangled, too. Yet I choose to home in on the city because cities make manifest, they conveniently concretize, their entanglements: they're full of networked infrastructures, layered histories, and multiple media forms. And given that cities are a common area of investigation for many scholars, and a common site of practice for many spatial practitioners, cities provide a pragmatic meeting point for interdisciplinary investigation, for scholars and practitioners to integrate their various disciplinary knowledges and critical sensibilities. Here, media and culture scholars, borrowing tools and techniques from archaeologists, can learn to look to the material landscape for evidence of temporal and spatial entanglements. Researchers and designers can learn from archaeologists' own history of self-reflexivity regarding the sensitive cultural politics of "rescuing" objects from the past, of sinking shovels into the dirt and isolating particular artifacts or sites for analysis. Our acts of excavation, whether metaphorical or literal, have ethical and political implications for those who occupy or have some investment in those sites—as well as for those who administer and design their futures. Those envisioned futures, informed by an archaeological sensibility, will ideally be something more richly layered than the tabula rasa techno-solutionism of sites like Songdo or Hudson Yards. A city that recognizes its dependence on both ether *and* ore—and appreciates their potentially complimentary logics of mediation—is better equipped to accommodate temporal entanglement, to acknowledge and amplify the immediate, and timeless, resonances and relevance of its pasts.

A Note on Multisensory Methods

I'd like to offer a final note on those resonances and how we can listen for them. "Cities are a product of time," Mumford writes.

> They are the molds in which men's lifetimes have cooled and congealed, giving lasting shape, by way of art, to moments that would otherwise vanish with the living and leave no means of renewal or wider participation behind them. In the city, time becomes visible: buildings and monuments and public ways, more open than the written record, more subject to the gaze of many men than the scattered artifacts of the countryside, leave an imprint upon the minds even of the ignorant or the indifferent.[70]

If we think of our cities themselves as historical media, or archaeological artifacts embodying their entangled temporalities of evolution, we have to acknowledge that they're not just historical texts to be read or artifacts to be gazed upon. They can also serve as resonance chambers in which we hear echoes of past conversations, oratory, radio static, clanging printing presses, and pens scratching on parchment. Our cities are textural environments in which we feel traces of architectural inscriptions and centuries' worth of public notices affixed to building facades, and where we shake with the vibrations of loud sonic media—today, a booming subwoofer in a passing car, centuries ago, the village bells. And that static we sometimes feel in the air on cold, dry days is the same electromagnetic activity that convinced early experimenters that the "ether" might support wireless communication.[71] We can even detect olfactory clues of the city's mediation; walking past a paper recycling plant in the Dumbo neighborhood of Brooklyn, or through a printing district in Seoul, reminds us that our historical publishing centers also smelled of ink and paper.

While there has been, over the past two decades, some excellent work in sensory history, particularly on the sounds of historical sites, much ex-

FIGURE 5. Young men breakdancing in front of a sound system, 1996, London. Photograph by Adrian Boot, 1996.

isting work on the media city presents it as a visual entity, and the urban dweller as first and foremost a spectator—a subject position that implies a particular, limited politics of engagement with the city.[72] In *Code and Clay, Data and Dirt*, and in a short volume that foreshadowed it, my *Deep Mapping the Media City*, I have hoped to redress both the limited historical and sensory scope of this existing work by demonstrating the copresence of media from myriad epochs, and by depicting cities past and present as spaces that are simultaneously aural, graphic, textual, electroacoustic, digital, and haptic. Clues in any one of these sensory modes might offer insights into other registers. Emily Thompson, in *The Soundscape of Modernity*, acknowledges that "everyday sounds" from the early twentieth century, her period of study, "are virtually always lost to the historian, who must necessarily turn to textual descriptions and silent photographs to elicit the lost reverberations of the past."[73] In his *The Acoustic World of Early Modern England*, Bruce R. Smith "assembled evidence from travelers' accounts, estate maps, letters, diaries, sermons, plays, poems, fictional narratives, ballads from oral tradition, and architectural remains, and interpreted that evidence in relation to sixteenth- and seventeenth-century ideas about sound and the human body, and in light of modern principles of acoustic ecology, psychoacoustics, architectural acoustics, and sociolinguistics."[74] We can't know precisely how the denizens of early modern England heard the cries of street barkers, or how the citizens of ancient Rome heard a public address in the forum; there's necessarily some speculation involved in piecing together the sensory dimensions of urban and media history. Architectural historian Diane Favro and classicist Christopher Johanson acknowledge that creating a model of an "entire urban space," and imaging its textures and colors and acoustic properties, "requires hypotheses and assumptions about many unknown aspects."[75] Such indeterminacy "is unpalatable to many scholars, but especially to archaeologists, who are trained to appreciate accuracy, not speculation"— particularly certain camps of archaeologists, like the processualists who value rigorous use of the scientific method.

But speculative methods do at least allow us to acknowledge our media cities as multisensory, and to appreciate that these myriad sensory registers are integral to mediation. Speculative models allow us to imagine, if not posit definitive claims regarding, what our historical media cities might've looked, sounded, and felt like—and how urban politics might have been exercised through these empirical and affective registers. Urban and architectural historians and archaeologists have much methodological insight to offer in this endeavor, in large part because they already appreciate what a historical and material understanding of media and infrastructure can offer to studies of the past. In their *Archaeology: The Discipline of Things*, Bjørnar Olsen, Michael Shanks, Timothy Webmoor, and Christopher Witmore speak of

> making manifest the past (or, crucially . . . allow[ing] the past to manifest itself) in its traces through practices and performances (writing, corresponding, visiting, touring, mapping, pacing, debating), artifacts (letter, notebook, manuscript, printed book, pamphlet, map, plan, plaster cast, model), instruments (pen, paint brushes, rule, Claude Glass, camera lucida, surveying instruments, boots, wheeled transport, spades, shovels, buckets), systems and standards (taxonomy, itinerary, grid), authorized algorithms (the new philology, legal witnessing), dreams and design (. . . of a nation's identity, of personal achievement). Making manifest came through manifold articulations.[76]

Olsen and his colleagues see these various disciplinary infrastructures—technologies, instruments, protocols, and standards—as modes of engaging with and manifesting the past. Different tools for record-keeping and representation manifest different aspects of that past, including those ineffable qualities that don't readily lend themselves to "accurate," standardized formats of representation. Witmore argues that using a mixture of media can allow archaeologists to "translate something of the sensory, physical presence of the material past" into the present.[77]

There are myriad artists and media-makers and writers—Dziga Vertov, Walter Benjamin, Constant Nieuwenhuys and the Situationists, Alighiero Boetti, Lize Mogel and Alexis Bhagat, Rebecca Solnit, Joyce Kozloff, and Julie Mehretu among them—who discerned a similar need for new tools and strategies to represent modern spaces, and the modern city in particular. The "literary montage" form of Benjamin's *Arcades Project*, and the reader's experience in engaging with it, are regarded as "city-like"; its textual passages resemble, in their pace and structure, the passages of urban exhibition halls, arcades, and train stations.[78] Cartographers and geographers, too, have experimented with various critical, counter, and radical cartographic approaches, including indigenous mapping and sensory mapping.[79] These approaches aim to illuminate the unavoidably subjective and political aspects of mapping, and to provide alternatives to hegemonic, authoritative—and often naturalized and reified—approaches to cartography.

In my *Deep Mapping the Media City* I explored the use of "deep mapping" as a means of capturing the *longue durée* of urban mediation. The deep map, as archaeologists Mike Pearson and Michael Shanks explain, "attempts to record and represent the grain and patina of place through juxtapositions and interpenetrations of the historical and the contemporary, the political and the poetic, the discursive and the sensual; the conflation of oral testimony, anthology, memoir, biography, natural history, and everything you might ever want to say about a place."[80] While Pearson's and Shanks's list of ingredients is rather literary, we can also layer in GIS and empirical data and satellite images, thus juxtaposing qualitative and quantitative conceptions of space, or balancing out GIS's seeming precision with the relative fuzziness of humanistic data.[81] My own mapping studios at The New School have adopted such a multimodal approach. Fellow archaeologist Cliff McLucas adds that deep maps are characterized not only by their layering of different media or registers, but also by their "engagement of both the insider and outsider," "the official and the unofficial."[82] Deep maps don't claim to be authoritative or objective; to the contrary, they're intentionally "fragile and temporary"—always evolving and evading stable representation, just like our media and the cities they inhabit and shape.

Our Materials of Investigation

Our investigation here, in *Code and Clay, Data and Dirt*, is less cartographic and more thematically topographic. In other words, we'll explore patterns in how particular media made themselves materially present in cities around the world, at various points in history. And we'll consider how those cities took shape in order to accommodate mediation. My own methodology in piecing together these histories over the past fifteen years has been similarly diverse and distributed. I've studied the evolution of urban media and urban form in various archival collections—at the New York Public Library; the New-York Historical Society; the U.S. National Archives; the Lemelson Center at the National Museum of American History; the Hagley Museum and Library in Wilmington, Delaware; and the Canadian Centre for Architecture, to name just a few (I've relied, too, on the published and publicly presented research of international colleagues who've employed primary resources in their own languages and regions of the world). And I've explored additional collections alongside my students, as they've mapped their own historical urban media infrastructures. I've organized and participated in walking tours of Internet and cell-phone infrastructures, and behind-the-scenes tours at knowledge institutions, sound labs, logistical centers, information hubs, and various media-cities-in-the-making.[83] I've studied artifacts ranging from cuneiform tablets to old pneumatic tubes to the history of record-keeping systems—both material and ethereal "things." I've welcomed architects, planners, acousticians, cartographers, anthropologists, sound artists, infrastructural stewards and scholars, and policy experts into my classes and into the many public events, speaker series, and exhibitions that I've helped to organize. I've also conducted interviews with those same folks, and visited their studios and examined the tools and techniques they use to design media for urban use, or to build cities to accommodate those media, or to understand how cities past have facilitated mediation. And all the while I've read as widely as possible across the disciplines, weaving together insights from classics, materials science, art history, geology, urban history, engineering, media studies, and elsewhere. I've attempted to teach myself a little something about everything from brick-making and ancient bookkeeping to cell-phone azimuths and acoustic modeling. Mine was not a systematic methodology; it was more of a dig across space and time, through ether and ore, that only after years of sifting and sorting has enabled me to recognize thematic, historical, and geographical patterns in urban intelligence and mediation.

Each chapter of the book moves progressively farther backward in time—from the radio city of the early twentieth century, to the early wired cities of the mid-nineteenth century, to typographic places of print that have spanned the past five centuries, to sites of urban inscription and record-keeping, to urban volumes of vocality from the ancient world through today. As Graeme Gilloch advises in his study of Walter Benjamin's writings on the city, "History itself is a construction of the present age and must always be read backward from the ruins which persist in the here and now."[84] Similarly, archaeologists Rodney Harrison and John Schofield state that doing archaeology on the "contemporary past"—on recent history, like our media cities of the telecommunications age—requires that we "approach the present as a surface layer, working 'backward' through time to explore the ways in which the past intervenes in the present."[85] While we are reading backward, we'll examine our old media infrastructures not as *ruins* but as "residual" media, as "effective element(s) of the present."[86] Thus *Code and Clay, Data and Dirt* isn't organized in a simple reverse-chronological order; each chapter examines not only how these historical media have shaped urban space in the days when they were "new," but also how they continue to do so in our time, and will continue to do so tomorrow.

I offer an "anonymous history" of urban mediation—one that, much like Heinrich Wölfflin's "art history without names," pays little attention to great men or specific sites and times of origin and invention. While some folks—typically, those deemed sufficiently important to have had their thoughts recorded for posterity—might have interesting things to say about cities and media, and might aid in our historical and archaeological tasks, I don't regard these figures as the sole, or even primary, catalysts for historical change. Ether and ore, mud bricks and paper, sound waves and electricity are all critical actants here—just as critical as the named and nameless people who learned to harness them, mold them, and maintain them. In aggregate, these "humble objects . . . have shaken our mode of living to its very roots . . . for, in the anonymous life, the particles accumulate into an explosive force."[87] So proclaimed Siegfried Giedion, who presented his own *Mechanization Takes Command*—in which he examined the history of mechanization through the hand and the hearth, soil and sanitation—as an anonymous history. While my history of media cities is similarly anonymous, and while I have drawn inspiration from a theoretical tradition that is known for its occasional anti-humanism and technofetishism, the history I present here is certainly not a nonhuman one. Our story is one of how various topographies, climates, things (both immaterial and material), and people (both named and unnamed) have, across the millennia, shaped cities that, at their best, represent humankind's greatest feats of engineering, its greatest repositories of media and culture in their myriad forms, and its greatest embodiment of a culture's core values and critical knowledges—and at their worst can become, by design or through neglect, sites of decay, erasure, oppression, and injustice.

Each chapter of the book will be structured around the search for a particular archaeological-infrastructural "emblem," a material "topos" or artifact, that we tend to associate with specific epochs in media history, but which we'll trace forward and backward in time, through cities around the world. Archaeologists and historians have long acknowledged the ideological significance of different building materials. Concrete, in the form of expressways, for instance, is thought to embody various modernist political visions, ranging from self-directed mobility and emancipation to the military-industrial "disciplining" of urban circulation. Likewise, many media archaeologists and historians, like Ernst and Gitelman, have addressed the importance of considering the specific material natures of our historical records and artifacts; our histories are shaped by the substrates they're etched into.

We'll start amidst the ether—that "mediating substance between technology, science, and spiritualism," "the source of all things," as Joe Milutis describes it.[88] Our first chapter, "Waves and Wires: Cities of Electric Sound," describes how, since the mid-nineteenth century, urban atmospheres have been charged with electric and electromagnetic telecommunications—telegraph and telephone wires and radio waves. We'll begin by looking and listening for the impact of radio on urban form and architecture, and how the medium made itself both seen and heard in the urban environment. We'll then study how radio's wired precursors, the telegraph and telephone, effected their own influence on urban form and built space, and how new fiber-optic and cellular technologies are doing the same. Ether and ore (or its metallurgic analogs) have long been intertwined in our radiophonic cities: then and now, these ethereal technologies have relied for their operation on a byzantine array of antennae, rivers of wires, and a constellation of transmitters and switches—all of which have remade the material urban landscape around themselves.

We then shift our scale of observation to focus on ore molded into much more modestly-sized forms—particularly the letterform. Chapter 2, "Steel and Ink: The Printed City," traces how, for over half a millennium, a humble assemblage of steel, ink, and paper has informed the way we've imagined, designed, constructed, inhabited, administered, and navigated our cities. We'll study how new printed urban and architectural treatises and documents transformed the way designers learned their craft and shaped the cities they created. We'll then map how those cities became centers of print production, distribution, and consumption; they generated literary cultures and public spheres of readers and writers, and their new print forms—maps, guidebooks, and publicly-accessible architectural texts and pattern books—shaped the way people interacted with their cities. We'll look then to newspapers' role in both rendering the modern city legible to its inhabitants and shaping the urban material landscape. The administration of modern cities was particularly printing-intensive: we'll study how urban governance necessitated the generation of mountains of printed forms and typewritten memos and punched cards, as well as the creation of homologous architectures—metal filing cabinets, municipal archives, and the "enormous file" of the skyscraper itself—to circulate and contain all those standardized printed artifacts. And while our current age of more "ethereal" texts might spell the diminishment of the press, we'll close by examining how the printed page persists, even thrives, in some places as a still-popular mass-circulated medium, or as the fulcrum of niche urban print cultures.

In chapter 3, we dig into an even more humbly and messily elemental medium: mud. In "Of Mud, Media, and the Metropolis: Aggregating Histories of Writing and Urbanization," we'll consider how mud and its material analogs—clay, stone, brick, concrete—have supplied the foundations for our human settlements and forms of symbolic communication, and have bound together our media, urban, architectural, and environmental histories. Some of the first writing surfaces, clay and stone, were the same materials used to construct ancient city walls and buildings, whose facades also frequently served as substrates for written texts. The formal properties of those scripts—the shapes they took on their clay (or, eventually, parchment and paper) foundations—were also in some cases reflected in urban form: how the city molded itself from the materials of the landscape. And those written documents have always been central to our cities' operation: their trade, accountancy, governance, and culture.

In chapter 4, we attend to the sounds and textures of the voice, arguably among our oldest of "media." In "Speaking Stones: Voicing the City," we'll consider how the city itself functions as a sounding board, resonance chamber, and transmission medium for vocality—for public address, interpersonal communication, and vocal expressions of affect. Such considerations have, either intentionally or accidentally, informed the design, construction, and inhabitation of cities for millennia. We'll consider what we might learn from the field of archaeoacoustics, particularly regarding how urban spaces—the Greek agora and Pnyx, the Roman forum, the Byzantine church—have created the acoustic conditions necessary for democratic deliberation and other forms of assembly. We'll then discern how the resounding or containment of voices (particularly the voices belonging to particular classes of society) has demarcated urban boundaries and established territory. For instance, the Muslim call to prayer and the activist's voice, engaged in urban demonstration, have both exploited the material city as their resonance chamber, and supplemented the "live" performance with other mediations, including amplification and radio broadcast. We'll then close by considering new opportunities for scripting the urban voice and carefully engineering bounded spaces for its resounding. While such sound design work can help us to build more acoustically efficient cities, those sanitized, rationalized spaces can also muffle the urban public voice by stripping away its resonant texture and muting the historical echoes that might mix with and amplify it, creating harmonies or productive discord.

And finally, in the Conclusion, we examine a recent archaeological project, the reconstruction of Palmyra's Arch of Triumph, that involved the use of a wide variety of media technologies as archaeological tools, and that ultimately transformed the archaeological object into a globally circulating media production. The project's entangled materialities, temporalities, and geographies will allow us to revisit many topoi we will have explored through each of the book's four chapters; to reassess the cultural politics of media archaeology and archaeology-proper; and to consider the potential implications of these past-oriented fields of exploration for our urban media futures.

These chapters don't reflect mutually exclusive archaeological periods. I'm not suggesting that the voice, writing, print, and electrified sound are the media equivalents of our bronze, iron, and stone ages. While our media technologies did rise to prominence at different times in different places, they don't reside in distinctive historical strata. Our urban media ages are productively mixed in their materialities. Our cities past and present have been simultaneously aural, graphic, textual, electroacoustic, digital, and haptic. They're made of electromagnetic waves and infrastructure formed from mud, metal, or silicon. They've *always* been both new and old, immaterial and material, wireless and wired. Our media cities have been, and still are, both ether *and* ore, code and clay.

1

Waves and Wires

CITIES OF ELECTRIC SOUND

Shortly after Web 2.0's "marvelous clouds" appeared on the horizon, a ray of illumination broke through: those folks reliant on smartphone apps and Web-based services came to the realization that their WiFi networks, cloud storage, and phone connections relied on a heavily material network—one with a complex architecture, a fixed geography, and a huge carbon footprint.[1] Artists and designers offered an abundance of maps, apps, soundwalks, installations, and field guides that "made visible" the "invisible" networks powering the wired world's digital economies, institutions, and lifestyles.[2] Late 2015 brought Richard Vijgen's Architecture of Radio iPad app, which visualized and sonified signals from the Wi-Fi routers, satellites, cell phone towers, and fixed cabling that together constitute the "infosphere."

A few years earlier, the Berg research and design group, in their attempt to understand "radio and wireless networks as one of the substrates essential to contemporary design practice," introduced its Immaterials project, a "light painting" or interactive public sculpture that registered the presence and strength of WiFi signals in particular urban spaces.[3] German composer/sound artist Christina Kubisch, meanwhile, had long been investigating electromagnetism, and in 2004 she began hosting her Electrical Walks. Using specially designed headphones that translate electromagnetic signals within the environment into sounds, she discloses for users the myriad waves and particles that not only make possible their ATM transactions and signal their surveillance by ubiquitous CCTV, but that also perpetually envelop and penetrate their bodies.[4] Her work materialized growing public concerns about the potential health effects of the ubiquity and invasiveness of electromagnetic signals—ever present in the universe, but now harnessed and targeted by the devices many of us regularly carry in our pockets or next to our brains.[5]

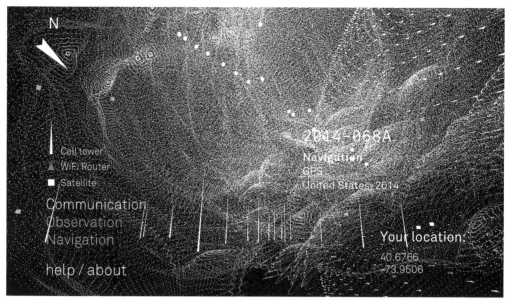

FIGURE 6. Still image from the Architecture of Radio iOS app, 2016. Image by Joshua McWhirter.

Such fascinations and fears echoed those from nearly a century before, when folks wondered how fledgling commercial radio managed to carry voices and melodies through the air. The rise of this new wireless medium, historian Michelle Hilmes argues, incited a host of utopian hopes and dystopian fears—including the simultaneously thrilling and threatening realization that "geographic and physical separation could be overcome by electrical agitations in the ether."[6] The ether: that same immaterial, conceptually murky medium that had, over the millennia, given residence to the gods and gravity, light and dark energy, mesmerism and Theosophy's auratic, etheric bodies. The landmark Michelson–Morley experiment of 1887, which sought to measure how "ether wind" impacted the speed of light, yielded a null result, challenging the very existence of ether. But early radio, Joe Milutis explains, "reenergized the etheric imagination."[7]

Since the mid-nineteenth century many cities' atmospheres have been charged with electric and electromagnetic telecommunications— telegraph and telephone wires and radio waves. These ethereal actants seemed to bend the laws of physics and raise profound existential and ontological questions about presence, temporality, and corporeality. As communications scholar James Carey has famously noted, the telegraph allowed for the separation of transmission from transportation; for the first time, a message could reach its recipient faster than a train or horse could deliver it.[8] The telegraph and radio were envisioned as conduits to the spirit world, and the telephone brought distant loved ones close enough to speak directly into our ears, leading early users to attach auratic qualities to these media. "From early radio on," Milutis claims, "ether became the context of the network universe—a space that has always been half fantastic, erected in the hopes of creating global simultaneity and cultural all-at-oneness."[9] Still, even ethereal technologies relied for their operation on a heavily material system of wires, tubes, transmitters, and switches. And these apparatae, when they took up residence in our cities, reorganized the material urban landscape around them. In this chapter we'll examine how the waves and wires of telecommunications shaped our cities of electric sound.

Moving backward in history, to peel away successive (but also intertwined) layers of mediation, we'll begin by examining the impact of radio on urban form and architecture, and how the medium made itself both seen and heard in the urban environment. We'll then study how radio's wired precursors, the telegraph and telephone, effected their own influence on urban form and built space. As we then consider the shift from copper wire to fiber optics and the repurposing of old infrastructural sites for new communications functions, we'll acknowledge the rivers of wires under the city streets that make possible our supposedly wireless urban mobility, as well as the heavy architecture that engenders the Cloud. And we'll close by examining new cellular wireless topologies within the urban environment, and how their often exclusionary politics compel some urban residents to adopt "old-school" approaches to reclaim the airwaves, to embed them in urban place.

Some archaeologists—particularly those engaged in contemporary and industrial archaeology—have attended to sites and artifacts critical to the evolution of telecommunications. Transoceanic telegraph landing points, old radio factories, central broadcasting buildings, television masts, telegraph poles, and military communications technology are among their sites and artifacts of investigation.[10] Likewise, massive microwave towers are a common site of study for amateur archaeologists and "infrastructural tourists" seeking to understand the material bases of our digital communication networks.[11] Those towers spread across the United States in the mid-twentieth century to transmit telephone and telegraph signals, but have been rendered ruins since the arrival of fiber optics. In recent years, however, some high-frequency traders have returned to microwave because it cuts valuable milliseconds off the transmission time for financial data.[12]

MediaCityUK, a center for digital media and broadcasting companies (including many units of the BBC), explored its own "urban media archaeology" in a 2012 conference.[13] Presenters examined infrastructural connections between canals, railways, printing technologies, radio, television, and the Internet, and considered how those earlier historical strata laid a foundation for their contemporary media production activities in Salford, near Manchester. In his look at the history of telegraphy and telephony, John Liffen, a curator from the Science Museum in London, focused on a number of sites and artifacts: broadcasting towers, switching racks, telephone poles, telegraph instrument factories, and telephone exchange buildings, where he "read" their successive renovations as evidence of evolving telephonic mechanics and labor practices. We'll visit many such sites later. While Liffen celebrates the widespread amateur enthusiasm for telecommunications history, he laments the *archaeological* methodological difficulties such a study presents. Most of early telecommunications' artifacts are gone: its poles have been ripped up, its pneumatic tubes decommissioned, its messenger boys retired or passed away, its buildings repurposed and renovated or razed.[14] Historical telegraph and telephone technologies "had, for the most part, extensive and highly visible infrastructure."

> As each technology was supplanted by the next, however, the equipment and its connecting networks have been dismantled and scrapped, and the survival of early features is poor. Telecommunications buildings have a better survival record because they can be adopted for other uses, but preservation of (for example) complex telephone exchanges with all equipment in working order is completely beyond the resources of amateurs.[15]

Digital communications archaeology presents similar challenges, according to Salford telecom scholar Nigel Linge: "the digital age is potentially one of the worst recorded and archived. The pace of change and commercial ethos of the markets is outstripping our ability or motivation to preserve what is in effect recent heritage."[16] Archivists and librarians know these challenges all too well.

Given the spottiness of the material record, the archaeology of telecommunications necessitates an integration of methods, resources, and intelligences. It requires fieldwork, archival work, oral history, forensic investigation, and interaction with communities of highly committed amateur historians, who are often former telecom employees themselves. As Liffen demonstrated, being a contemporary archaeologist of the media city requires knowing regulatory and business history, communications and cultural history, electrical engineering and physics (among other disciplinary knowledges)—all of which are needed to help us piece together why things are *where* they are, *as* they are, and *when* they are. An archaeology of wires and waves is necessarily an interdisciplinary affair. In this chapter we turn to architectural historians and designers, technologists, technological and cultural historians, media scholars, telecom workers and executives, and city officials. And as we'll see, such a multi-perspectival investigation into our past mediated environments can ultimately help us to identify recurring and divergent formal patterns—architectural, urban, topological—and the aspirations and ideologies that undergird them.

Radiating Space: Radio's Distributed Urban Forms

Radio emerged into an urban atmosphere often clogged with smog and newly punctuated with skyscrapers.[17] The first radio broadcast centers were in cities—which, ironically, presented many material barriers to a radio signal. Speaking in 1935 of the New York City Police Department's early adoption of a radio communication system, chief engineer Thomas Rochester explained how the city's mass of tall buildings functioned both as an infrastructure for transmission, and as an impediment to it:

> A single 500-watt transmitter station would be hopelessly inadequate for New York because of the absorbing effects of the many tall, steel-framed buildings, elevated railways and bridges, and because of the area to be served. The interference caused by electrical systems and devices adds to the difficulty.[18]

Because signal strength and the location of stations' transmitters determined their broadcasting range, allowing radio waves to either penetrate or circumvent tall buildings, many early broadcasts were relayed from their cities' highest points, on the top floors of their tallest buildings, which were sometimes hotel rooms. In 1922 WMAQ began broadcasting in Chicago from the La Salle Hotel, then the tallest downtown building, and WGN started up in the Wrigley Building.[19] Meanwhile, radio stations in New York were broadcasting from the Metropolitan Life Building and making use of the Chrysler and Empire State Buildings' antenna spires.

Since the turn of the twentieth century, this new structural typology—the radio mast—quickly boosted the altitude of the world's tallest buildings. Lee de Forest and Guglielmo Marconi, warring radio pioneers, visually broadcast their battle for superiority through the progressively increasing heights of their New York City radio masts.[20] It was a radio mast that saved Paris's tallest structure, too. Constructed for the 1889 World's Fair, the Eiffel Tower was to be dismantled after twenty years, but when engineer Gustave Eiffel installed an antenna in 1903 he established his one-time architectural folly as a critical node within a military radio network. Taking inspiration from the Parisian icon, many designers and artists of the Russian avant-garde—Vladimir Tatlin, Vladimir Shukhov, Ivan Leonidov, Alexander Rodchenko, László Moholy-Nagy—embraced radio as a polemical tool (as we'll see in chapter 4) and aestheticized the infrastructure's latticed geometry and heavily wired crowns. Meanwhile, audiences around the world witnessed an explosion of commercial imagery—ads, logos, animations—depicting planetary-scale towers.[21] The classic RKO Radio Pictures opening logo that played before the studio's films between the 1930s and the 1950s portrayed an elegantly gargantuan Eiffel-esque radio tower tooting out a Morse code message (purported translation: VVVV AN RKO RADIO PICTURE VVVV).[22] Wireless telegraphy is represented here as a halo of lightning bolts, which transform into spherical waves that radiate over a spinning globe.

The "spatial ontology" of radio is radiant, spherical, and lends itself to graphic representation in the form of expanding rings or ripples. While neither the radial city, a city radiating outward from its civic center, nor the circular city, an alternative to the iconic urban grid, was a novel urban form in the early twentieth century, communications scholar James Hay argues that radio's radiant electromagnetic waves reaffirmed the rationality and efficiency of this urban morphology: "Over the 1920s and 1930s, radio became the invisible but audible and felt connectivity of the city as communicative space."[23] The architect Le Corbusier suggested in 1925 that radio, in concert with the telegraph and telephone—all forms of "apparatus for abolishing time and space"—would allow urban activity to be concentrated in the high-rise business hub.[24] Telecommunications would undergird the capitalist grid. Others have claimed to hear—or rather, see—radio in other urban and architectural forms of the early twentieth

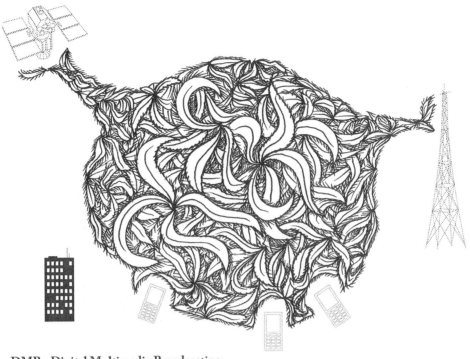

DMB - Digital Multimedia Broadcasting
Spherum Elektrum Multanum

Field: radio transmission using satellites and radio towers
Uses: mobile devices
Range: potentially worldwide, FM Coverage
Capacity: 1 Mbps at max. 200 km/h

FIGURE 7. Visualization of Digital Multimedia Broadcasting (DMB) from *The Bubbles of Radio*, 2007, by Ingeborg Marie Dehs Thomas. Image courtesy of the artist.

century. Eric Gordon, author of *The Urban Spectator*, finds that designer Hugh Ferriss's iconic drawings of New York adopt the "same formal logic as network radio."[25] In Ferriss's *Metropolis of Tomorrow*, Gordon writes, "the city is divided into multiple centers. These 'centers' function as broadcasting stations, each emanating out to its proximate cluster of buildings, and each connected through a singular network." Empty space, or ether, has been assimilated into the "structural mass of the city."[26] Rather than depicting densely packed skyscrapers or the *radial* "radio city" Hay describes, Ferriss's charcoal drawings show "each great mass . . . surrounded by great spaciousness," affording citizens "ample vistas" and rendering the city "visible and possessable." In making space for sound, the city thus opened up new modes of looking. For Frank Lloyd Wright, the city was "possessable" through a generous plan of land distribution: a minimum

FIGURE 8. Illustration from *The Metropolis of Tomorrow*, 1929, by Hugh Ferriss. Reproduced by permission of the heirs of Hugh Ferriss.

of one acre for every family. Radio—again alongside the telephone, the telegraph, and the automobile—was "at work building" his decentralized Broadacre City, which presaged the rise of our now-ubiquitous suburbs.[27]

Architect and critic Sam Jacob observed radio rendering itself visible at the architectural scale. The new topography of radio, one oscillating "between the physical and invisible, between media and architecture," was reflected in new architectural forms: the "open plan and the glazed curtain wall . . . connecting spaces that were once separate, dissolving physical boundaries . . . in ways that echo the electronic dissolution of space."[28] Buckminster Fuller, who regularly celebrated his own biographical connections with radio (as a young man, he worked aboard a naval ship where de Forest established the first successful radio communication between a ship and a plane), also sought to reimagine shelter for the radio age—to open space up to electromagnetic waves. As architectural historian Mark Wigley describes, "Fuller's lifelong project was to thin buildings down to minimize the difference between the object and the space of radiation." His geodesic domes, plastic structures, and radome antenna shelters for the U.S. Marine Corps "became transceivers" suited for the age of "global mobility."[29] While these architectures and networks of dispersal and dissolution seemed to celebrate the triumph of communicative space over geographic space (a *topos* touched upon frequently by designers, planners, and futurists of the day, and repeated by communication historians), traditional, terrestrial architecture and zoning provided convenient metaphors for making sense of the newly charged ether. This atmospheric geography could still be colonized, owned, auctioned, and controlled through regulation; as many historians have noted, the Radio Act of 1927 transformed the electromagnetic spectrum into real-estate parcels ripe for development and ownership.

Yet what supposedly distinguishes "radio space"—its radial organization, multiple connected centers, open plans, ample vistas, material lightness—does, in some cases, *precede* radio, and is equally representative of other media or cultural logics and aesthetics. Renaissance architects favored the radial plan; centuries of sea travel and the construction of road and rail networks in the eighteenth and nineteenth centuries made possible the connection of multiple urban centers; and new steel and glass construction made possible the opening up of interior spaces. Many ancient cities had designed vistas, and nomadic societies have long used light, mobile architectures. Radial and radiant cities are always-already new. Perhaps what distinguishes our radio cities, then, is not so much their macro-scale visual form as their *sound*, and how that sound is shaped by the city as a material resonance chamber and transmission medium. Sound is, paradoxically, one urban dimension that is neglected in many of the aforementioned studies, in which radio logic manifests primarily as a visual or infrastructural form. But what about radio as a *sounding* medium, and the city as its instrument? Certainly we can hear radio's influence in the urban landscape.

Urban planners, administrators, and public health advocates were well aware of the city's role as a sonic medium, and they sought to colonize and control it through regulation—specifically through zoning. Acoustic zoning has a long history that we can trace back to the separation of the "hammering trades from the learned professions" and to calls, including those from Hippocrates in the fifth century BCE, to protect the infirm from urban din.[30] The home had historically been a site of labor, and laborers' residences were often located in close proximity to the shops and factories where they worked. Businessmen and real-estate developers

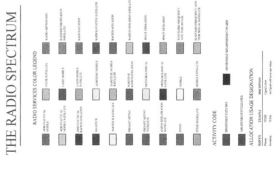

UNITED
STATES
FREQUENCY
ALLOCATIONS
THE RADIO SPECTRUM

RADIO SERVICES COLOR LEGEND

AERONAUTICAL MOBILE
AERONAUTICAL MOBILE SATELLITE
AERONAUTICAL RADIONAVIGATION
AMATEUR
AMATEUR SATELLITE
BROADCASTING
BROADCASTING SATELLITE
EARTH EXPLORATION SATELLITE
FIXED
FIXED SATELLITE

FIXED-SATELLITE
LAND MOBILE
LAND MOBILE SATELLITE
MARITIME MOBILE
MARITIME MOBILE SATELLITE
MARITIME RADIONAVIGATION
METEOROLOGICAL
METEOROLOGICAL SATELLITE
MOBILE
MOBILE SATELLITE

RADIO ASTRONOMY
RADIODETERMINATION SATELLITE
RADIOLOCATION
RADIOLOCATION SATELLITE
RADIONAVIGATION
RADIONAVIGATION SATELLITE
SPACE OPERATION
SPACE RESEARCH
STANDARD FREQUENCY AND TIME SIGNAL
STANDARD FREQUENCY AND TIME SIGNAL SATELLITE

ACTIVITY CODE

GOVERNMENT EXCLUSIVE
GOVERNMENT/NON-GOVERNMENT SHARED
NON-GOVERNMENT EXCLUSIVE

ALLOCATION USAGE DESIGNATION

SERVICE	EXAMPLE	DESCRIPTION
Primary	FIXED	Capital Letters
Secondary	Mobile	1st Capital with lower case letters

U.S. DEPARTMENT OF COMMERCE
National Telecommunications and Information Administration
Office of Spectrum Management

August 2011

3 kHz
300 kHz
3 MHz
30 MHz
300 MHz
3 GHz
30 GHz
300 GHz

resisted zoning, but they faced rising opposition from noise abatement and public health advocates, Progressive economists, landscape architects, and City Beautiful proponents, who advocated for improved urban circulation—of air, light, waste, and noise. Asphalt and cement began to replace cobblestone- and wood-paved streets, dampening sound and transforming resurfaced regions into *"ipso facto* zones, as much by environing sounds as by echelons of class."[31]

And with the arrival of new acoustic meters and an agreed-upon unit of measure, the decibel, cities began to define acoustic zones by maximum noise levels.[32] That noise could be created by traffic, airplanes—or, in the early twentieth century, by family pianos, gramophones, and radios. A 1930 survey initiated by the New York Noise Abatement Commission identified the radio as the third most frequently cited annoyance.[33] (Interestingly, the Commission also asked the city's radio stations—a part of the problem—to become part of the solution: to aid in a "campaign to educate radio listeners in noise etiquette" by broadcasting, at 10:30 each night, a reminder to listeners to turn down their loudspeakers "as an act of good sportsmanship."[34]) In the mid-1930s, New York mayor Fiorello La Guardia declared a "war on noise" and framed unwanted sound not as a behavioral or technological problem, but as a "spatial problem," which led to the city's first noise ordinance. Later, in the sixties and seventies, Mayor John Lindsey helped to pass the city's first comprehensive noise code.[35] Yet zoning laws, Hillel Schwartz argues, were rarely "accompanied by revisions of building codes toward the better insulation of floors, ceilings, and walls."[36]

Radio thus emerged into urban environments that presented both material supports for and impediments to its own broadcast. Contemporary and future archaeologists will likely find that electromagnetic waves have had variable impacts—both decentralizing and centralizing—on concrete urban and architectural form. But they'll likely agree that this ethereal force certainly did shape designers', engineers', and city officials' *conceptions* of the city and its regulation, and those conceptions shaped material spatial practice. Radio's signals resounded, both audibly and intellectually, to inform the way city-builders deployed antennae and administrative policies, open space and, as we'll soon see, iron ore and other building materials throughout their metropoles.

Opposite page:

FIGURE 9. Chart of radio spectrum frequency allocations in the United States. U.S. Department of Commerce: National Telecommunications and Information Administration—Office of Spectrum Management. Public domain.

Radio Waves and Brick Walls: Designing Sonic Architectures

Radio gave rise to new purpose-built architectures, which revolutionized the spatial "containment" and production of sound, and then released those sounds back out into the urban environment. That evolving environment became the subject of many early radio broadcasts. From 1927 to 1933, Walter Benjamin took to the airwaves of Berliner Funkstunde and the Südwestdeutscher Rundfunk to share strategies for coping with the stresses of modern urban life, and to steel children with stories of great global catastrophes (perhaps an early attempt to instill "grit"?). Many of his programs focused on the city itself—specifically, Berlin. "Reflecting on particular urban conditions, describing architectural works, and, most interestingly, calling on the listener to visit specific sites within the city," Alexander Eisenschmidt reports, "Benjamin's radio talks encouraged an active engagement with the city and its architecture."[37] Meanwhile, from 1927 to 1945, BBC radio aired more than six hundred programs about the built environment: about land-use politics and taxation, domestic do-it-yourself projects, and the roles of architects and local councils in shaping country estates and urban development—all framed as a means of egalitarian aesthetic and moral education.[38] Shundana Yusaf, in her study of the BBC, wonders what happened to the built environment, "with its physical and visual mode of knowledge and exercising power," when it was "subjected to the productive, reproductive, and diffusive logic of an electronic medium?"[39] How to make the urban environment radiophonic? Benjamin's participatory broadcasts presented the city as a terrain to be explored. Other broadcasters chose to translate abstract topics into concrete, applied, quotidian concerns: thus, architectural heritage was examined through the lens of tourism, and contemporary design was made accessible through lessons on good housekeeping and home repair. Radiophonic discourse seemed to favor the active and concrete (although there are plenty of examples of radio, "transmission," and sound artists who capture a city's character or sense of place via more abstract, ambient approaches).[40]

Broadcasting House, the space in which the BBC's broadcasting took place, likewise translated diffusive waves and dispersed publics into an architectural form. Much like Hans Poelzig's Haus des Rundfunks (House of Broadcasting) in Berlin, completed in 1931, the BBC's London headquarters situated its broadcasting rooms at the building's core and surrounded them with offices, thus shielding the studios from street noise. The architects

FIGURE 10. BBC Broadcasting House and Church of All Souls, view northward from Upper Regent Street, 1940, London. Photograph courtesy of Ben Brooksbank / CC-BY-SA-2.0.

and engineers developing this new architectural type were designing for both humans and machines. As architectural historian John Harwood notes, the new "radio architecture" had to synthesize "conventional architecture (e.g., a building with walls, floor, and ceiling, useful and habitable for human beings)" with "the vastly complex electromagnetic apparatus required," which included studios, transmission towers, relays, and receivers.[41] This calibration of allegiances, to people and equipment—which we also see in contemporary data centers and telco hotels—was apparent in Broadcasting House. "Since studios had to conform to strict acoustical requirements," Yusaf writes, "the choice of materials was almost entirely determined by their capacities for absorption, resonance, or reverberation; furnishings, equipment, and the layout were calculated in terms of music, singing, and speaking."[42] Wells Coates's rubber-walled effects studio "embraced radiophony's disquieting grafting of mechanical, electric, and electronic possibilities over orality"; Coates created an infrastructure of microphones, loudspeakers, telephones, control rooms, and accouterments for sound effects, which allowed for the mixing of activity in ten different studios.[43] Yet the broadcasters, "the talent," insisted also on "studio designs that mitigated the psychological obstacles" of performing live, and of "speaking aloud to [often] imaginary, mute interlocutors."[44] Thus, in talks studio 3D, designer Dorothy Trotter gave the BBC's hosts fake fireplaces, leather chairs, bookshelves, wall clocks, and portraits—a familiarly domestic study-like environment to help them "overcome the new artificiality" of chatting on air with invisible interlocutors.[45]

Up on the roof, within view of John Nash's 1824 All Souls Church next door, the broadcaster's steel lattices, electrical cables, and booster towers seemed to rewrite Victor Hugo's proclamation that "this will kill that" for the radio age: rather than portending the triumph of print over architecture, as Hugo foretold, the BBC's wires and waves "had robbed church bells of the function of calling the faithful. They had reduced spires to pure visual ornaments and nostalgic reminders of a bygone sonic era."[46] Yet George Val Myer's Broadcasting House design was not without its own mythology: the fortress-like building's "watered-down art deco vocabulary" featured stone reliefs and sculptures depicting Ariel and Prospero, soaring birds, airwaves, and light rays.[47]

A similar mythical sensibility (another recurring topos) resonated—in sound and stone—in New York, where, at roughly the same time, the Radio Corporation of America (RCA), including its affiliates RKO and NBC, converged on a newly developed complex in Midtown Manhattan. As historian Emily Thompson describes it, Rockefeller Center was an "unprecedented concentration of facilities for the dissemination of sight and sound by radio and by record—through the air, the film, and the disk."[48] Architect Raymond Hood and his associates ornamented the building with broadcasting-themed mosaics, depicting humankind's mastery of the material universe and conquest of space in service of the transmission of knowledge. Donald Deskey's interior design for Radio City Music Hall, with its ceiling featuring eight enormous bands that radiated from the stage, seemed "to pulsate and throb."[49] Meanwhile, industrial designer John Vassos, who regularly consulted for RCA, designed radio studios and transmitter buildings for cities and towns around the country; those steel, cement, glass, and aluminum structures, with their streamlined designs that resembled the smooth forms of a radio tube, were meant to "express the tempo and spirit" of the radio age.[50]

The radio aesthetic was more than visual. As Rem Koolhaas famously noted, Rockefeller Center offered "the first architecture that can be broadcast." The RKO building was equipped with an Antenaplex system, which allowed all tenants to plug their radio receivers into special outlets and receive guaranteed efficient reception; windows were fitted with Maxim-Campbell Silencer and Air Filter units; and offices were isolated with soundproof partitions.[51] The NBC studios, meanwhile, with their movable acoustic units, were "heralded as 'a temple to glorify the radio voice,' a 'gigantic cathedral of sound.'"[52] Radio City was the apotheosis of modern sonic developments; with its state-of-the-art acoustical design, microphones, and loudspeakers, it represented the ultimate sonically controlled space. Yet its precise calibration may have instead cultivated an uncomfortable artificiality. Walter Lippman, rather than comparing Radio City to a temple or cathedral, as the designers of this state-of-the-art facility might have expected, likened it to a "monument to a culture in which material power and technical skill have been divorced from human values and the control of reason."[53] In other words, its designers had taken the spatialization and sonification of "radio logic" too far; presaging Friedrich Kittler and Wolfgang Ernst, they regarded architecture as a tunable "signal-processing" machine and engineered the environment right out of the acoustics, stripped the space out of sound.

In the years leading up to Rockefeller Center's arrival, a host of technical and cultural shifts had shaped the "soundscape" of the modern city and set the stage for its new radio architecture. Those developments included the emergence of new sound recording and broadcast technologies and new acoustical architectural materials; the rise of the field of acoustical engineering, and the cultivation of new techniques and tastes in the "culture of listening," including new definitions of what constituted "noise" and what passed as "music." This assemblage of developments collectively "[reformulated] the relationship between sound and space."[54] Steen Eiler Rasmussen, in his classic *Experiencing Architecture* of 1959, also explained that radio impacted the design of space at the architectural and interior scale, too: "Radio transmission created new interest in acoustic problems. Architects began to study acoustical laws and learned how a room's resonance could be changed—especially how to absorb sound and shorten the period of reverberation."[55] Products like Akoustolith, Acousti-Celotex, Acoustone, Sanacoustic Tile, Sabinite, and Sprayo-Flake created architectural spaces characterized by a lack of reverberation.[56] Rooms no longer had a signature sound based on their dimensions and materials. Instead, the new architectural materials of which they were composed signaled "the power of human ingenuity over the physical environment."[57] Radio and record producers could then engineer *back in* the simulated sounds of particular performance spaces, just as we can today manipulate the EQ settings on our stereos and iPhones. Later, architects and engineers extended these techniques to other building types, installing double-paned windows and acoustic ceilings, and exploiting the white noise in heating and ventilation ducts, to provide "acoustic perfume" that would mask the sounds of noisy office technology and coworkers' chatter.[58]

Urban Sounds: Listening to Radio in the City

The arrival of radio didn't always command such monumental and measured architectural design and infrastructural engineering. Plenty of radio stations and transmission buildings were housed in purely functional, nondescript steel and concrete boxes, or in repurposed structures. In those cases, where radio had little discernible visual presence in the urban landscape, it signaled its arrival as a new addition to the soundscape. In Africa, colonial governments began building radio stations in the 1920s, and much of that early programming was not broadcast, but transmitted via wired subscription services. Anthropologist Brian Larkin writes about the sonic consequences of radio's arrival in Nigeria in the 1940s:

> In 1944, engineers in Kano began to erect loudspeakers on the walls outside the emirate council office, the public library, the post office, and other prominent public places. The words and music coming from these speakers were radio broadcasts, mainly from England, which were captured by a central receiver and amplifier, relayed by wire to individual households and public loudspeakers, and then discharged into urban space for any in earshot to hear. Radio [thus] . . . began its life in Nigeria as a public technology.[59]

Urban streets and houses were filled with new, foreign sounds—typically propagandistic messages, uttered in British accents, intended to win Nigerians over to the "power and promise of modern life" offered by their colonizers.[60] "Loudspeakers thus formed part of the tactile, everyday world of colonial urban life and created channels of radio waves, cables, receiving sets, and sound waves that connected that world to a larger network."[61] Eventually the arrival of wireless moved radio indoors, but then, in the 1960s, the availability of cheap transistor radios—and, equally significantly, *batteries*—brought it back outdoors again, in portable form. This shifting site of listening reminds us that radio sounded in a "tactile,"

FIGURE 11A. Loudspeakers attached to a mosque minaret, location unspecified. Photograph by Bev Sykes / CC-BY-2.0.

FIGURE 11B. Women listening to radio on a rooftop garden, 1926, Berlin. bpk, Berlin/Art Resource, N.Y.

multisensory world; the city provided a variety of multisensory ambiences, infused with smell and taste and rhythm, in which those electromagnetic waves resounded.

Different cities in different eras have provided distinctive material contexts in which radio and public broadcast could resonate, and the local residents employed different culturally, historically, and generationally-informed techniques for making and listening to those sounds. By the 1930s, Buenos Aires had been reshaped by a regimented urban grid, subways and trams, electrical cables, and telephone poles. Radio was yet another infrastructural development that, according to literary and cultural critic Beatriz Sarlo, distinguished the city from others in Latin America, and that enabled its inhabitants to develop a unifying mass culture and see their city as one that was uniquely "modern, regular, socially balanced."[62] By the late twentieth century, in the favelas of Rio, warring strains of world music and evangelical music bled through the thin walls of precariously stacked apartments and wound down reverberant narrow alleyways and concrete stairs, sonically signaling clashing cultural identities; and in Durban, South Africa, "swanking taxis" blasted kwaito music to stake a claim on urban space as they passed through white, black, and Indian neighborhoods.[63] For centuries in the Islamic world the call to prayer and, more recently, recorded sermons have resounded, mixing with the urban din, providing a means of spiritual orientation for the faithful and, particularly in spiritually diverse cultures, inciting debates over spatial and sound politics (more about this in chapter 4).[64] Architectural building materials, road surfaces, the massing of buildings—and even climatic conditions, like heat and humidity—affect how such amplified sounds spread throughout each of these cities.

In Kathmandu, where both telephone calls and radio broadcasts were rare or nonexistent before the democratic revolution of 1990, the FM radio program *Rumpum Connection* broadcasts calls between Nepalis and their friends and relatives abroad, uniting a diaspora through the ether, "figuratively drawing [the dispersed] into the public space of the nation's capital."[65] State-run Radio Nepal had been broadcasting on AM airwaves since the 1950s, and when FM stations came into existence in 1996, they "quickly became a symbol of a new democratic movement and its promises of 'free speech.'"[66] Many Nepalis regard AM and FM as completely different media, according to anthropologist Laura Kunreuther; they claim: "I don't listen to radio. I listen to FM." Meanwhile, phones were a rarity in Nepali households in 1990, but by the middle of the decade they had become a common household technology, symbolizing families' middle-class arrival. "As a material object," Kunreuther says, "telephones entered most homes after they had acquired televisions and at the same time as refrigerators." This isn't the normative Western timeline of technological adoption. Such a chronology reminds us that there is no consistent, global pattern of technological *or* urban development. To put it reductively, one community's "old" medium or urban form is another's "new." Consider also the case of Iraq, where pirate broadcasters and government officials launched radio stations in 2016 to help the residents of Mosul resist and perhaps escape the tyranny of Islamic State; here, "old" media represents a critical tool for self-preservation.[67]

And even in cities defined by their breathless pursuit of the ever-new, the old medium of radio continues to shape the urban environment. From my living room window I look out upon the new One World Trade Center in downtown Manhattan, currently the tallest building in the Western hemisphere. In the spring of 2015, technicians climbed to the top and tested the strength and coverage of a set of antennae that could potentially accommodate up to eleven TV stations and twenty-one radio stations. Thus, even in a city that's replacing its payphones with public WiFi hotspots and embedding sensors in its streets, radio still resonates (as does over-the-air television, as more families "cut the cord" from cable).[68] We still recognize our cities as broadcasting centers, and their urban ether as a realm where electromagnetic waves confront architecture. We still seek the highest peaks from which to broadcast, and concede that the density of the terrain below—with all of its steel, glass, and concrete barriers and competing electromagnetic signals—presents a treacherous obstacle course for radio, WiFi, and cell signals alike.

Wired Monuments: Poles, Cables, and Telegraphic Architectures

Antennae themselves changed the visual and material character of the urban landscape. As we noted earlier, many cities acquired landmark broadcasting towers, or extended their tallest buildings with crowns of transmission apparatae. Radio's *wired* precursors in telecommunications, the telegraph and telephone, had a more terrestrial, and thus, in most cases, more immediately perceptible, more tactile, impact on the city.[69] Telephone exchanges, for instance, were capped with a metal frame, a derrick, that carried a wire to *each* subscriber's home; as the number of subscribers increased, so too did the size of the derricks.[70]

FIGURE 12A. Overhead wiring in Delhi, 2010; Photograph by Louise Goggin / CC-BY-NC-2.0.

FIGURE 12B. Overhead wiring in New York City, after the Great Blizzard of 1888. Courtesy of the New-York Historical Society.

Some communities used their corner telephone poles as vital communication hubs, to post neighborhood news and advertise their services. As Franz Kafka relates in a 1911 diary entry, the Jewish community in Warsaw used overhead wires to demarcate within the city a bounded area, a delimited communal zone—what the Talmud refers to as an eruv—in which Jews can move about freely on the Sabbath.[71] Despite the fact that some publics resourcefully appropriated the new infrastructure (and contemporary Orthodox communities still use phone and power lines to demarcate eruvin), most late nineteenth-century urban denizens lamented the security and aesthetics of these ubiquitous poles and overhead wires. While many of his early twentieth-century successors celebrated the sublime engineering of their graceful new radio towers, Victorian-era electrical engineer William H. Preece was no fan of the wires:

Decidedly the most striking feature in New York to my professional eye is the poles that disfigure the streets in every direction. How such an enormity can have been perpetrated is simply incredible. Hideous crooked poles carrying twenty or thirty wires are fixed down the principal streets and sometimes three different lines of poles run down the same street.[72]

When the installation of a new IRT subway afforded the opportunity to bury the wires in the subway tubes—to embed one infrastructure within another—the city's mayor, Hugh Grant, began cutting down that "forest of poles," which had "literally darkened the sky."[73]

In the 1870s and '80s other cities' mayors, driven not only by aesthetic preferences, but also by practical concerns—the harm posed to wires by inclement weather or natural disasters, for instance—also mandated the burial of their telecommunications infrastructures.[74] In Philadelphia, Western Union's president, William Orton, promised in 1876 to connect the company's Third and Tenth Street offices via underground wires and pneumatic tubes, which would be laid in a trench between the railroad tracks and the street curb.[75] "Cable-management" strategies and policies have evolved at different rates and in different patterns around the world. It wasn't until 2010, for example, that the city of Dhaka, in Bangladesh, mandated the burial of its Internet and television cables (which had been in use only since 1998), and even as recently as 2015 San Francisco officials lamented that it would take six hundred years to bury its one hundred fifty years' worth of utility lines.[76]

Still, some found beauty in the wires—if not in their visual aesthetic, then in their song: "As I went under the new telegraph wire, I heard it vibrating like a harp high overhead. It was as the sound of a far-off glorious life, a supernal life, which came down to us, and vibrated the lattice-work of this life of ours," opined Thoreau in his journal. To him, the wire song was both celestial *and* classical: "How much the ancients would have made of it! To have a harp on so great a scale, girdling the very earth, and played on by the winds of every latitude and longitude"[77] (and as we saw earlier, architects of the following radio age embedded similar poetic allusions into their broadcasting buildings, with all their mythical ornamentation). Yet the celestial wasn't a mere metaphor. Sound scholar Douglas Kahn suggests that those early telephone company men, as they strung their lines across rooftops in cities around the globe, were unwittingly "building a huge sensing array to observe and study the effects of atmospheric electricity, electrical storms, magnetic storms, earth currents, and electromagnetic fields and waves, some of them originating from the distant reaches of the earth's magnetosphere."[78]

These wires, unsightly though they were, extended terrestrial architecture into the electromagnetic ether. And accompanying the wires' song was another new infrastructural sound: the hiss of pneumatic tube systems, which many cities, like Philadelphia and London, installed to handle inefficiencies in telegraph logistics and to aid in postal delivery (and at city shipyards and department stores they helped to shuttle small goods).[79]

In urban downtowns, those wires converged at the central office or exchange building, which constituted a new architectural type: a building where human operators interfaced between both machines and people, connecting wires to switchboards and distributed callers to one another. While in most towns the central office was a purely functional building (which, Liffen says, nevertheless occasionally became a local landmark), some major cities housed their exchanges in buildings of regal design—like Ralph Walker's 1932 art deco AT&T Long Distance Building in New York—which celebrated the impressive machinery and technological wizardry inside, as well as the feats of structural and electrical engineering necessary to accommodate such a complex and weighty assemblage of equipment (Walker also designed Western Union's headquarters at 60 Hudson Street).[80] Yet their interior working environments were typically stark and cacophonous, as writer and technologist Paul Ford explains:

> [You] picked up the phone and the suddenly broken circuit animated some light in an unseen switching station; soon would come an operator, a real woman . . . would say: "Number please?" Or something along those lines. . . . On the other end of that wire was a relay—a large heavy ozone-smelling device that heard the clicks. Or rather it didn't hear as much as register modulating electric pulses. These are beautiful, abstract, incredibly dumb devices that clack. Anything that they could do a matchbox-sized computer can do today.[81]

The arrival of automatic exchanges in the early 1900s (and their gradual phasing-in over the following decades) dramatically decreased the need

Opposite page:

FIGURE 13A. Sectional view of a telephone building, ca. 1900, from *The Wonder Book of Knowledge* (1921) by Henry Chase Hill. Public domain.

FIGURE 13B. Night rendering of 33 Thomas Street, New York, by Marc Feldman, from "Designed for Machines but Mindful of People," *Architectural Record* 146 (1969). Courtesy of John Carl Warnecke Archives.

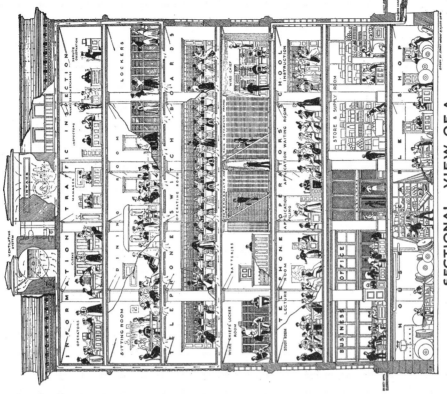

SECTIONAL VIEW OF A
TELEPHONE BUILDING

A Typical American Central Office Building, Showing the Efficient Arrangement of the Various Departments

for human laborers (just as pneumatic tubes were championed as a means to decrease the reliance on noisy, unreliable messenger boys), which meant that the offices became primarily "post-human" workspaces. Operators "were replaced by vast [electronic switching system] banks and the much smaller contingent of technically skilled, largely male workers who designed, programmed, manufactured, installed, and maintained them."[82] These were, for the most part, Kittlerian and Ernst-ian signal-processing machines writ large, despite the humanist grandeur of many such buildings' facades. Like the radio buildings that came after them, these stations constituted architecture for machines. And unlike many other equipment-heavy facilities like factories, which were moved to outlying areas of the city, utilitarian telecommunications architecture was purposefully sited downtown because its central location allowed for interconnection among the facilities, and facilitated speedy service to its business customers.

AT&T opened its Long Lines Building at 33 Thomas Street in 1974. It was so densely packed with machinery that some of its twenty-nine floors could accommodate only five or ten human bodies. And it, like the facilities at 811 Tenth Avenue and 375 Pearl Street before it, was windowless. As new switching technology emerged, the exchanges' internal architecture evolved; with the increased use of vertical channels of cables, the decreased presence of human beings, and concern about equipment's sensitivity to heat and dust, windows went by the wayside. Many urban areas feature similar windowless monoliths among their corporate and residential skyscrapers, and perhaps they, like 33 Thomas, also alter their surrounding soundscapes. Here, the building seems to create an acoustic vacuum in the bleak plaza outside. That eerie calm hints at another of the building's purported functions: fallout prevention. These windowless facilities were often promoted as bunkers protecting the nation's telecommunications networks from nuclear attack. And through their visual, sonic, and palpable prominence, they materially communicated a sense of security and preparedness.

In more quotidian contexts, those wires were to serve as an invisible source of convenience. Hidden behind walls, they were to afford each housewife, each hotel guest, each executive and office worker a line to the outside world. "The desirability of planning in advance for telephones in residences is generally recognized by architects, engineers, and builders," the Bell Telephone Company noted in *Planning for Home Telephone Conveniences*, a 1928 guide it created for its regional subsidiaries to distribute to residential builders.[83] The company was not aiming to sell their services, they claimed, but to help the building trades corral wires and apparatae so that "telephone arrangements may be readily provided commensurate with other household conveniences." Meanwhile, the General Post Office in London published a guide for architects, surveyors, and engineers to promote the inclusion of cable "runs" in buildings that would allow for easy access by maintenance workers.[84] And perhaps the most humble telephone architecture of them all—the phone booth—emerged from the payphone, which, as legend has it, was born in Hartford, Connecticut, in 1889. The first patent for a booth, however, was issued in the United States in 1883, but it didn't arrive on city streets until 1903, in London—or in 1881, in Berlin, or somewhere else at some other time. The tiny booth is stuffed with countless disparate genealogies.[85]

Centripetal and Centrifugal Circuits: Telecommunications' Urban Forms

Booths and other nodes in the telephonic network all linked up to the central exchange. Wires converged upon and diverged from these buildings— either above or below ground—from all across the city. The evolution of these telecommunications networks is a much larger subject than we can examine here; what's most relevant for our purposes is how those developing networks interacted with the material space of the city. The first telegraph lines followed existing railway lines in connecting urban business centers, and they were critical to the development, invigoration, and normalization of financial markets.[86] But their network structure didn't prioritize links *within* the cities themselves. Businesses and residents thus relied on huge teams of telegraph messenger boys, who undoubtedly completed their rounds with a clamor, to deliver intra-city messages. As businesses expanded (aided by the simultaneous expansion of other media infrastructures, including the typewriters and filing systems required for records management), they were often squeezed out of their downtown headquarters, forcing them to distribute their administrative, production, sales, and warehousing operations across different facilities. These newly distributed companies created private telegraph lines to allow for communication among their various units.

While it can't be proven that the telegraph *effected* this separation of offices and factories, Tarr, Finholt, and Goodman acknowledge that the technology "theoretically allowed for" and "demonstrated the feasibility of" such distribution. The company office could remain downtown, in what would become the city's central business district, in proximity to other businesses, its suppliers, and customers, while the factories could move to cheaper plots of land on the urban fringe.[87] With the emergence of a reliable printing telegraph in 1867, which eliminated the need for trained operators (and which also changed the soundscape of the telegraph office by replacing "sounder" machines, and the humans who transcribed their messages, with printing versions), those private telegraph lines expanded. Some even linked to the central offices of companies like Western Union, which allowed for long-distance communication. Those firms that couldn't afford private lines likely concentrated downtown, near the central telegraph office. All these connections allowed for the swift flow of financial information throughout the city and between urban areas. By the latter half of the nineteenth century, the telegraph had begun to knit individual cities together via an internal communication network, which included telegraph-based (or, more likely, combined telegraph-and-telephone-based) fire and police alarm systems. These public services eventually evolved into more professional and bureaucratic organizations, which proved responsive to a systematic, centralized communications network.

Telephone networks also began as small local systems that were then interconnected and expanded into citywide, and then nationwide, networks granting "universal" coverage.[88] Individual phones connected to exchanges at the company office, which in turn linked to a central switching station downtown. Unlike the telegraph, most telephone service until the 1890s was distinctly *intra*-urban, largely because signal attenuation problems made long-distance calling infeasible. For its first fifty years, Stephen Graham and Simon Marvin argue, the telephone "facilitated the development of centralized cities with specialist functions located in urban downtowns"; while there was evidence that the telephone also allowed for dispersion, its force was primarily centripetal.[89] The shapes those networks took depended on a variety of factors, including, for instance, the business decisions of the monopolies that owned the lines, the autonomy of local and regional providers, those monopolies' capacity to convince customers that they were part of a nationally unifying network, the degree of engagement of local municipalities in shaping their own networks, and their ability to negotiate with competing service providers.[90]

Plenty of urban historians and historians of technology tell conflicting tales about the telephone's centripetal and/or centrifugal influences on urbanization. As we've heard before in regard to the telegraph, the telephone, too, supposedly allowed businesses to concentrate their offices downtown, while relocating their factories, warehouses, and shipping facilities outside the city.[91] Phones also freed city residents to move out to the end of the streetcar lines with reassurance that the news and activity of the city was only a phone call away. Some claim that telephones incited significant growth in suburban residential construction.[92] These newly networked neighbors then needed an index to find one another, which engendered a new print form: the phone book, a successor to the old city directories that listed local businesses, residents, and their addresses.[93] The phone book, Ford says, effectively "described a town . . . . Progress was a phone book released every year, a cycle of civic rebirth."[94] The phone also purportedly contributed to the development of the skyscraper; without phones for inter-floor communication, the theory goes, we would've needed countless bays of elevators to shuttle messenger boys delivering paperwork by foot.

Sociologist Claude Fischer argues that there's insufficient evidence to support most of these claims.[95] Still, we can say with confidence that architects and urban and regional planners were conscious of the telephone's—and other communication and transportation technologies'—impact on their work. As we saw earlier, Le Corbusier's and Frank Lloyd Wright's urban visions were shaped by these technologies. Architectural historian Carlotta Daro argues that the "professional practice of telecommunications engineering was absorbed by modernist architects and urban planners and synthesized as a new kind of technological vision of both town and country." Lewis Mumford represented one such group of planners: the Regional Planning Association of America (RPAA). In 1937, he wrote in *Architectural Record*: "The area of potential urban settlement has been vastly increased by the motor car and the airplane; but, the necessity for solid contiguous growth, for the purposes of intercourse, has in turn been lessened by the telephone and the radio."[96] These new, liberating technologies—what he called *neotechnics*—have afforded planners an opportunity to consider alternatives to increasing urban concentration. Mumford, and the RPAA of which he was a cofounder and spokesperson, advocated instead for *planned* decentralization.

Los Angeles is regarded as one model—albeit, according to some critics, a dystopian one—of planned decentralization. The city has long been emblematic of a new form of post-Fordist urbanism, sprawl, ostensibly effected by car-centric urban planning. The so-called Los Angeles school of urbanism, fronted by Edward Soja and Mike Davis in the 1980s and '90s, took an "outside-in" look at L.A. urbanism, examining how peripheral units shaped the urban core. Yet urban studies scholars' traditional focus on the exceptionalism, prescience, or paradigm-breaking radicalism of Los Angeles—and cinema and media studies' overwhelming focus on L.A. as a *cinematic* city, in particular—has eclipsed Los Angeles's relationship with other, older communication technologies, many of which have shaped the city's form and laid the groundwork for future "automotive," "cinematic" and "networked" layers of urbanity. Architectural historian Emily Bills extends the L.A. school's work by demonstrating how the establishment of Los Angeles's telephone networks in the late 1800s "wired" the city's future development and gave rise to spatial qualities that are commonly attributed to later developments. She argues that the telephone "should be recognized as the first form of infrastructure to efficiently and effectively bind the greater Los Angeles area into a comprehensive, multinucleated whole."[97]

L.A. incorporated its first phone company, Los Angeles Telephone, in 1881, and by 1895 the company was experiencing greater phone use per capita than in any other domestic or international city. Long before the city had paved streets and trolleys, Bills writes, "telephone poles and wires marked the area as the heart of a modernizing city."[98] Those phone connections enabled companies like Union Oil to keep their business offices downtown, and their production facilities in the outskirts. The city relied on production in those outlying areas, which in turn relied on the downtown for financial services, cultural activity, and connections to communication networks. Sunset Telephone had organized a hub-and-spoke model network that connected L.A.'s outlying agricultural areas to the downtown, but didn't connect them to each other. Yet these farming communities and growers' associations needed to share information with one another about weather, harvests, freight transportation, and other agricultural and business concerns, so they created their own phone lines. Communities grew around them. L.A.'s signature sprawl, we see, is attributable not only to its car-centric planning, as the well-rehearsed stories have told us, but also to its farm-grown phone networks. "Multifarious intraregional telephone routes," which connected communities like Pomona and Toluca but didn't necessarily connect to downtown L.A., emerged, establishing a pattern for the multinucleated development of Los Angeles itself.

Merlyna Lim tells a parallel tale about Bandung, the capital of West Java in Indonesia: While the telegraph was first installed downtown, the city's first phone company originated in 1895 in the rural *kabupaten*, or regency districts, at the plantation of KAR Bosscha, and it served 157 subscribers, mostly from other plantations. This pattern of development, Lim argues, "had implications [for] how the physical structure of the city was developed." Rather than making it possible for the plantation landlords to conduct business with downtown clients without leaving the plantation, Lim says, the phone increased these businessmen's contacts and thus increased the frequency of their travel to the city center, where a network of restaurants and hotels existed to accommodate them.[99] The fact that Bandung then emerged as a high-tech center is attributable in part to its early installation of telegraph, telephone, and radio networks. Lim, like many scholars before her, finds that telecommunications—not only old-school telegraphy and telephony, but also new digital technologies—have had both centralizing and decentralizing, centripetal and centrifugal impacts. "The city and telecommunications interact in many ways: reinforcing the centrality of the city, facilitating the decentralization of some particular activities, shifting some physical flows into electronic flows, and mediating access to physical space, thus removing the barriers to further urban growth."[100] Here again, amidst the recurrence of particular urban development topoi, we see urban forms and media infrastructures evolving at different paces, in accordance with distinctive contextual variables. There have been, and continue to be, multiple ways to wire the wired city. And that city persists, in varying degrees of wired-ness, even in this wireless age.

Rewiring and Recalibrating: Copper Wire to Fiber Optics

Many of our early telecommunications entrepreneurs had aspirations of transgressing time and space, of collapsing geographic distances and effecting new patterns of living. Silicon Valley's pioneers are of like mind. But in recent years, as we noted at the beginning of this chapter, many of the world's most plugged-in consumers have come to recognize that their supposedly placeless, ubiquitous, immaterial, instantaneous, always-on digital networks *do* have a fixed geography—one that's both centralized *and* distributed, and impacted by their place within a material urban landscape. Urban density and finite bandwidth, flooded data centers and solar flares are among the myriad factors that impact our Internet traffic and cell connections. Precedent infrastructures also inform how these digital networks take shape. As technicians swapped out copper wires for fiber optics, they tended to follow the pathways carved out by the old conduits: they stuffed new cables into existing water and gas ducts or old pneumatic tubes, and exploited existing right-of-way easements along railways and roads. As architectural historian Kazys Varnelis explains, "new infrastructures do not so much supersede old ones as ride on top of them, forming physical and organizational palimpsests—telephone lines follow railway lines, and over time these pathways have not been diffused, but rather etched more deeply into the urban landscape."[101] Such "path-dependent" evolution tends to reinforce familiar urban development patterns. Varnelis describes fiber optics' development in terms that should by now be familiar to us:

> The historical role that telecommunications has played in shaping the American city demonstrates that, although new technologies have made possible the increasing sprawl of the city since the late nineteenth century, they have also concentrated urban density. Today, low- and medium-bandwidth connections allow employees to live and work far from their offices and for offices to disperse into cheaper land on the periphery. At the same time, however, telecommunications technology and strategic resources continue to concentrate in urban cores that increasingly take the form of megacities, which act as command points in the world economy.[102]

While cities retain their "command point" status, many of their "minor" telecommunications architectures are changing to reflect new patterns of use, new network architectures, new political economies. For example, given the saturation of cell phones in many parts of the world, there's not much use for phone booths anymore.[103] In many cities those familiar media-architectures are either grossly and tragically neglected, in line for replacement or removal, or already gone. In New York a company called Intersection—which formed when Alphabet's (née Google) Sidewalk Labs acquired Control Group, a technology and design company, and Titan, an outdoor advertising company—began working in 2016 to transform the city's eight thousand–plus payphones into "Links," ad-supported pylons offering super-fast WiFi, free calls, and charging stations. As the *New Yorker*'s Ian Frazier described them:

> The Link stands nine feet six inches tall—a little higher than the average "Don't Walk" sign. It is made mostly of shiny, extra-tough

aluminum, has the shape of a hockey-stick blade, and gleams like a futuristic monolith that primitive humans might worship in a movie. Perpendicular to passing traffic, its sides will light up with advertisements, about four feet high by three feet wide, that change every fifteen seconds.[104]

The Link is the minimalist-monolithic telecom architecture of a new age, an age in which the future of the wired-and-wireless city belongs not to Western Union, Bell Telephone, or AT&T, but to Alphabet.[105] This post-telecom conglomerate already has a significant footprint in myriad cities around the world, where its extensive office spaces are often prominently and proudly branded, much like the early telephone buildings. But its wider presence, in the form of data centers, isn't meant to be conspicuous. Rivers of wires enter these centers through their "cable vaults," and zetta-bytes of data flow in and out, yet rather than serving as public-facing civic hubs, these facilities adopt a form of conspicuously self-effacing, anti-monumental monumentality. As Varnelis explains, "The space of global technological flows does not desire to become visual or apparent: perhaps only some spray-paint or a flag in the ground marks the presence of fiber below, and sometimes even that is elusive."[106]

While the machinery of old-school telecommunications has evolved, its terrestrial mark on the urban landscape has diminished. No longer needing legions of electromechanical switches and operators, the phone companies' architectural footprint has shrunk dramatically, and, aside from a few pockets of persistence (in India, for instance), the presence of the telegraph has all but completely faded from city streets across the globe. Lots of grand old art deco telephone buildings—as well as abandoned malls and printing plants and other outmoded facilities with heavy load-bearing capacity—have been transformed into data centers and luxury condominiums, reflecting the ascendance of a new (but perhaps not so different) regime.[107] Sixty Hudson Street, the former Western Union headquarters, and 32 Avenue of the Americas, the former AT&T Long Distance Building, now house data centers, and the former Long Lines building at 33 Thomas reportedly houses data facilities for Verizon and a surveillance hub for the National Security Administration.[108] As architecture scholar Addison Godel notes, "Many of the features of a hardened telephone exchange—space, connections, structural capacity, and the impression of security—are attractive to entities handling vast quantities of Internet traffic."[109] The facilities' proximity and interconnection is also a boon. The Telx company owns collocation space at 60 Hudson, 32 Avenue of the Americas, and 111 Eighth Avenue (owned by Google), all of which are interconnected; this "Telx Trifecta" allows for "low latency and superior redundancy."[110] What's more, these fiber-optic companies that are repurposing architectures of the copper-wire age probably take some pride in their opulent art deco lobbies, lovingly restored, with murals reflecting early telecom's hubristic aspirations to conquer time and space. Those rhetorical topoi continue to resonate (although Silicon Valley's "social entrepreneurs" might replace latter-day allusions to "conquering space" with new promises to "save the world").

Despite its widespread diminishment, telephony still stakes some claim on urban space. Architects are still designing and building call centers, including MVRDV's Teletech center in Dijon, France; and Estudio Lamela's Banco Santander call center in Querétaro, Mexico. Skidmore, Owings & Merrill's lightly-fenestrated, blast-resistant Public Safety Answering Center II in the Bronx—a highly visible manifestation of New York's commitment to upgrading its emergency services after 9/11—is a 2015 take on the telecom-infrastructure-as-bunker approach adopted at 33 Thomas. Yet telecom "regime change" has a different face in other parts of the world. Myanmar, for instance, has witnessed the waning of its roadside phone rental shops and, with them, the typewriter clerks who sat outside courthouses and government offices, waiting to take transcription (also disappearing: the men who manually carved rubber stamps).[111] The echoes of telephony dissipate at different speeds, and in different patterns, in different urban landscapes.

Meanwhile, we've witnessed the continual rebirth of one of telephony's most elemental, and iconic, architectures: the telephone pole. The old-school pole was "like a tree undone," Lisa Gitelman says: "chopped down, shorn of bark and branches, dipped in creosote, and transplanted to a city block, where an occasional street tree grows in counterpoint."[112] When the utility pole was then made to support cell phone antennae, it had an opportunity to reclaim its shorn branches, to become a "tree re-done"—an antenna tree. These cell towers disguised as trees (which, by the way, fool no one) "have been designed to soften the severity of the steel tower with botanical plastics."[113] Their function is both aesthetic and political: making the infrastructure more aesthetically palatable in an attempt to circumvent NIMBYism. And now even *living* trees—those neither chopped down nor shorn—can self-actualize as full-body arboreal

FIGURE 14. Cell phone tower disguised as palm tree, 2009, Dubai. Photograph by Peter Dowley / CC-BY-2.0.

antennae, thanks to the development of spray-on nanocapacitors that can transform pretty much any surface into an antenna.[114]

Vectors to Cells: New Communications Topologies

While the idea of an aerosol connection might lead us to believe that contemporary network architectures are like a Sloterdijkian "foam," our cell phones actually rely, as their name implies, on cells—a honeycomb-shaped, airborne network that we attempt to impose on uneven urban topographies.[115] Architect Michael Chen, who, in 2011, led one of my classes on a walking tour of New York's phone infrastructure, explains how the cell network works:

> At the most fundamental level, a mobile phone is a two-way radio. The phone contains an antenna that communicates with a mobile base station nearby. A base station generally includes a series or array of antennas that receive and transmit signals, and a computer that coordinates the communication and interfaces with the cabled phone system. The structure of mobile networks is generally comprised of sectors or cells, defined as the overlapping region of three base stations. At its simplest, a cellular network can be imagined as a continuously tiled set of hexagonal cells, with base stations located at every other vertex. An individual user making or receiving a call communicates with a nearby base station. As that user moves out of range, the signal is shared between other base stations within range until the most optimum base station is identified and the call is handed over.[116]

Just as with early radio broadcast, the city itself presents physical obstructions, and its volume of users can overtax the network. Network architects have to negotiate between the idealized "cell" architecture, the not-so-geometrically-uniform urban terrain, and the potentially variable user demand in order to calibrate their installations—to determine where to place base stations, and how many to put there. In an urban environment defined by extreme verticality, the coverage area is three-dimensional, so the installations have to be tuned for specific strata—mostly mid-rise building rooftops and dedicated towers—and in accordance with the interior square footage of buildings within each antenna's broadcast radius. The high building volume and user volume in many dense urban centers thus requires an extraordinarily high number of base stations.

This material network is continually evolving. Because each base station can serve only a limited number of users, phone providers, to keep up with growing demand, catalyze fission (they "sectorize" the terrain into smaller cells) and add more and more antennae. Those accumulating antennae are increasingly moving into new environments, including indoors (where they often raise questions regarding their potential health effects). Their base stations can employ spatial algorithms and probabilistic modeling to determine their optimal placement, interpret interference, and anticipate their transmission quality in particular contexts. But given the complexity of variables affecting their performance, their position and specific calibration also rely on on-site experimentation—real-time interaction between the electromagnetic spectrum and the material landscape and its inhabitants. That material landscape now also includes billions of "things"—street sensors, trash cans, "smart" building systems, Fitbits—that also use cellular technology (low-band radio) to link together the Internet (or, in Chicago, the "Array") of Things. And here, again, poles—for traffic lights and utilities—have become integral, and sometimes highly contested, supports for all the fiber-optic cables and transmission boxes necessary for the IoT.[117]

This amalgam of equipment, architecture, vectors and volumes, electromagnetic waves, user location and behavior, and technicians' intelligence and labor is what ultimately comes together to constitute "signal space." Chen claims that signal space constitutes a "fundamentally new form of space"—one representing a break from centralization and consolidation, from a "model of broadcast involving a single elevated point, blanketing the city with transmission," as we see atop One World Trade Center. Signal space operates instead on "multiple, simultaneous strata."[118] Some designers and think tanks (many with commercial interests in promoting particular approaches to urban development) think this new spatial ontology has the potential to revolutionize urban planning, to allow designers and officials to track populations via their cell data, and to build urban spaces and systems that respond to, and perhaps even redirect, those flows. Daniel Doctoroff of Alphabet's Sidewalk Labs, the urban think-tank, is a strong proponent of "performance-based" zoning: using sensors and cell phones (and Alphabet's own Link kiosks and traffic management platforms) to automatically monitor residents' behaviors; they can do as they please in their homes and businesses, so long as they don't exceed certain thresholds for noise, toxic emissions, and so forth.[119] Passive regulation via "signal space" thus, ostensibly, allows for more flexible use of the

Hello?

What is the mobile phone infrastructure and where do we find it? The mobile phone infrastructure is at once public and secret. Despite being hidden in plain sight on the rooftops and sides of buildings, there are no publicly available maps of all of the mobile phone base stations in New York City. The Federal Communications Commission and the Federal Aviation Administration publish information about antenna registrations, and the New York City Department of Buildings maintains a current record of building permits associated with mobile phone antennas.

Here the antenna data has been isolated and located in three dimensions, creating a comprehensive view of the cloud of antennas that service all five boroughs of the city. It's a cloud that has been calibrated to the shape of the city and the distribution of its population.

ANTENNA HEIGHT   24'   1220'

BUILDING AGE   1890   2011

ANTENNA COUNT   4   1

physical spaces it knits together. Ethereal activity drives the redeployment of ore, or more fixed infrastructures.

Yet such sensoring and signaling methods can also easily be applied in targeted advertising, or in surveillance and profiling. As we've seen on many occasions in previous eras of our electromagnetically mediated cities, every decentralizing force seems to be joined by a corresponding centralizing tendency. While "signal space" might enable greater flexibility of human motion, it also facilitates a greater centralization of information regarding users' data use and whereabouts, and potentially the ability to predict their trajectories and behaviors. These moving bodies can flow through the city streets with "seamless" coverage, never suffering a lost connection, because of a byzantine array of hard-wired antennae bolted to rooftops and facades, knit together with millions of seams, beaming imperceptible, but still very much material, waves at all that inhabits the streets below. As sociologist Adrian Mackenzie reminds us, "the notion of wireless networks implies that there are fewer wires, [but] it could easily be argued that actually there are more wires"—billions of chipsets, billions of cables stuffed behind walls and snaking down building facades.[120] What urban planners or technicians see as "signal space" is then experienced phenomenologically by urban inhabitants, who might not be privy to the existence of the tangle of behind-the-scenes wires (or where they lead, or who's intercepting them), as a "protocological surround."[121] This surround is defined by various levels of intersecting protocols that direct our connections, facilitate or close off access, and thus subtly shape the geographies—both informational and physical—we are then able to explore. In short, our seeming unfetteredness is actually quite fettered—by fixed, seam-full infrastructures and complex protocols.

Amidst such indecipherable, proprietary, and even exploitative co-optations of the electromagnetic spectrum, we find some communities staking a claim to their own frequencies. Steve Goodman, musician, DJ, and music producer, has written about the many scales at which sonic resistance, or even "sonic warfare," can be executed. While police might use technologies like the LRAD Sound Cannon in crowd control, disenfranchised populations might adopt their own acoustic strategies to resist, and perhaps create new forms of social interaction, particularly within public

Opposite page:

FIGURE 15. Map of antenna data in New York City. Courtesy Michael K Chen Architecture.

FIGURE 16. DJs at the Notting Hill Carnival, 1979, London. Photograph by Adrian Boot.

spaces. He asks: "What vibrations are emitted when slum, ghetto, shanty-town, favela, project, and housing estate rub up against hypercapital? And what kind of harbinger of urban affect do such cultures constitute within contemporary global capitalism?"[122] He uses the example of Jamaican sound systems, with their "intense vibrational environments," that effect "sonic dominance"—a condition in which sound is both "physical and for-mal, feeling and hearing, content and form, substance and code, particle and pattern, embodying and disembodying, tactile and sonic"—in order to "attract and congeal populations."[123] An architecture of waves: Bucky Fuller revisited.

Many cities have also noted a resurgence of low-powered radio amidst the increasing conglomeration and syndication of commercial radio sta-tions, and despite the relative ease of broadcasting online.[124] Of course people have been "unlawfully" broadcasting since they were capable of marshaling the airwaves, and "pirate" and "free" radio were particularly prevalent in the 1960s—but evolving legislative and political-economic contexts have changed the nature of current "narrow-casting" activity. In 2000 the U.S. Federal Communication Commission began issuing

low-power licenses for noncommercial stations, after years of antago-
nizing these broadcasters. The U.K.'s Office of Communications (Ofcom)
regulatory authority started issuing community radio licenses in 2005,
and in 2011 the U.S. federal government passed the Local Community
Radio Act, opening the door to still more small stations. Predictably, tech
start-ups have gotten in on the game: RootIO offers a solar panel, battery,
15-meter-tall transmitter tower, and Android app that allow users to set
up "micropower" stations from their smartphones.[125] The project, which
has been unfolding throughout Uganda, is intended to allow broadcasters
to share community-specific information and discussion among a hyper-
local audience, many of whom are illiterate and thus especially dependent
upon aural media.

   Although some of these once-illegal activities have won official sanc-
tion, there are still actual pirates out there—both on the high seas and on
city rooftops, engaging in what Goodman calls a "rhymachinic takeover
of space-time."[126] They, unlike their authorized low-powered compatriots,
present a threat, according to officials, because they interfere with vital

FIGURE 17A. Still image of rooftop pirate
radio transmitters in London, from
Palladium Boots Presents: Uneven Terrain,
"Exploration #6."

FIGURE 17B. Red Sands offshore forts in the
Thames Estuary, 2008, formerly occupied by
pirate radio stations throughout the 1960s.
Photograph by diamond geezer / CC-BY-NC-
ND-2.0.

communications and compromise emergency services. London officials seized over four hundred pirate radio setups between 2013 and 2015.[127] Tenacious broadcasters are often motivated by their commitment to specific material practices of production, particular material urban spaces, and particular marginalized urban communities. When they climb to the rooftop and put up the aerial, they're signaling to the neighbors that it's time to tune in. Last Moyo describes how pirate radio stations in Zimbabwe have embedded in their local ward communities, enabling community members to hear their own voices on the air and occasionally contribute to the station's operation.[128] The simple love of music—particularly home-grown music—is an equally powerful motivator. Pirate DJ/MC's play "thousands of songs that will never be heard anywhere else," rhapsodizes the *Guardian*'s Sam Wolfson; through this "musical alchemy, . . . whole genres are created in a few hours on air. To shut them down seems perverse, but it is also what keeps pirates alive—without the cat-and-mouse chase with the police, these stations can lose their urgency."[129] On the other hand, in places like Mosul the urgency is life and death, and pirate radio itself helps keep threatened populations alive.

The continual suppression and rebirth of pirate radio demonstrates that this "old" medium still resonates in, and gives form to, contemporary urban landscapes. Media artist and scholar Matthew Fuller (this chapter is full of Fullers!) lists the material components of piracy's counter-signal space:

> Pirate radio: transmitter, microwave link, antennae, transmission and studio sites; records, record shops, studios, dub plates; turntables, mixers, amplifiers, headphones; microphones; mobile phones, SMS, voice; reception technologies, reception locations, DJ tapes; drugs; clubs, parties; flyers, stickers, posters. . . . As all the various elements organize in combination within the sound, across the city, through a jumble of available media, there is also a sense in which the polyphony traversing the signal echoes a wider sense of connective disjuncture as a crucial term of composition . . . . The media ecology is synthesized by the broke-up combination of parts.[130]

The urban residential tower block is another integral part of this combination: "The thicker the forest of towers, the more antennae perched above the city, the more the Radiant City, botched, radiates."[131] These are the artifacts and environments future archaeologists will have at their disposal to re-sound the marginal signals—to some ears, the "noise"—within today's urban soundscapes.

Pirate radio's apparatus is no algorithmically tuned multimillion-dollar antenna installation atop the highest building in the Western hemisphere. But even for these more home-grown installations, broadcasters still climb to the highest perch they can find and search for the most direct "line of sight" to potential listeners below—the same principle (another repeated topos) that's been behind so many historical telecommunications devices, from smoke signals and early "optical" telegraphs to microwave signals and contemporary hobbyist drone piloting. For pirate broadcasters, there are no open plans, open vistas, or "predictive algorithms" that aid in the calibration of their antennae. In the "botched" Radiant City—the city where so much of the world's population lives—pirate radio cities sound out the disjuncture, mismatch, time-slippage, grafting, and hacking that characterize urban survival. Their city might be "botched," "broke-up"—but still, it resounds. Wired or unwired, concentrated or dispersed, smooth or striated, the media city resounds, as it has for millennia.

2

Steel and Ink

THE PRINTED CITY

As I wait to cross busy Eastern Parkway in Brooklyn I learn about an upcoming community board meeting, a lost dog, a found dog, a guitar teacher seeking new students, and yet another new neighborhood yoga studio. The news reaches me not through my phone, which is back at home across the street, but through paper flyers typed up in Helvetica or Times New Roman, adorned with photos and clip art, printed out on an ink-jet printer in someone's home office, and affixed to a utility pole that wears, beneath its paper trimmings, an under-armor of tacks and staples from missives past.

Social reformer, journalist, and photographer Jacob Riis, in his 1890 classic *How the Other Half Lives,* noted that telegraph poles everywhere played an integral role in disseminating public intelligence. But in New York's Chinatown, he noted, it was the "wrong end" of those poles—that is, the poles themselves from street level to eye level—that served as the neighborhood's "real official organ." "Every day yellow and red notices are posted upon it by unseen hands, announcing that in such and such a cellar a fan tan game will be running that night, or warning the faithful that a raid is intended on this or that game."[1] While the "right end" of the pole held aloft the wires that transmitted electrical signals, connecting nodes into a widely distributed communication network (the subjects of our previous chapter), the "wrong end" supported paper notices tailored for a hyper-local community and tacked to weathered wood for casual encounters by passersby.

In some parts of the world, including in New York's Chinatown, most of those poles have since been eliminated and the wires buried, but elsewhere they continue to carry communities' electrical, telephone, cable television (and Internet) wires; their streetlamps; sometimes their solar panels and various accouterments of the "smart city," including gunshot

FIGURE 18. Stereograph of flyers attached to a telegraph pole, late nineteenth century, in Chinatown, New York. Photograph by Jacob Riis. Courtesy of the Museum of the City of New York.

detection sensors—in short, a whole host of entangled infrastructures.[2] But what strikes media scholar Lisa Gitelman are the physical and social infrastructures that rally around the pole's *other* end, including "all of the hardware at eye level, all of the rusty staples and leftover tacks" that once secured home-printed flyers and advertisements. Those staples, tacked to a creosote-coated pole, "publish to a neighborhood eye." Their printed notices "address a local more local than telephone area codes; they articulate a neighborhood at the scale dreamt by Jane Jacobs, say, rather than the one capitalized by either Craigslist or Groupon."[3]

Wood, steel, paper, ink: these materials compose the humble infrastructure for our home-grown, print-based systems of hyper-local urban communication—models of which we can see in cities around the world. The posting of printings in public space is certainly nothing new, nor is this particular assemblage of materials. Whether or not, as legend has it, Martin Luther nailed his Ninety-Five Theses to the wooden door of the Castle Church in Wittenberg, Germany, in 1517, thus inciting the Protestant Reformation, those wooden doors did commonly feature nailed-up public notices. Minute metallic instruments—from type to tacks—have long played a central role in producing and publishing, or publicizing, printed matter throughout the world's cities.

Archaeologists have also studied texts' material substrates and the tools used to make them. Paleographers, for instance, examine the forms, customs, and material instruments of ancient and historical handwriting. Codicologists focus on books as physical objects, especially those composed of manuscripts written on paper or parchment. Papyrologists study ancient literature and records written on papyrus, while other archaeologists study *pothi*, or loose-leaf texts written on palm leaves; these particular substrates are specific to particular geographic regions, which means that studies of such writings are also necessarily studies of place. Writing is the focus of our next chapter. But what do archaeologists have to say about print?

The printed world has been a subject of study in a wide array of disciplines—among them book, art, media, design, cultural, intellectual, economic, and religious history (and many other histories); bibliography; library and archival science; literary and language studies; sociology; and "area studies," where scholars focus on the print of specific geographic regions. Architectural and urban historians have also examined the place of print in the built world, print *about* the built world, and print's influence in *shaping* the built world. These folks typically rely on printed (or written) sources—published and archival materials—to do their work; after all, one might expect to find traces of print's history in, well, print. Yet many of these scholars also draw on material culture studies and the work of historical archaeology, whose practitioners study past societies that left behind both material remains *and* documentary records in other forms—printed, written, oral, architectural, and so on.[4] Examining the entwined histories of print and the city requires such a material mix of resources because, as we discussed in the introduction, media are the products of their urban environments and human creators and users; and media, in turn, script and shape those places and people. Looking only to printed sources to recount the "printed city's" history leaves out some important human and nonhuman actors—particularly those whose voices and lives weren't deemed "fit to print" (you might recall our discussion, from the introduction, about the inevitable incompleteness of the archive)—and offers only a partial story.

Consider one such story: Gutenberg's printing press, with its movable type, has been heralded as a catalyst of cultural and political revolution—

and, thanks to Luther, religious reformation—in Western Europe. Yet the first movable type was made not of metal in Germany in the mid-fifteenth century, as the prevailing story has it, but of wood and clay in Asia centuries earlier. The Chinese were using ceramic letterforms as early as the eleventh century CE; then, two or three centuries later, adopted bronze, copper, and tin type (China's history of woodblock printing spans over two millennia).[5] Korea followed a similar typographic trajectory. This mixture of typographic materials—wood, clay, and metal—is manifested in the production of the letterforms themselves, as sixteenth-century Korean scholar Sŏng Hyŏn explains:

> At first, one cuts letters in beech wood. One fills a trough level with fine sandy [clay] of the reed-growing seashore. Wood-cut letters are pressed into the sand, then the impressions become negative and form letters [molds]. At this step, placing one trough together with another, one pours the molten bronze down into an opening. The fluid flows in, filling these negative molds, one by one becoming type. Lastly, one scrapes and files off the irregularities, and piles them up to be arranged.[6]

Those metal letterforms, locked in a wooden chase and inked, produce a textual artifact that, as Marshall McLuhan, Elizabeth Eisenstein, Walter Ong, and other media theorists and historians have argued, is defined by its rigid structure, its sense of finality and completeness on the page, its "fixity."[7] Print historians like Adrian Johns have challenged this claim, citing piracy, plagiarism, printing errors (particularly with the use of woodcuts or copper plates), and the publication of multiple editions of a text—all sources of potential error and variation.[8]

What's more, structural "fixity," however mythical, isn't exclusively print's domain. Print's predecessor, the handwritten manuscript (which we'll examine more fully in our next chapter), had an architectonics of its own. Scribes and illustrators frequently inserted architectural references—columns, arches, vaults, tracery, and niches—in the margins of their medieval manuscripts, as a means to impart both structure and symbolism to the page.[9] In the New World, colonial documents also featured *frontispicios* and *portadas*—illustrations facing the title page and throughout the book—that resembled doorways, gates, or portals and represented an "entrance into knowledge."[10] These manuscripts were architectural-scriptural hybrids.

FIGURE 19. Engraved title page for *I qvattro libri dell'architettvra,* 1570, by Andrea Palladio. Via Houghton Library at Harvard University. Public domain.

While architecture made its appearance in the medieval illuminated manuscript, giving shape to the page, there were few visible letterforms in and on the medieval city itself (although, as we'll see in chapter 3, public writing was quite prominent in ancient cities). Armando Petrucci attributes this absence to the waning of literacy, and to an urban form that wasn't readily written upon or read from: "the intentional closing of spaces, the narrow, winding streets, the dizzying vertical perspectives of the city walls interrupted here and there by architraves and protuberances" simply didn't lend themselves to architectural inscription.[11] Then in the eleventh century, as Italy's population, its northern urban centers, and its commercial culture grew, public writing reemerged. At that time, and for subsequent centuries, much of this epigraphy took the bound manuscript as its model, mimicking the codex's leaves and layout, or employing bookwork-based Gothic script.

Over the next few centuries, shifting political regimes, increased trade and exploration, the rise of humanism and religious reform, and the spread of universities and print fomented a renaissance in Italy and, later, Northern Europe. As part of a broader rediscovery of Greco-Roman ideals and cultural forms, artists revived classical epigraphic scripts—with their adherence to geometric patterns and proportions—everywhere from the walls of public spaces to tombstones.[12] These epigraphs, too, often mimicked the form of a book cover or title page. And their classical scripts and layouts then began to exert mutual influence on the design of printed literature, in what Petrucci calls "the intentional blending of two graphic systems—the epigraphic and the textual."

We witness that blending not only on cities' inscribed walls and in their printed texts. As we'll see in the following pages, the evidence and influence of print has informed, and continues to inform, the way we imagine, design, construct, inhabit, administer, and navigate our cities. Since their early installation in the presses of Europe, those metal letterforms generated printed urban and architectural treatises and documents that transformed the way designers learned their craft and shaped the cities they created. Those cities became centers of print production, distribution, and consumption; they generated literary cultures and public spheres of readers and writers. And they provided alleyways and underground hideaways where those readers and writers could continue to read and write when their work, and its promise of intellectual freedom, threatened the ruling class. New print forms—maps, guidebooks, and publicly accessible architectural texts and pattern books—shaped the way people interacted with, and sought to influence the design of, their own cities. Later, newspapers both helped to render the modern city legible to its inhabitants, including particularly those (im)migrating from afar; and to shape the urban material landscape. In cities like New York and Chicago, newspaper publishers were among the most prominent and ambitious architectural clients of the late nineteenth and twentieth centuries.

Through their half-millennium of employment, those letterforms gradually filled cities around the world with printed texts. Those texts eventually found themselves stored in new steel-framed buildings and metal bookstacks, and read in train cars and trollies gliding atop steel rails. The administration of modern cities was particularly printing-intensive: urban governance necessitated the generation of mountains of printed forms and typewritten memos and punched cards, as well as the creation of homologous architectures—metal filing cabinets, municipal archives, and the "enormous file" of the skyscraper itself—to circulate and contain all those standardized printed artifacts. And while this age of data-driven governance and e-readers and "paperless offices" has seemingly diminished the presence and status of print, the printed page persists, even thrives in some places as a still-popular mass-circulated medium. Elsewhere, amid the decline of print's heavy infrastructures, including its massive iron-framed presses and delivery logistics, those tiny metal letterforms continue to incite and inspire niche urban print cultures. Meanwhile, in the world's cutting-edge design labs, architects and urban designers are experimenting with new technologies to "print" structures of steel and polymeric "stone."

All this is to say: the printed city is no mere metaphor. What's at stake here are nothing less than the shape and size of the urban public sphere and the state of public literacy; determinations of who's entitled to see their words and images typeset and printed, and where that work is published and disseminated; how urban public affairs are made public; how publics understand and navigate their cities; how a city's tools of administration shape its administrative practices; and how design tools shape urban form. In short, the city in print gives typographic form to urban perceptions, practices, and politics.

Cities in Printed Form: Typography and Topography

There are myriad literary and artistic references and methodological models that behold the city as a legible text, a system of signs, a spatial narrative.[13] In most cases, though, this "urban text" is regarded figuratively; the city is taken to be something we can decode or interpret. Yet there's more to the metaphor: the rise of the printed page and book trade had a formal, material impact on the shape of the city and its plazas, streets, and buildings. Some have imagined that impact to be revolutionary, even catastrophic. Claude Frollo famously proclaimed in Victor Hugo's *The Hunchback of Notre Dame,* "This will kill that. The book will kill the edifice." The arrival of the printing press, with its movable type of lead, tin, and antimony, struck fear in "the pulpit and the manuscript" because it represented "the future," a new intellectual and political regime: "intelligence sapping faith, opinion dethroning belief, the world shaking off Rome." Each generation has its own dominant mode of expression, Hugo noted, and the press incited a changing of the guard. The era of the "book of stone"—the cathedral, a structural medium that not only contained "The Word" in its pulpits and oratory but also codified the culture's core beliefs in its architectural form and ornamentation—was coming to an end. "The press will kill the church."[14]

Lewis Mumford read Frollo's prediction literally: "The real misdemeanor of the printing press was not that it took literary values away from architecture, but that it caused architecture to derive its values from literature."[15] New forms of Renaissance architectural literature, specifically the architectural treatise, compelled architecture to "live . . . by the book," and this rigid adherence to formal rules, Mumford claimed, depleted architecture's vitality, originality, and local variety. According to architectural historian Mario Carpo, Mumford's literalism reflects a historical reality: architecture in the age of printing, much like the epigraphy carved into its facades, did come to "live by the book," and it reflected the formal and intellectual qualities of those treatises in its built form.

In the Gothic period, which began around the twelfth century, before the spread of print and reliably reproduced images, architectural theory was disseminated primarily through speech and memory, Carpo says. The medieval guilds required that builders travel to see ancient monuments and canonical cultural sites (via the noble tradition of Grand Tours and antiquarian study), but their ability to record or relay their experience was limited by what they could describe ekphrastically or sketch out. Medieval architectural instruction thus emphasized general rules and abstract forms, in the Aristotelian sense; medieval builders' discourse "propitiated a normative architectural theory founded on geometric rules that were transmitted orally and kept secret by initiates."[16]

But starting in the sixteenth century, Carpo argues, "architectural treatises began to diffuse a new, media-savvy architectural theory that was consciously developed in response to the new means of communication": the printed book, with its "trustworthy, portable, and [relatively] inexpensive printed images of architecture," which obviated the need to see the depicted buildings *in situ* and allowed for the representation of architectural detail.[17] Hélène Lipstadt explains how this new media form shaped its content:

> Pictorial representation and forms of synthetic views were developed to illustrate cities, total buildings, spaces, and sites and to adapt them to the structure and "space of the book." For the reproduction of figurations, however, plans, sections, and elevations—each with their own order—had to be fitted to the logic of the page and the order of the book. . . . The typographic composition of the page and the placement of images, together with the different techniques required to print text and illustration, provided not only a *concrete* but also a *conceptual* framework into which architectural figurations had to be fitted as forms and as conceptions.[18]

That concrete framework readily lent itself to the promotion of the classical conceptual framework of the Roman architectural orders: Tuscan, Doric, Ionic, Corinthian, and Composite.[19] Sebastiano Serlio's *Five Books of Architecture* (published in installments between 1537 and 1551) highlighted the orders, offering a "catalog of graphic components that were standardized and repeatable" and subject to many of the same rules as a language: grammatical, syntactical, rhetorical.[20] Architects could replicate and reassemble those components. Publications like Serlio's, which both built upon and departed from the classical theories of Vitruvius, the ancient Roman architect and engineer, normalized architectural education: "For many architects, the Pantheon and the Colosseum were not places in Rome. They were places in books."[21] We might assume that this standardization of references led to a homogenization of architectural and urban form.

Yet architectural historian Michael J. Waters suggests that things weren't quite so rigid and derivative. Such a conception of Renaissance architecture—that of a practice based on the imitation of a limited number of permissible forms—is rooted in the fallacy of print's fixity.[22] He argues that the age of print also gave rise to forms *other* than the architectural

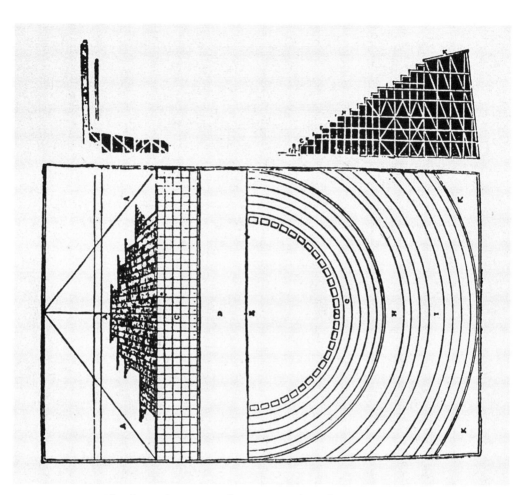

FIGURE 20. Plan for auditorium and stage, 1545, by Sebastiano Serlio. Public domain.

treatise and the ordered column. Serlio's work appeared in a century that saw the production of over three hundred multifarious architectural publications and at least two hundred single-sheet prints of architectural details. Typically derived from architects' sketchbook drawings, those single sheets were untethered from the codex. They "remained malleable"— available for copying, cutting, reorganizing, annotating, and pasting into printed books, albums, and scrapbooks. And consequently they "unleashed a plethora of varied models that defied systematization, traveled widely," and lent themselves to architectural reinvention.[23] They "became an active part of a fluid practice of transmediation in which drawings were made into prints, prints were remade into drawings, and both were translated into built architecture, possibly through another medium such as a model."[24] These acts of translation, transcription, and remixing cultivated more variety in design than Carpo acknowledges.

Perhaps early architectural publications didn't give rise to any particular rigidly proscribed built forms, but through their mechanically reproduced images, they did inform architectural discourse and practice, and thereby shaped the built environment. According to Mumford, the potency of these printed forms extended for centuries: "the last phase of the baroque," in the mid-eighteenth century, was "an age of paper patterns, paper plans, paper constitutions." This new order "sacrificed the craft autonomy of the workers to the vanity of the architect" and "the uses of life to the formalities of plan and elevation."[25] (We'll hear more in the next chapter about the standardization and formalization of design and building, particularly construction with brick and concrete.) The following century was then characterized by "crazy copybook simulacra," with "measurement and imitation tak[ing] the place of intelligent design."[26]

Those paper plans of the early nineteenth century sometimes depicted "paper cities" on the American frontier: hypothetical towns—like Cairo, Illinois, the projected "Metropolis of the West"—that were a product of not-so-measured speculative development. Even without any inhabitants or infrastructure, such cities-to-be

> articulated their urban status through an impressive array of paper documents, including the survey that subdivided the township into sections and subsections, the plat that laid out and even named its streets . . . , and the charter submitted to the state legislature, followed by freshly minted real-estate certificates and local bank notes, and the lithographs and prospectuses that promoted them.[27]

Those aspirational architectures often inspired the circulation of another kind of printed matter: money; these urban projections generated real investment and real hope, both ultimately rendered fruitless. Thomas L. Nichols tells of his arrival at Cairo, at the confluence of the Ohio and Mississippi Rivers:

> Whoever looks upon the map with a utilitarian eye sees at the confluence of these great rivers a favorable point for a great city. A few years since an English company took possession of or purchased this site, and, with a capital of nearly a million of pounds sterling, commenced

operations. They lithographed plans of the city and views of the public buildings. There were domes, spires, and cupolas, hotels, warehouses, and lines of steamboats along both rivers. How fair—how magnificent it all looked on the India paper! You should see the result as I saw it in the misty miasma, by the pale moonlight. Cairo is a swamp, overflowed by every rise of either river.[28]

While Cairo's reality may not have lived up to its "reading," the real French city of Paris was simultaneously "editing" itself into a legible urban form. Architectural historian and theorist Anthony Vidler, acknowledging the general "Enlightenment aspiration for the city to read like an open book," writes of mid-eighteenth-century urban reformers' desires to "render [their renewed] city legible to its citizens, as if it were a three-dimensional treatise in civic virtue written on the facades of its institutions."[29] Architects and planners envisioned monuments, buildings, and streets that denoted their "role, nature, and moral status."[30] The city and its component parts were to clearly communicate what they were "about"—much like a modern-day book cover.

By the late eighteenth century, ideas around one particular building type, the library, had coalesced into a materially—and morally—legible urban form. The metallurgical insight that over three hundred years earlier generated Gutenberg's type was now producing iron in mass quantities for use in constructing machines, bridges, and buildings.[31] Architect Henri Labrouste's Bibliothèque Sainte-Geneviève in Paris, completed in 1850, was among the first buildings to use cast and wrought iron from foundation to roof, and to incorporate a large reading room—one made all the more open, bright, and grand thanks to the building's iron structure. With its gas lighting and central heating, the library was unprecedentedly hospitable to the reading of books. But it was also designed to embody its own form of architectural legibility. As architectural historian Neil Levine explains,

Labrouste's own perspective rendering of the library . . . makes the building look as if it had just rolled off the presses. The continuous surface that wraps around the volume is rigidly compartmented. An overall grid of vertical and horizontal lines contains the composition like a "form" arranged and locked in a "chase." Within each bay thin vertical "rules" divide the surface into "columns" of print. These are enclosed in "boxes" by vertical "margins" and horizontal decora-

FIGURE 21. Reading room of the Bibliothèque Sainte-Geneviève, Paris, architect Henri Labrouste. Photograph by Marie-Lan Nguyen / CC-BY-2.0-FR.

tive "slugs." . . . Black iron dots in the spandrels make a line of punctuation above. . . . [A] series of 810 names of authors [is] inscribed in chronological order on the tables set in the arcade.[32]

The building itself is thus a book: the facade, with all its literary ornamentation, functions as a sort of library catalog; and the interior, with its work tables between parallel rows of books, functions as one big, inhabitable bookcase.[33] When I visited, I found myself reading the entire assemblage as a massive, immersive text, with the architecture functioning as a concordance to the collection, and my eyes, ears, and movement enacting the textual connections. Labrouste's later Bibliothèque nationale de France, completed in 1868, also in Paris, incorporated a four-story iron bookstack—regarded as the first of its kind—with skylights and grilled floors that allow natural light to penetrate to the lower levels. A glass wall separated the stacks from the reading room, granting patrons a glimpse of two technological and cultural marvels: the metallic marvel of engineering, illuminated to dramatic effect; and an astounding display of books, borne of the convergence of metal, ink, and paper.

Today, even in this age of Google and smartphones and computer-aided design, cities around the world are still constructing grand libraries—many of which prominently feature the printed book, and some of which even fetishize the stack.[34] And cities are still "published" by other means. Real-estate developers print aspirational images of prospective developments, modern-day "paper cities" with market-research-tested names, and plaster them on construction barriers, hinting at the utopic urban futures arising just behind the fence.[35] Architects and urban planners still use "plotters" to print large-format plans on paper, vellum, or Mylar; and with 3D printers, they're transforming their drawings into polymeric printed models—and even experimenting with printing full-scale building materials in steel and "sandstone." We could soon be literally printing our cities into existence. Such a development would be merely the next phase in a centuries-long history of "printed" cities: urban and architectural design shaped by the printed forms that inspired and educated their creators; future-cities projected in print; urban plans and building facades read as if they were printed texts; and urban structures made to house, circulate, and perhaps, as Labrouste sought to do, celebrate those growing stacks of books and digital files.

Urban Printing Centers: Sites of Textual Production

Modern cities haven't merely been shaped by print forms; they've also been the primary generators of printed material. Eminent book historian James Raven has documented how and why, up through the late-eighteenth century, printers, binders, stationers, and booksellers congregated in particular neighborhoods in London—St. Paul's Churchyard, Paternoster Row, and Little Britain, for instance—where they could share resources and enjoy access to nearby markets and other useful urban infrastructures.[36] Those publishers were the prime providers of print for the British provinces and colonies, and eventually a chief supplier for readers around the world. Historian John Hicks acknowledges that "book production and distribution were primarily urban activities," yet he focuses his attention on a more microcosmic case study: medieval Leicester, a growing town roughly a hundred miles from London.[37] Its Augustinian Abbey of St. Mary, which schooled some of the local boys, had a sizable library, and its scriptorium produced administrative documents and manuscript books, many of which were traded locally. Here we find "evidence of literacy, of education, of book ownership, and of the demand for books in connection with the governance of the town and religious affairs"—which explains why two stationer-booksellers set up shop in Leicester before 1600. The town's printers began to source paper from continental Europe, rather than using locally produced parchment, and trade of their printed copies of paper books reached rural populations, some of whom may have been drawn into town by its markets and seasonal fairs. Still, printers in smaller cities and towns like Leicester had to acquire many of their raw materials from, and ship their sellable wares to, London, which remained Britain's center of book production and the hub of its distribution network. Yet even London, removed from the continent and its print centers in France, Germany, and Northern Italy, was considered peripheral in the European book trade of the fifteenth and sixteenth centuries.

As Gutenberg's "trade secrets"—particularly the "ingredients" and process for casting metal type—spread from Germany throughout Europe, those cities that established vibrant print trades grew much more rapidly than those without, according to economist Jeremiah Dittmar. "The printer's workshop brought scholars, merchants, craftsmen, and mechanics together," and cultivated new economic activity and a diverse, dynamic urban culture that attracted migrants, promoted further gains in literacy, and gave rise to a new class of professionals that included merchants, lawyers, doctors, and teachers.[38] Dittmar focuses primarily on Europe, but we can identify similar economic and cultural patterns in other parts of the world. Tobie Meyer-Fong laments that, "in spite of the voluminous output of Asian publishers, past and present," East Asia represents "a mere footnote in most world histories of the book."[39] She surveys city-specific research on historical Ming dynasty Chinese publishing centers, including Jianyang, Yangzhou, and Nanjing. This regrettably marginal research (which does draw to a small degree on archaeological research on Asian antiquity) examines how "a place and its books are mutually productive"; how "publishers capitalized on their environment and its raw materials, whether natural or social"; and how publishing shaped cities' reputations, cultivated urban literate and literary cultures, and extended their communications and commercial networks.[40]

Similar economic and cultural growth was taking place around the book markets in the Middle East and South Asia; while this activity owed much to the book, it sometimes had little to do with print. In Lahore,

Pakistan, as in Leicester, a commercial publishing market arose alongside sacred space: starting in the second half of the seventeenth century, the Kashmiri Bazaar grew around the Wazir Khan Mosque, and among its merchants were publishers, bookbinders and booksellers, calligraphers, and shops selling paper and papier-mâchè decorations. Resident "qissa khawans," or storytellers, inscribed tales in calligraphic script on fine Lahori paper, often handmade by women in their homes. "It was a tradition that stretched across the Indian subcontinent and Central Asia," writes Majid Sheikh: "the mosque, the market square and the storytellers. Specialist editions of the classics were produced and the caravans purchased them to sell in the markets of Central Asia" and beyond.[41] Thus, while urban markets and cultures and regional trade were flourishing around the printing press throughout Europe, the handwritten manuscript on handmade paper engendered similar urban growth in some parts of Asia—and those manuscripts often eventually made their way to the libraries and museums of Europe. Once again, we see media following disparate evolutionary paths in different parts of the world, and we watch those paths converge when Pakistani manuscripts share storage space with European incunabula in a Parisian or Roman library.

Leipzig and Lyon, Boston and Beirut are among those cities that evolved, over the centuries, into printing centers. In South Korea, Seoul had traditionally been the hub of book publishing, but in the late 1980s a group of prominent publishers, led by Yi Ki-ung of the Youlhwadang publishing company, sketched out a plan to relocate the country's publishers and printers to Paju, a half-hour drive north of the city, in the marshes next to a highway near the Korean Demilitarized Zone.[42] A response to rapacious twentieth-century growth, blind technological progress, and Seoul's bigness and commercialism, Bookcity was conceived to preserve "the spiritual culture of Korea" and to bequeath "the value and importance of the Book to the next generation."[43] This was to be no generic industrial estate. Bookcity would be just that: a city—a World-Famous City of Books and Publishing dedicated to modernizing the industry; an Eco-Friendly Industrial City, modeling the integration of technology with nature; a Permanent Architectural Exhibition, showcasing innovative designs by leading architects (alongside traditional wooden architecture); and an Educational City, an experimental prototype for community-focused urban developments.[44]

"This is no different [than] if we were editing a huge and beautiful book called 'Bookcity' on a wide expanse of land," Yi said, referencing the long lineage of "legible" cities.[45] Similarly, landscape and urban designers Florian Beigel and Philip Christou, of the London-based firm Architecture Research Unit, claim to have "written the city into the river landscape like a text," creating a "landscape script" that takes its inspiration from historical Korean maps, as well as Paul Klee's painting *A Leaf from the Book of Cites*. This "paper city," or at least its first chapter, became real in 2007.

I visited in the summer of 2012, as Bookcity was in its second phase of development. I found that while many of the architectural gems—including buildings by Byung-yoon, Kim In-cheurl, Seung H-Sang, Stan Allen, and Alvaro Siza—shine independently, their radiance is due in large part to the way they're situated on the streets, with sufficient distance from their neighbors. While this atomization might be appropriate for the city as *architectural* exhibition, it weakens the *urban* coherence of Bookcity. Its urban format—an *ex*-urban city-in-box; a segregated, monofunctional industrial estate—also compromises its ability to serve its intended function: to generate creative collaboration and business efficiencies, and thereby provide what we might call a "nature preserve" for print. It's not enough simply to "script" this city into glass-and-steel existence, and to thereby program a vibrant literary culture.

Special economic zones like Paju constitute a "relatively dumb form of urban software," says architectural theorist Keller Easterling, using a postprint metaphor.[46] In this home of Samsung and super-high-speed Internet and "smart" urban developments like Songdo, in a country that prides itself on its digital prowess, it seems unlikely that a city could sustain itself by print alone. Yet Bookcity was always intended, from the very beginning, as an "integrated media city," with the book taking pride of place. Thus its phase two development involved the incorporation of film, animation, and software companies.[47] And as I noted in my 2013 article on Bookcity, its future chapters could unfold in myriad ways:

> It could develop into a hub for media research and education, for cross-industry collaboration, for experimental production driven more by the spirit of innovation than the pursuit of profit. It could be a bastion for the book, for the "rigor" of print, reflecting a dedication to Korea's publishing history and the continued value of printing, on paper, those books that demand material manifestation. It could turn out to be a model of sustainable urban development or an example of the wrongheadedness of the "enclave" model of industrial zone urbanization.[48]

One thing is for sure: as the printing industry evolves, as boutique book-sellers rise up to take on the great Amazon, and as niche publishers emerge amid the tech startups, the urban landscapes in which printed matter is made and traded and read will necessarily evolve in response.

New Urban Print Forms and Public Spheres

Just as typewritten scripts and JavaScript intermingle at Paju and other contemporary printing hubs, early printing centers accommodated various forms of urban script. Armando Petrucci noted the arrival, during the late Renaissance, of new types of display texts—shop signs, playbills, notices, advertisements—alongside the continued appearance of informal hand-written inscriptions on facades and walls.[49] In Rome, from the sixteenth century through today, even the statues of Pasquino, Madama Lucrezia, Il Babuino, and Abbott Luigi have sported poems, witticisms, or critiques; these famous "talking statues" have transformed the city's static ornamentation into an organ for public address. We see from these examples that, contra Hugo, print certainly didn't kill hand-inscription or other symbolic media like sculpture and architecture. And as we noted earlier, print even took formal and aesthetic cues from architecture, incorporating pedestals, columns, statues, and ancient ruins into its title pages and frontispieces.

Yet print, with its greater speed of production and its capacity for the reproduction of images, did have a qualitatively and quantitatively different impact on these cities, with their mixture of media, new and old. Print ultimately generated a flood of new publication forms for new reading publics. The more than 450 printers, publishers, and booksellers in sixteenth-century Venice created printed maps, atlases, and travel chronicles that made use of innovative techniques of geometry, surveying, and rendering perspective; as well as chronicles of ceremonial processions, costume books, portrait books, and a host of other fresh formats. Art historian Bronwen Wilson examines the "materiality of [these printed] objects themselves: what their format, scale, conventions, novelty, predictability, vocabularies, sources, texts, historicity, and order indicate about their function and how these encouraged new viewing practices."[50] These new modes of visual representation informed how cities portrayed themselves to their own citizens and to outsiders, like tourists and pilgrims. And the new modes of looking that these publications encouraged likewise informed how people explored, experienced, and understood their cities, and how they comported themselves and adopted appropriate urban subjectivities befitting their station of nobility, race, gender, or piousness.

EDITTO

Sopra le Scritture, e Libri manuscritti.

250

GIO: BATTISTA SPINOLA Prete Cardinale di S. Cesareo, della S. Romana Chiesa Camerlengo .

Remendo sommamente alla Paterna carità, e zelo di Nostro Signore, che si conseruino i libri manuscritti, & altre scritture tanto publiche, quanto priuate, e che non sia lecito agl'Artefici, & altre Persone di Roma comprare, e vendere respettiuamente simili scritture senza le douute licenze: Per tanto d'ordine espresso di Sua Santità datoci à bocca, e per autorità del nostro Officio di Camerlengo rinouando, confermando, & ampliando i Bandi altre volte da Nostri Antecessori, e da noi publicati, e particolarmente quello in data delli 30. Settembre 1704.

Di nouo dichiariamo, & ordiniamo, che nessuna persona di qualsiuoglia grado, conditione, sesso, e qualità, ardisca di vendere, e comprare sotto alcun pretesto qualsiuoglia sorte di libri scritti à mano tanto volgari, e latini, quanto Greci, Hebraici, e di qualunque altra lingua così in carta pecora, come in carta bambacina, tanto intieri, quanto diuisi, rotti, e sciolti, come pure Instromenti, Processi, Inuentarij, lettere, Bolle, Breui, diplomi, e qualunque altra sorte di carte, ouero pergamene manoscritte sotto che nome, ò titolo siano se non ne hauerà ottenuta particolar licenza in scritto da Monsignor Domenico Riuiera Prefetto dell'Archiuio Apostolico di Castel S. Angelo, ouero dal Sig. Canonico Giacomo Antonio de Pretis Custode dell'Archiuio Vaticano, quali la daranno gratis in nome nostro prima, che si stabilisca la vendita, ò almeno auanti, che si consegnino al Compratore le scritture, e libri sudetti sottopena à quelli, che contrauerranno tanto nel comprare, quanto nel vendere, senza licenza come sopra, di esser tenuti insolido alla rifezzione di tutti li danni, & interessi, che per occasione di tal compra, e vendita patiranno li Padroni delle scritture, ò altri, che in quelle habbino interesse, & in oltre di tre tratti di corda da darseli subito in publico, e di scudi duecento da applicarsi alla Reu. Camera Apostolica, de quali si promette, e si darà la metà à chi renelarà le compre, e vendite di simili libri, e scritture fatte senza licenza, & esso riuelante sarà tenuto segreto.

Per l'istesse raggioni ordiniamo, e commandiamo à tutti i Librari, Pizzicaroli, Battilori, Cartolari, Dipintori, Tamburrari, & altri Artegiani, che dentro il termine di otto giorni prossimi dopo la publicatione del presente Editto debbano auer notificato al sudetto Monsignor Riuiera Prefetto dell'Archiuio di Castel S. Angelo, ò vero al detto Signor Canonico de Pretis Custode dell'Archiuio segreto Vaticano quei libri, e scritture di sopra descritte, che si troueranno di hauere nelle loro Botteghe, ò altroue per vso, e seruitio delle loro arti, e che non ardischino, nè presumino sotto qualsiuoglia pretesto di sciogliere, diuidere, rompere, ò guastare detti libri, e scritture tanto ad effetto di venderle, ò valersene per legare altri libri, quanto per adoperarli ad vso delle loro Arti, senza licenza di detto Monsignor Riuiera Prefetto dell' Archiuio di Castel S. Angelo, ouero del detto Sig. Canonico de Pretis Custode dell'Archiuio Segreto Vaticano sotto le pene stabilite in detto secondo Capitolo da eseguirsi irremissibilmente contro li Trasgressori .

In tutti li casi di sopra espressi vogliamo, che s'intendano comprese anche le Persone Ecclesiastiche tanto Secolari quanto Regolari, & ogn'altra persona quantunque priuilegiata, e degna di special mentione, dichiarando, che contro li disubbedienti si procederà rigorosamente anche ex officio ad istanza del Fisco. Dato in Camera Apostolica questo dì 14. Maggio 1712.

G. B. Card. Spinola Camer.

Gaspar Turchi Comm. Gen.

Domenico Antonio Galosi Segr. e Cancelliere della R.C.A.

Die, Mens. & anno quibus supra supradictum Edictum affixum, & publicatum fuit ad Valuas Curiæ Innocentianæ, & in Acie Campi Floræ, ac in alijs locis solitis, & consuetis Vrbis, vt moris est per me Antonium Placentinum Apost. Cursorem.
Sebastianus Vasellus Mag. Curs.

IN ROMA, Nella Stamperia della Reu. Camera Apostolica 1712.

1712.
14. Maggio

FIGURE 22. Roman *bando* on scriptures and book manuscripts, 1712. Via Biblioteca Casanatense Scaffaldi Digitali. Public domain.

Rose Marie San Juan offers a similar characterization of early modern Rome, paying particular attention to how print—guidebooks; topical pamphlets; and *bandos,* or street posters—and its interplay with the city "proved a crucial site for reworking early modern subjectivities," organizing the movement of different groups, determining who had access to different parts of the city, and negotiating conflicts.[51] Some new print forms arose primarily to welcome tourists and religious pilgrims. Pope Sixtus V even commissioned his scribe, Luca Horfei, to create new epigraphs at key sites in the city, both to celebrate his grand urban reformations and to welcome the flocks of faithful pilgrims from across Europe. Those very same publications may have meanwhile constrained the movement of others, particularly women, merchants, and Jews.[52] Likewise, maps mediated their readers' perceived positions within their environment, as they conceived it at various scales. Wilson argues that new printed maps "condensed the world, making it legible and compact," while at the same time cultivating a sharpened awareness of borders and distinctions between "here and there, familiar and unfamiliar, city and landscape."[53] Of particular note is how these maps gave prominence to the city as a spatial unit: "Since borders between countries were subject to change in the sixteenth century, these were rarely demarcated in printed maps. Instead it was cities that provided a stable point of reference, to which the appearance of printed collections of city maps in the second half of the century attests."[54] Similarly, *Portrait of Modern Rome,* a guidebook first published in 1638, enabled its tourist-reader to "order the outer world," but only by making choices from Rome's "overwhelming range of possibilities" and developing an itinerary that produced a seemingly "coherent modern city."[55] Print's ordering of the city as its primary typographic unit helped readers then make sense of the world beyond.

These texts not only mediated access to the city and defined their readers' subjectivities within it; they also used the city as their "theatre." The posting of each *bando* in Rome was followed by a public reading of the order or notification printed on it, and the specific location of each poster was an integral part of its meaning. "Urban print" had to be read in context. And even though printing presses were scarce in the Spanish colonial New World, the printed page, imported from Europe, was "ever present." But it, like the *bando,* "was something that was to be read aloud, perhaps even to be copied . . . by hand."[56] Again, we see that "old" and "new" media forms—print, manuscript, the voice—intermingle, and that the sites in which these readings and transcriptions, and perhaps the ensuing discussion, took place mattered in how they made meaning (these

SECOND EDITION.

THE

LONDON GUIDE,

AND

STRANGER'S SAFEGUARD

AGAINST THE

Cheats, Swindlers, and Pickpockets

THAT ABOUND WITHIN

THE BILLS OF MORTALITY;

FORMING A

PICTURE OF LONDON,

AS REGARDS

ACTIVE LIFE.

COLLECTED FROM THE VERBAL COMMUNICATIONS OF

WILLIAM PERRY, AND OTHERS.

TO WHICH IS ADDED,

A GLOSSARY OF CANT TERMS.

BY A GENTLEMAN,

WHO HAS MADE

THE POLICE OF THE METROPOLIS,

AN OBJECT OF ENQUIRY TWENTY-TWO YEARS.

LONDON:

PRINTED FOR J. BUMPUS, 6, HOLBORN BARS,
W. SHARPE, KING STREET; T. HUGHES, T. FISHER, J. CRANWELL;
J. RIELLY, LIVERPOOL; AND SOLD BY ALL BOOKSELLERS.

1819.

Price 3s. 6d. bound in red.

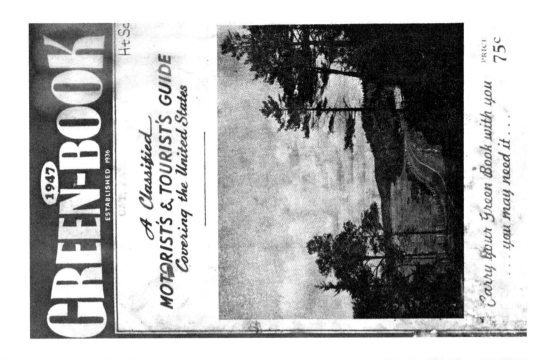

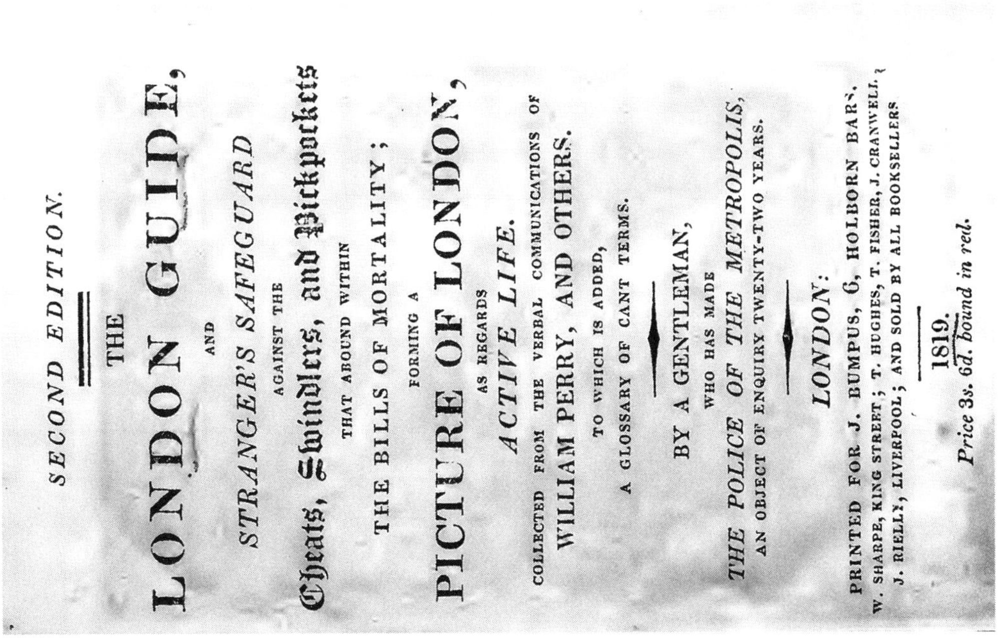

FIGURE 23A. Title page of *The London Guide, and Stranger's Safeguard,* 1819. Via the British Library. Public domain.

FIGURE 23B. Front cover of *The Negro Motorist Green Book,* 1947. New York Public Library digital collections. Public domain.

themes reappear in the next chapter). These particular sites of reading were places of unbalanced power: the *bando* was a decree from a political or religious leader "published" to his subjects in a "public" space, where it was clear which readers were privileged; and colonial print was recited by an indigenous reader in an imposed second language, then transcribed onto paper, an "alien surface" imported "with great labor and expense" from afar.[57]

The European coffeehouses and salons frequented by the bourgeoisie in the seventeenth and eighteenth centuries represented the site of a different political order: here, intellectuals and aristocracy exchanged and debated new printed materials: novels, "moral weeklies" like the *Tatler* and the *Spectator*, critical journals, and other periodicals. "The salon," Jürgen Habermas writes, "held the monopoly of first publication: a new work, even a musical one, had to legitimate itself first in this forum."[58] Here, too, the urban site offered a stage for print: the existence of print media played a critical role in transforming these social and commercial spaces into places for rational-critical debate—at least as Habermas envisions it in his idealized model (one that's been roundly criticized, especially by feminist and queer scholars). And these urban forums served as a testing ground for new, publishable ideas and works of art. Meanwhile, more marginalized communities made use of their own media forms—pamphlets, radical papers, little magazines, and, later, zines—and their own marginal urban gathering spaces to compose their own *counter*-publics.[59]

Nevertheless, many widely distributed printed materials and widely accessible urban forums offered a means for "normalizing and codifying a coherent body of public opinion on matters hitherto considered to be largely subjective," including art and architecture. "As these texts came increasingly to shape the public reception of architecture," argues architectural historian and theorist Sylvia Lavin, "architecture was transformed into one of the public sphere's most significant means of self-definition."[60] Architecture's "indiscriminate availability"—the fact that it is accessible to and used by nearly everyone—means that many readers and discussants deemed themselves qualified and entitled to have an opinion on their material urban environment (excluded, of course, were the illiterate, the impecunious, the homeless and unwelcome).[61] Lavin, evoking Kant, says that critical readers—particularly those who availed themselves of newly available travel books, archaeological studies, essays on aesthetics, and architectural treatises—could "transfer the use of private reason from the act of reading the book to that of reading the most peculiarly public of texts, buildings themselves."[62]

Having *opinions* about their city and its architecture prepared some readers to shape that environment by designing and building their own homes—particularly just outside the city, in the countryside, and eventually in the suburbs. The eighteenth and nineteenth centuries brought new "villa books" and series like Humphry Repton's *Red Books* for exclusive clients; builder's guides and pattern books by the likes of Asher Benjamin, Andrew Jackson Downing, and Alexander Jackson Davis; catalogs like Sears, Roebuck and Company that sold "kit homes"; and architectural magazines.[63] These were accompanied by new women's books and periodicals, like Lydia Maria Francis Child's *The Frugal Housewife* and *Ladies' Home Journal*, that focused on home management and interior design—especially the moral dimensions and ideologies of such practices, which are ideally based in frugality and simultaneous commitments to community and family privacy.[64] These print materials—like Serlio's treatise, the "paper cities" of nineteenth-century speculative developers, and Labrouste's adoption of the book as his architectural model—generated material landscapes in their own image. And they cultivated urban subjects who negotiated and navigated their cities, their neighborhoods, their homes, and their own identities through the printed page.

Mass Circulation: Newspapers and the Modern Material City

The nineteenth century brought the rotary press, the telegraph and news wire services, new papermaking techniques based on pulping wood, the mimeograph, newspaper presses capable of double-sided printing, linotype, and automatic sheet feeders. All were tools and techniques that relied heavily on metal machinery and served to generate piles of papers that stocked the city's shelves, stuffed its pockets, clogged its desks, coated its walls, and lined its streets and sidewalks. Once again, new forms of print—this time, produced in unprecedentedly large quantities and distributed via new telecommunication and transportation technologies, including telegraphs and trains and, later on, trucks—mixed with old and new forms of public writing to reaffirm the city's streets "as a site of public reading, a palimpsest of shared information," as was the case even in ancient Rome.[65] In antebellum New York, historian David Henkin explains, urban texts including street signs, house numbers, and commercial signage—which often occupied the highest perch on the street—served as points of orientation and aided in navigation.[66] Meanwhile, printed posters, broadsides, sandwich boards, banners, handbills, circulars, paper money, and newspapers were ephemeral (rather than locationally "fixed") urban

FIGURE 24. Striking workers in front of an advertising column, 1932, Berlin.
Photograph by Friedrich Seidenstuecker. bpk, Berlin/Art Resource, N.Y.

printed texts, joining people together temporarily into a public of private readers; and fashioning the city's public spaces into "strikingly inclusive arena(s) for impersonal communication."[67] In Berlin, brightly colored art nouveau posters plastered the city's *Litfaßsäulen*, or advertising columns. Installed in the mid-nineteenth century in the hope that they'd provide a site for the orderly organization of the city's scattered posters and printed proclamations, the columns' physical form—"two meters taller than anyone in the crowd, topped with a green crown of wrought iron"—attracted attention.[68] These screaming urban "exclamation marks," as two contemporary writers described them, became a magnet for unauthorized notes and notices.[69]

Given the wide variety of texts—at all scales and altitudes, in myriad fonts and formats—vying for their attention, urban readers had to be able to "peruse, select, discard and reassemble a range of messages" (much like the readers of *Portrait of Modern Rome*, who had to find coherence in their city's overwhelming array of choices).[70] Those copious texts carried disparate messages through the city, but they also embodied, in their material form, disparate messages *about* the city. Consider first the handbill, whose evanescence and modesty befit that of a "floating signifier," and which momentarily reified the city's dynamism. Contrast this with New York City's paper "contract" for its own indefinite growth: the 1811 Commissioners' Plan, the famous grid plan of Manhattan, which mapped from river to river, up to 155th Street, well before New York had enough inhabitants to fill in the grid. This "paper city," Henkin suggests, represented the "displacement of brick by paper. . . . Physical buildings depend on plans to give them spatial meaning, on dollars and price quotations to give them value, and on print technology to give them durability."[71] Texts of permanence and evanescence reflected different aspects of urban temporality.

Yet it was newspapers, with their vertical orientation, columnar layout, density, verbosity, heteroglossia, mobility, and rapidity of circulation, that best embodied the turn-of-the-twentieth-century industrialized city. The Chicago school sociologists have shown how urban newspapers helped newcomers, particularly immigrants, make sense of the city and cultivate new urban communities (and newsprint also functioned as an improvisational form of shelter for those without communities and homes). Yet for all readers, city natives and implants and those merely passing through, "popular newspapers did more than introduce the metropolis," historian Peter Fritzsche notes; "they calibrated readers to its tremendous, machine-tempered rhythms."[72] The newsroom and presses also echoed the city in

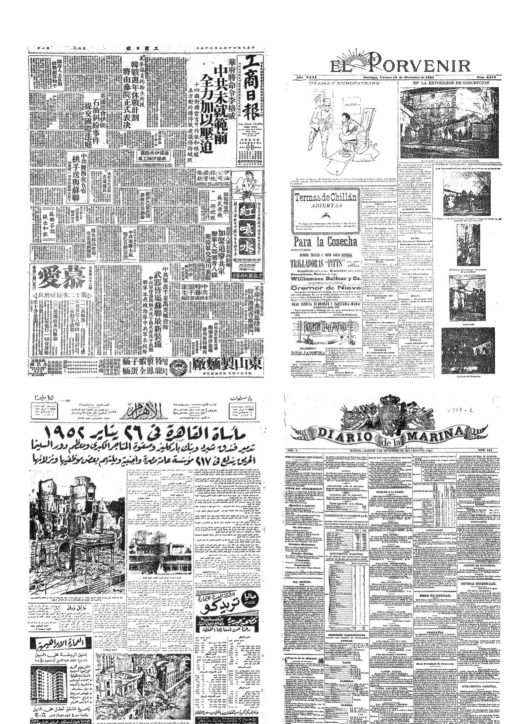

FIGURE 25. Quadriptych of newspaper front pages (clockwise from top left):

FIGURE 25A. Kung Sheung Yat Po, 1951, Hong Kong. Via Hong Kong Public Libraries. Public domain.

FIGURE 25B. El Porvenir, 1904, Chile. Public domain.

FIGURE 25C. Diario de la Marina, 1844, Cuba. Public domain.

FIGURE 25D. Al-ahram, 1952, Egypt. Public domain.

their sonic and kinesthetic cacophony. In 1906, in his *In the Days of the Comet*, H. G. Wells describes "a newspaper day":

> Figure first, then, a hastily erected and still more hastily designed building in a dirty, paper-littered back street of old London, and a number of shabbily dressed men coming and going in this with projectile swiftness, and within this factory companies of printers, tensely active with nimble fingers—they were always speeding up the printers—ply their type-setting machines, and cast and arrange masses of metal in a sort of kitchen inferno, above which, in a beehive of little brightly lit rooms, disheveled men sit and scribble. There is a throbbing of telephones and a clicking of telegraph needles, a rushing of messengers, a running to and fro of heated men, clutching proofs and copy. Then begins a clatter roar of machinery catching the infection, going faster and faster, and whizzing and banging—engineers, who have never had time to wash since their birth, flying about with oil-cans, while paper runs off its rolls with a shudder of haste.[73]

The city's spaces of modern print production engendered, and demanded, a multisensory mania, with humans and machines working together at breakneck speed.

Journalistic writing styles and graphic formats—bold headlines and attention-seeking front-page layouts—captured the tempo, volume, and provisionality of urban activity. And just as the Bibliothèque Sainte-Geneviève and the books it housed "cited" one another, the newspaper's graphic and material forms have had a homologous relationship with the streetscapes, facades, and topographies of the city. Both New York City and its newspapers, Henkin suggests, are characterized by a "grid of uniform columns juxtaposing a broad range of discrete elements," and the "symbolic relationship between rectilinear city and rectilinear print columns was reciprocally clarifying."[74] They helped to make sense of one another. The paper's supporting infrastructures likewise announced their presence in the urban streets. Newsboys, once a fixture on street corners, gave voice to the mute, but graphically loud, front page. And newsstands were recognizable urban fixtures, sometimes even hubs of neighborhood life, that, according to Henkin, "arrayed social difference in public view and transformed personal habits into public spectacle."[75]

Newspaper buildings—originally homes to the newsrooms, printing facilities, and loading docks that launched the dissemination of their product throughout the city—loomed especially large in the urban landscape.

Media historian Aurora Wallace agrees with Henkin and Fritzsche that the newspaper and the city shaped one another via their mutual interests in "industrial capitalism, specialization of labor, [and] geographic concentration"—but she suggests that the two were also linked through their growing interest in real estate.[76] The nineteenth-century rivalry between New York's many newspapers "manifested itself in increasingly tall and bold purpose-built structures."[77] We saw a similar battle for supremacy in de Forest and Marconi's construction of ever-taller radio masts, but while radio's architects constructed structural novelties, newspaper's architects sought to associate themselves with grand tradition. Wallace continues:

> Publishers chose the most important architects of their day to design large, classical structures with towers, domes, columns, and pilasters based on Italian Renaissance campaniles, French Second Empire chateaus, and Gothic churches. By evoking the classical past of architecture, publishers intended to convey permanence, authority, and stability to their readers, and to lend much-needed credibility to their enterprises.[78]

And the same materials that anchored their presses—cast iron or steel—also scaffolded their elevated architectures. The iron frame, first used in the mid-nineteenth century, and later the steel frame made it possible to build higher without relying on a building's thick walls to support its weight. The elevator, too, was necessary to make vertical circulation possible in these ever-taller structures. Increasing land values also fueled the drive to build upward. By the twentieth century, art historian Anthony King argues, the skyscraper had become the "paradigmatic statement, not only of American architecture and urbanism, but of the economic ideology, mode of production, and ethos from which it was largely (if not entirely) produced: capitalist land values, speculative office development and big business materialism."[79] But as the towers "exceeded the limits of functional efficiency"—once they grew taller than ten stories and had to devote a large proportion of their floorplates to the elevators necessary to reach the upper floors—"their market becomes increasingly based in symbolic capital."[80] The buildings functioned as corporate communications.

"The earliest industry to translate its promotional needs and notions of corporate imagery into tall structures," argues geographer Mona Domosh, "was the newspaper industry," particularly in New York and Chicago.[81] The area around Park Row in Lower Manhattan—near City Hall, the courts,

FIGURE 26A. Park Row, also known as Newspaper Row, 1936, from the Federal Art Project's *Changing New York* collection. Photograph by Berenice Abbott, via the New York Public Library digital collection. Public domain.

FIGURE 26B. Office of the *Wahkiakum County Eagle,* Cathlamet, Washington. Photograph by Joe Mabel / CC-BY-SA-2.0.

the financial district, the Western Union building at Broadway and Dey, and the telephone exchanges at 82 Nassau—was home to the first collection of tall buildings in nineteenth-century New York. Here, at Printing House Square, we would find the headquarters of the *New York Tribune*, the *New York World*, and the *New York Times*. Wallace explains how George Browne Post's design for the *New York Times* building, much like Labrouste's libraries, represented its occupant in form, material, and ornament:

> [The building] was an architectural translation of the Aristotelian principle that all forms should have a beginning, middle, and end. The base was clearly differentiated from the middle shaft, and the capital was an ornamental and climactic finish, typical of classical buildings of the period. . . . For a newspaper building, this conscious adaptation of narrative structure added yet more layers of meaning to the design, a play on the words "story" and "storey."[82]

Its "serious exterior of olive granite" also reflected the paper's "somber grey pages."

What's more, the buildings themselves served as a platform for news.

When the papers sought to make major announcements in between the publications of their multiple daily editions, they wrote messages on chalkboards in front of their buildings, or posted prefabricated block letters or handwritten messages. And later—after an 1893 street-sweeping campaign removed the permanent billboards, along with other impediments to free circulation—they used stereopticons to project photos, cartoons, maps, and other images and messages onto large canvases strung across their facades.[83] Wallace notes that the various tall buildings around the square created a partial enclosure, which fashioned the space in between, where the public gathered, into an amphitheater.[84] That crowd made noise. In gathering to read and respond to these live updates—sports scores, financial reports, breaking news about elections or wars—the newspaper's "ambient" readers, often a disparate "imagined community," reformed as a physically proximate public, audibly and tangibly aware of one another's presence.[85] This single urban plot thus accommodated an entanglement of media forms: print, inscription, image projection, conversation.

When the railroad terminals, theaters, and banks headed uptown in the early twentieth century, New York's newspapers soon followed. The *Herald* moved to a new home on Thirty-Fourth Street—a long, two-story classical building designed by noted architect Stanford White (of McKim, Mead & White). Rather than highlighting the power of steel to gain height, this building celebrated the potential of another new building technology: sizable sheets of glass. The facade of White's decidedly non-skyscraperesque building featured large windows that afforded views down into the basement presses, where feats of iron engineering were again on display. These machines of textual production, rather than architecture-as-monumental-text, became the new spectacle.

Newspapers made their mark on the late nineteenth- and twentieth-century city. Their legacy was writ both large (through magnificent buildings, structural and machinic marvels of engineering, and large-scale public texts) and small (through tiny type on printed page, via the presses' metal plates) on urban forms and facades, and in its streets, offices, and apartments.

The Enormous File: Print and Urban Administration

The period's print production wasn't all meant for public consumption and dissemination in the streets. The administration of the city, and of its businesses and institutions, generated a great deal of paperwork, too.

"The swish and crackle of paper is the underlying sound of the metropolis," writes Lewis Mumford.

> What is visible and real in this world is only what has been transferred to paper. . . . All the major activities of the metropolis are directly connected with paper; and printing and packaging are among its principal industries. The activities pursued in the offices of the metropolis are directly connected with paper: the tabulating machines, the journals, the ledgers, the card-catalogues, the deeds, the contracts, the mortgages . . .[86]

The offices of city governments were particularly print and paper intensive. "Population surveys, police records, sanitary reports, statistics, muck-raking journalism, and photography" rendered the city "an object of knowledge, and so an object of government."[87] City administrations generated standardized forms on which officials collected mountains of data, and that data was then compiled into files and registries; perhaps later transferred to punched cards; and processed and analyzed by statisticians.[88] This statistical understanding of the city—one enabled by massive paper files—didn't merely offer a rational picture of the city; it actually played a role in reshaping the city in its own image. "The use of statistical approaches to social problems posed the problem of finding forms through which to present this understanding," Paul Rabinow writes, "just as the century-long search for new architectural forms was perplexed about the norms of modern society that these forms were supposed to embody and represent."[89]

Those new architectures—which both stored all the city's printed materials and embodied the logic of its statistics-based administration— were often small scale: they included wood and metal filing cabinets, metal vaults, metal safety deposit boxes, and paper shredders.[90] But as architectural historian Alexandra Lange suggests, the architectures of scientific management were building sized, too. Office Taylorism, or scientific management, she says, privileged "clean surfaces, the open plan, global surveillance, and efficiency of movement for its product—white, thin, weightless paper." The aesthetics of early modernist architecture happened to value those same qualities.[91] "The filing cabinet (and its resident papers) can be seen as a building block for the twentieth-century design of offices and, by extension, white-collar lifestyles."[92] C. Wright Mills said as much in 1951: "Each office within the skyscraper is a segment of the enormous file, a part of the symbol factory that produces the billion slips of paper that gear modern society into its daily shape."[93]

Again, we find homologies between paper, the file, and the skyscraper, where steel frames allowed for taller buildings and open floorplans, unobstructed by columns and unobstructing to the free flow of files. Should there ever be a fire in a skyscraper, though, its upper floors would be beyond the reach of the fire truck's ladder and hose, Lange writes; thus, "the market grew for all-steel office furniture, replacing heavy, flammable wooden cabinets."[94] And in those steel cabinets, "cold-drawn" steel mechanisms supported smoothly gliding drawers, and steel frames scaffolded hanging files. The Steelcase office furniture company, founded in 1912, began to offer a variety of desks with interchangeable drawers that could be tailored to hold typewriters, stationery, receipts, and invoices. "Office manuals of the early twenties," Lange reports, "devoted themselves to the arrangement of cabinets, desks, and departments in relation to their place in the paper-processing hierarchy. . . . Private offices were eliminated in the attempt to create a true assembly line of signatures, stamps, or other addenda."[95] Architect Le Corbusier, whom we met in the previous chapter, adopted a similar strategy; his *Casiers*—lockers, or metal storage units—partly inspired his ideas for office design: both the cabinet and the office design were "generated from the inside out, dimensioned by the path of standardized white paper."[96]

What was printed or written on those sheets of paper was often beside the point. It was the processes of printing and filing that created the semblance of productivity; these actions gave form to those "statistical approaches to social problems" that Rabinow noted, and to parallel "scientific" approaches to business management. The architectural and urban forms then created to store that paperwork enabled city administrators, businesses, and other institutions to demonstrate to their stakeholders, to the city at large—and to themselves—that they upheld the "norms of modern society": order, accountability, efficiency.

The Late Age of Urban Print: Long Live Paper

Today, in much of the postindustrial West, we supposedly work in "paperless offices," and architects design workplaces to facilitate mobility and collaboration and the flow of digital information. The large windows of White's *Herald* building prefigured the dominant design element of today's workplace: ubiquitous screens, pervasive glowing glass rectangles.

SHAW-WALKER STEEL LETTER FILES

"Built Like a Skyscraper"

Channel Steel Skyscraper Construction as shown in the famous Woolworth Building, New York, and in the Shaw-Walker Steel Letter File.

FIGURE 27. Excerpt from the Shaw-Walker Company's *Pocket Catalog of Steel Filing Cabinets, Wood Filing Cabinets, and Supplies for All Files, Third Edition,* 1917. Public domain.

The inhabitants of these new spaces of digital labor—white-collar workers, or, more likely, tattooed *no*-collar workers—rarely arrive at the office with a newspaper tucked under their gray-flannel-suited arms. Those newspaper publishers that have weathered the digital storm have long since moved their presses to cheaper real estate outside the city, leaving the downtown staff to spend much of their time contemplating digital strategy and paywall policies. Still, print persists—both in societies driven by information capitalism and on its margins.[97] The printed book is still a vital part of many urban economies and cultures, and in this section we'll take a global tour of cities that continue to make room for the book and the printed periodical.

Printing came relatively late to the Islamic world, where scribal traditions flourished until the nineteenth century. Because most publishers, both inside and outside the Islamic world, had little knowledge of the region's languages or religious traditions, their work was often marred with printing errors, which generated popular resistance to the publishing of religious material.[98] The area around Baghdad's Al-Mutanabbi Street had long been home to scribes' markets and bookshops.[99] After the Gulf War, the street quickly resumed its role as a center of literary culture, hosting many book vendors dedicated to selling their own books or liberating those once banned. Shortly after a car bomb devastated the street's bookshops in March of 2007, printed broadsides expressing solidarity and hope for renewal started to appear in the district, and the books began to re-emerge the following year.[100] "These days," Borzou Daragahi writes in the *Financial Times*, "most of the highly religious enforcers are on the front fighting against ISIS, and have less time to harass people selling books or drinking alcohol."[101] So, Al-Mutanabbi—now, as always, a mixture of high and low, of Korans and pirated DVDs—is again thriving, serving for some as an ongoing urban "festival . . . of ideas."[102]

Khartoum, Sudan, has likewise been a longtime center of Arabic literary culture. Those behind the nationalist movement after World War I were avid readers. In the ensuing years the country experienced a cultural renaissance, during which Khartoum boasted nearly four hundred bookstores, including one that claimed to be the largest in the Arab world. But with Omar al-Bashir's rise to power in 1989, the city's libraries were closed and their books destroyed. The Sudanese Writers Union was banned, too, then reinstated in 2005, after the signing of the Sudanese peace treaty. Meanwhile, the *Guardian*'s Alia Gilbert reports, "along the back alleys" and "in the dark corners of bookstores or underneath dusty floorboards

FIGURE 28. Iraqi men look at books displayed at the Mutanabbi book market, 2007, Baghdad. AP photograph by Khalid Mohammed.

an underground market of used books resiliently persisted" (in the next chapter, we'll learn about similarly "dusty" modes of survival among manuscript-based communities).[103] In recent years, activists sought to incite yet another literary renaissance; the writers' union championed books, and the Work Culture Group, an arts and culture organization, instituted the vibrant monthly Mafroush used book fair. Then, in early 2015, al-Bashir again banned the union and shuttered the fair.[104] Mafroush returned the following month. Such volatility has characterized literary culture in a Sudan plagued by oppression, poverty, and censorship. "Books and reading are embedded profoundly in Khartoum's self-image and the country's history," reports Isma'il Kushkush in the *New York Times*, "and there is growing worry that the collapse of book culture is a direct mirror of the country's overall decline."[105]

Caravans have long linked these various literary centers into a vast network of manuscript and book trade. Across the Islamic world, members of the book's "imagined community" have celebrated their literary ties: "Cairo writes, Beirut publishes, Baghdad reads," the saying goes. By the turn of the millennium, however, reading had declined dramatically in the Arab world: books selling only five thousand copies made it to the bestseller list; Arabic translations were scarce; book distribution was greatly attenuated; censorship was prevalent, and its codes varied from country to country; and poor education and religious fundamentalism had diminished literacy.[106] Yet, as we've seen, many cities of the region are still home to publishers and booksellers "who've persisted in their trade despite wars, repression, [and] tough economic times," occasionally, as in Baghdad and Khartoum, "accidentally ending up at the epicenter of a revolution."[107] "The very concentration" of activity in these cities has created "particularly intense, unique places: neighborhoods whose identities are vividly defined by the book business," much like New York's old Book Row near Union Square.[108] Trevor Naylor, director of distribution for the American University in Cairo Press, cites his own city, the contemporary center of Arabic publishing, and also acknowledges vibrant bibliophilic activity in Beirut and at Ansari Road and Connaught Place in Delhi, where booksellers serve both Indians and displaced Pakistanis who, after the partition, relocated from Lahore, whose own book culture once flourished. Istanbul and Tehran have not fared as well.[109]

Meanwhile, Mumbai's book market has been driven, since the 1970s, by piracy—by children, most of whom are themselves illiterate, selling shrink-wrapped black-market paperbacks on the streets. Publishing consultant Akshay Pathak attributes the situation in part to publishers' territory rights, which "package" the U.K. with all of its Commonwealth countries, including India, and which typically favor British publishers.[110] Consequently, in India, as Sonia Faleiro reports in the *New York Times*, "It is far easier to buy a pirated book than it is to find a bookstore or library," and many authors even regard it as a badge of honor—a sign of popularity—to find their books available in pirated form.[111]

Conditions are quite different across the globe in Argentina, where there is no sales tax on domestic books, and the government imposes heavy import taxes and surcharges for online book purchases. Consequently, Buenos Aires has more bookstores per capita than any other city: twenty-five shops for every hundred thousand people.[112] The prevalence of booksellers is also attributable in part to a cultural history that has favored publishing. In the late nineteenth and early twentieth centuries Latin American cities like Buenos Aires had experienced dramatic modernization. The colonial cityscape made way for a city of steel bones: a street grid that served both as a means to discipline urban growth and as a "symbolically unifying ideal"; new infrastructural systems powering this "geometric machine"; and migrants arriving from around the world.[113] The "written word came to the rescue," Angel Rama says, to help make sense of this rapid transformation.[114] Writers, who sought to chronicle the now-lost premodern city, generated a "veritable super-production of books," many of which recast that past in light of the ideologies of the present modernization.[115] "As the *real* city was destroyed and then reconstituted on a new basis, the city of letters found the opportunity to encode it anew in words and images."[116]

Yet across South America, in the "lettered mountains" of Peru, which we will explore further in our next chapter, colonialism has left a different literary legacy. "Officialdom does send a lot of print to the village," but it's locked away in the public school and the municipal building.[117] Towns and cities throughout the Andes function as nodes in an informal logistical system for the circulation of a wide variety of more ephemeral printed matter. Bus depots, where villagers head to and from Lima, serve as de facto post offices and bulletin boards, where locals post notices and deposit letters for the bus driver to deliver at his various stops.[118] Truckers bring tabloid papers from Lima, and those printed pages "pass from hand to hand for weeks until finally recycled as insulation for adobe houses."[119] Here, the printed word literally creates a framework for inhabitation. Electricity didn't arrive in Tupicocha, the site of Frank Solomon and Mercedes Niño-Murcia's fieldwork, until 2001, well after the wired world already experienced its first dot-com boom and bust. As of 2011, the Internet still hadn't reached Peru's "lettered mountain." Meanwhile, its stores were doing a booming business in stationery and office supplies, and its "manuscript culture of notebooks and ledgers remain[ed] as active as ever."[120] Here, again, we witness the disparate and entangled temporalities of various media distribution infrastructures.

While electricity and the Internet have yet to reach many of India's inhabitants as well, such lacks have generated a national resurgence of the printed newspaper. As of 2012, there were an estimated eighty thousand individual newspapers, 85 percent of which were published in one of India's twenty-two vernacular languages.[121] Particularly in India's smaller cities, the growing middle class—literate and financially secure, though often lacking reliable Internet access—preferred to read papers in their native languages, "rather than in the English favored by much of the former British colony's Westernized elite."[122] Many of the leading English-language publishers, like Bennett Coleman & Co., meanwhile, were launching local-language editions to tap into this growing market. Papers are typically cheap; delivered free of charge to people's homes; and recycled monthly by raddiwallahs, who pay customers for their retrieval. The local-language papers were also extremely popular with advertisers, who regard them as a key conduit to this attractive and expanding consumer base. Yet those advertisers have also been known to wield disproportionate editorial control. Many of India's papers are notorious for their receptivity to paid news, private treatises, and celebrity PR.

In places like New York, where digital newspaper distribution—and digital *alternatives* to the newspaper—have upset the publishing market, these changes have had a material impact on the streetscape. A city that, in 1950, hosted roughly fifteen hundred newsstands now has about three hundred, very few of which are outside of Manhattan. As Berenice Abbott's photos from the 1930s document, those corner shops were once *wunderkammern* of print's abundance, markers in their patrons' daily routines, vital, if underappreciated, participants in their neighborhood cultures. Today, newsstands' paper sales have fallen 80 to 90 percent.[123] As fewer people stop by to purchase a pack of heavily taxed cigarettes, and pick up a paper while they're at it, owners rely on lottery tickets and candy to make a modest living.

Inspired by Eugène Atget, who chronicled the endangered elements of a turn-of-the-twentieth-century Paris in transformation, artist Moyra Davey set out in the mid-1990s to create a series of photos based on New York's idiosyncratic, derelict newsstands. She noted parallels between the ephemerality of their merchandise and the imperiled architecture itself:

> Newsstands are from the age of paper, soon to be eclipsed by microchip technology, and as I photograph these little dark rooms on the streets I can't help but be reminded of, and see the analogy between, other small, dark rooms which also traffic in paper products, and seem equally stranded in the machine age—namely photographers' laboratories and darkrooms.[124]

In 2007 New York's old-school newsstands began to be replaced by standardized stainless-steel and tempered-glass boxes. They were installed by Spanish advertising company Cemusa, which manages advertising space on the city's stands and bus shelters; and designed by Grimshaw Architects, a firm well known for their "high-tech" work with steel, including several rail stations, a museum of steel in Mexico, and, appropriately, the *Financial Times* print works.[125] Some have criticized the new structures, in all their modern, metallic monotony, as devoid of character, and charged

FIGURE 29. "Newsstand, 32nd Street and Third Avenue, Manhattan," 1935, from the Federal Art Project's *Changing New York* collection. Photograph by Berenice Abbott, via the New York Public Library digital collections. Public domain.

that their only distinctive design feature is their functionality as "advertising boxes."[126] In this regard, we might say, they're merely following in the footsteps of the self-promotional towers at Printing House Square.

In 2013 artist Lele Saveri opened his own newsstand in the Metropolitan Avenue subway station in Williamsburg, Brooklyn, yet this stand's merchandise was perfectly tailored to reflect its neighborhood character. His independent magazines, books, comics, and zines were supplied by McNally Jackson, Dashwood Books, Desert Island, and Ohwow, among New York's top specialty bookshops, and supplemented with material submitted by local artists. Saveri built ephemerality into his business model: the stand was open only from June to January—just long enough to feature two issues of a quarterly publication, just long enough to establish itself as a recognizable landmark in patrons' commuting routines, then disappear.[127]

FIGURE 30. "Newsstand #19, 1994," by Moyra Davey. © Moyra Davey, courtesy Murray Guy, New York.

The newsstand-as-art-installation reflects a revival of print not unlike that among India's local-language newspapers. Here in Brooklyn, though, both publishers and readers typically have ready access to digital alternatives, but their preference for print represents an aesthetic and political choice: print embodies qualities that some find lacking in their digital and urban experiences—qualities like slowness, focus, tactility, selectivity. Those who advertised their services or pled for the return of their lost pets via my utility pole on Eastern Parkway likewise chose the printed medium because of its immediacy and locality. Designer Dan Hill argues that "print, as a medium for the reproduction and dissemination of information, is thriving. Paper is suddenly"—or, rather, has always been—"rich in innovation and experimentation."

> Often originating from the culture of the Web rather than the traditional media, paper-based formats are fusing physical outcomes with digital infrastructures in entirely new ways. The affordances of paper are being harnessed to the content, conversations and context of the Internet, and it works.[128]

He cites two examples: the monumental newspaper-formatted *San Francisco Panorama* 2009 issue of the *McSweeney's* literary journal, and the DIY newspaper-designing and printing service Newspaper Club (newspaperclub.com), which "builds on the (existing) physical and social infrastructure of newspapers," relying on an existing network of printers to disseminate niche or special-interest ideas in a form long associated with commercial mass communication. (The "culture of the Web" has also given a boost to other networks of distribution: shipping networks, and another paper product: cardboard boxes. Google Express, Amazon Prime, UberRUSH and other personalized freight services have dramatically increased demand for cardboard boxes—and increased energy expenditures for product delivery and package recycling.[129] All the plastic and paper packages and bubble wrap that *aren't* recycled will leave future archaeologists much to sort through in our landfills.)

In recent years we've seen, around the world, a resurgence of small presses and inventive print forms, a revival of independent bookstores and letterpress print shops, and the emergence of new urban print enclaves. Witness the popularity of art book fairs and zine swaps, the rise of "little magazines," and the emergence of internationally renowned wheatpaste street artists like JR, COST, and La Wife. In the mid-2000s, as much design discourse was moving to blogs, several design historians turned their attention to the history of architecture's "little magazines," modest publishing ventures typically committed to representing marginal voices and experimenting with innovative formats. By the time of the financial crisis in 2007–2008, as most design commissions dried up, many practicing architects channeled their energy into the "architecting" of their own new print forms. The late aughts saw an explosion of new architecture and urbanism magazines and broadsheets—and a host of international exhibitions, events, and catalogs to celebrate and debate them.[130] It seems that when glass-and-steel construction proved scarce, paper lent *itself* to architectural experimentation.

The following decade, in the shadow of the Arab Spring and Occupy movements, new "little architectures" for print began popping up around the globe.[131] Cities from Colombia to India to Germany to the United States witnessed the arrival of many mini, pop-up, guerilla, ad-hoc, street-level libraries. They came in various forms, including the People's Library, the Little Free Library, the library-as-exhibition, the micro book exchange, the mini street corner library, the reborn storefront library, and the DIY branch library. And, for the most part, they were all motivated by shared frustrations and concerns with the urban realm and its cultural sphere: the privatization of public space; the weakening of public institutions; and the spreading corporate or state control of media, both its contents and conduits. Nostalgia undoubtedly played a role, too; some little-librarians and their patrons lamented the loss of tactile media; of real-time, face-to-face social interaction; of a visible, print-based public sphere.

We again observe the profound politics of small things: tiny metal letterforms, the standardized sheet of paper, the bookshelf. These humble enclaves of wood and nails and recycled books raise important questions about protocols of access, ideals of knowledge and rules of intellectual property, the health of public institutions, the viability of public spaces and public life, the definitions of civic values. These architectures of print, these public spheres incarnate, represent an effort to reclaim a small corner of public space for the commons. They are merely among the latter chapters in the continually unfolding story of the printed city—a city shaped by print, filled with print, governed by print, illustrated and immortalized in print, and perhaps soon, printed itself.

3

Of Mud, Media, and the Metropolis

AGGREGATING HISTORIES OF WRITING AND URBANIZATION

Over 6,500 years ago, not far from where the radicals of Islamic State have been bulldozing ancient mud-brick temples and sacrilegious shrines; sledge-hammering idolatrous stone statues; burning "haram," or un-Islamic, manuscripts; and smuggling clay cuneiform tablets and mosaics for sale on the black market, a civilization was born—a civilization built upon many of those very same humble materials: mud, stone, and clay. Small farming villages in the fertile Mesopotamian region had made way for what are widely regarded as some of the first cities, Eridu and Uruk—settlements whose proximity to the Euphrates River made possible the production of a reliable agricultural surplus. In Uruk, those bountiful grains fed a large population—up to eighty thousand at the city's peak around 2900 BCE—who had learned to build mud-brick temples and a mosaic-adorned ziggurat, craft stone sculptures and clay pottery, pursue a wide variety of professions, and design complex political and administrative structures to manage their affairs. All that administration required a system for keeping records.

Bureaucracy, many believe, begat writing sometime in the fourth millennium BCE.[1] The presumption is that our written languages, our chirographic cultures, are rooted not in noble literary traditions, but in accountancy (although it was the *Epic of Gilgamesh*, which survived on a set of clay tablets, that tells us much of what we know about Uruk's mythical history). "It has been suggested," economist Harold Innis writes, "that writing was invented in Sumer to keep tallies and to make lists and hence was an outgrowth of mathematics. The earliest [records] include large numbers of legal contracts, deeds of sale, and land transfers, and reflect a secular and utilitarian interest."[2] Yet all this "proto-paperwork" was part of a larger constellation of developments that extended beyond the merely managerial. As Innis explains, "The development of writing, mathematics, the standardization of weights and measures, and adjustments of the calendar were a part of an urban revolution"—a new way of living with others, a new way of organizing and inhabiting space.[3]

We needn't commit to the origin story. Our goal here is not to substantiate claims of writing's invention or provenance; as we've seen in previous chapters, media follow different paths of evolution in different geographic and cultural contexts. And many of those claims (often published under titles that tellingly acknowledge the *origins*, plural, of writing) depend in large part on how different researchers define "writing." Some paleographers argue that nonrepresentational marks like dots, lines, and geometric shapes in Paleolithic cave paintings suggest the potential for symbolic communication.[4] Others regard Ice Age rock engravings, wood carvings, and Cro-Magnon bone tools, believed to depict lunar cycles, as examples of proto-writing.[5] Still other archaeologists suggest that societies in Syria and Turkey may have been writing in proto-cuneiform script as early as the mid-fourth millennium BCE, before the practice took hold in Sumer.[6] For the purposes of this chapter, however, and in keeping with the central inquiry throughout this book, we'll follow the line of thinking inspired by the bureaucracy-and-urbanization theory (which roughly parallels Kittler's focus on information processing) and explore how writing's pasts might have been entangled with the pasts of cities.

It so happened that Uruk's urban "revolution" was fortified by the most archaic of natural resources: mud. The Tigris and Euphrates rivers yielded not only excess crops; their regular floods also offered plenty of alluvial clay—unconsolidated silt, sand, clay, and gravel, mixed in with organic matter—deposited on the river banks. That fine-grained clay was blended with chaff from the threshing floor, formed into molds, and dried in the sun, yielding the mud bricks that constructed most of ancient Mesopotamia's buildings and city walls. Those bricks were typically "faced" with a thick coating of mud and then sometimes gaudily painted.[7] Or the clay was fashioned into multiform tokens that were used for accounting, and into the clay envelopes that organized them.[8] Or it was strained and shaped into tablets, on which a reed stylus then impressed a wedge-shaped cuneiform script (or on which a hard-stone cylinder seal rolled out an impression, a script or a figurative scene, that served as a form of authorial notarization), after which the tablet was sun- or kiln-baked, or recycled.[9] These alluvial documents constituted the new urban register, and they serve us today as a valuable archaeological archive.[10]

FIGURE 31. Triptych of cuneiform tablet, mud bricks, and the ancient city of Al-Qasr in Egypt. Photograph by Vassil / CC-Zero; Photograph by Ian Scott / CC-BY-SA-2.0; Photograph by isawnyu / CC-BY-2.0.

We have access to writing's history largely because of the material properties of the historical record, of writing itself. Olof Pedersén et al. note that "it is a great advantage to archaeologists when texts are written on clay tablets."[11] Clay, as Innis would say, is a time-biased medium: it has permanence; it both cultivates lasting civilizations and sticks around to make itself available for historical study.[12] Of course early writing and proto-writing appeared on a variety of substrates: stone walls, shards of bone or wood, wax tablets, cloth, and metal, some of which are similarly durable. Yet the materiality of the archaeological record has implications that extend beyond the mere availability of artifacts; the forms of those artifacts inform their historical interpretation, because they also shape the civilizations that used them.[13] As Innis, Lewis Mumford, Denise Schmandt-Besserat, and a host of other historians and archaeologists argue, a civilization's prevailing media formats cultivate its habits of mind, its economy, its modes of governance, and its culture.

Urban and architectural history are likewise informed by the materiality of their historical records. Some early construction used stone: consider the megalithic temples of Malta and even Uruk's own stone temples, built of limestone and bitumen on a rammed-earth podium. But as archaeologist Seton Lloyd acknowledges, "The raw material that epitomized Mesopotamian civilization was clay."[14] For millennia clay and mud have together accounted for a significant proportion of the earth's built environment: wattle-and-daub structures (woven sticks or reeds coated with mud), cob houses (chunks of clay tempered with straw, manure, or sand, stacked and smoothed into walls), adobe bricks (tempered bricks, sun dried, stacked and mortared), rammed-earth buildings (sand, gravel, and clay compressed into a molded wall), and fired-brick structures span the globe and the ages.[15]

Those ancient architectures serve as more than archaeological remains; they're often historical *texts*, too. As we will see later, civilizations the world over—in Mesopotamia, ancient Rome, precolonial Mesoamerica, Fatimid-era Cairo, present-day Calcutta—have written *on* their material environments, as well—through architectural inscriptions or epigraphy, for example—which provides another set of historical writings for future archaeologists to consult. These various recorded formats—tablets containing urban administrative records, and the material city *itself* as a written text—are often entangled, which complicates archaeologists' attempts at periodization and historical dating. Christopher Woods, in his history of writing in the ancient Middle East, acknowledges that most Mesopotamian tablets were found in "rubbish heaps," in no clear historical strata. "The sun-hardened clay tablets, having obviously outlived their usefulness, were used along with other waste, such as potsherds, clay sealings, and broken mud-bricks, as fill in leveling the foundation of new constructions."[16] Writing thus provided not only a cultural and economic basis for urban development, but a structural foundation as well.

For millennia mud and its geologic analogs have bound together our media, urban, architectural, and environmental histories. Some of the first writing surfaces, clay and stone, were the same materials used to construct ancient city walls and buildings, whose facades also frequently served as substrates for written texts. The formal properties of those scripts—the shapes they took on their clay (or, eventually, parchment and paper) foundations—were also in some cases reflected in urban form: how the city molded itself from the materials of the landscape. And those written documents have always been central to nearly all cities' operation: their trade, accountancy, governance, and culture.

Of course mud has been both a constructive and a destructive force throughout urban history—actually, throughout all of human and even geologic history. Floods and mudslides have remade landscapes and destroyed many settlements and cities. Lutetia, the ancient Paris, sited amidst the marshes, most likely derived its name from *lutum*, the Latin term for mud; and both Drummer (Drusemere) Street in Cambridge, U.K., and Lothmere in Norwich were named after the stagnant pools of mud and refuse that festered there.[17] Mud has long been a public health concern, particularly in the medieval city, where some administrators sought to enforce the paving and regular sweeping of streets, the flushing of waterways and maintenance of aqueducts and wells, and the periodic testing of potable water (public health officials sought to tame other forms of disorder, too, by regulating particular undesirable sounds and smells). But our primary concern here is the mud that's been contained and molded for use.[18]

The long history of mud's applications as both a writing substrate and an architectural medium shows us how we can integrate both the historical and contemporary meanings of the term *Kulturtechnik*, or "cultural technique," a framework very much *en vogue* in media theory (despite its un-sexy agrarian roots). As Bernhard Siegert explains, "The very word *culture*, derived from Latin *colere* and *cultura*, refers to the development and practical usage of means of cultivating and settling the soil with homesteads and cities."[19] Since the late nineteenth century the term *Kulturtechnik* has been associated with agricultural or rural engineering—although there is, as we've seen and will see, a much deeper history to the *practices* that term refers to.[20] "Starting in the 1970s," Siegert continues, "*Kulturtechniken* also came to refer to elementary *Kulturtechniken* or basic skills such as reading, writing, and arithmetic."[21] The blending of these agrarian and literary etymologies, he suggests, enables us to recognize the existence of cultural techniques in realms that extend well beyond the book and culture-with-a-capital-C. Culture, in our case, even extends to techniques of settlement, urban planning and administration, and the practices of everyday urban life. Geoffrey Winthrop-Young proposes that *Kulturtechnik*'s genealogical ties to husbandry permit us to recognize culture as "that which is ameliorated, nurtured, rendered habitable and, as a consequence, structurally opposed to nature, which is seen as actively resistant . . . or indifferent."[22] Yet in examining the place of *mud* in the *Kulturtechniken* of city-making and record keeping, we recognize that urban and administrative culture are utterly dependent on "nature's" geological resources. Writing and urbanization are both muddy businesses, and they're messily entwined.

Aggregating these often-separate historical lineages has the potential to enrich the disparate disciplinary knowledges that are bound together here. Particularly in light of recent attempts to understand what kinds of intelligence are embodied in the world's emerging "smart cities," the comparatively "dumb" histories of mud and mark-making demonstrate that calculation, coding, and "embedded" technologies have long been integral to urban infrastructures.[23] But there's more at stake than historiography.

The public squares, city walls, building facades, urban archives, and sandy stores where earthen materials and writing intersect: these are the humble city sites where politics play out at myriad scales—where the entanglement of global and local political-economic forces enter people's lives through the material, the geological, and the aesthetic. Building and writing materials, extracted locally or sourced and distributed from afar, converge in our settlements and cities, where designers and laborers, often informed by internationally codified and inscribed protocols and standards, give them urban and architectural form. These same construction materials then become public media. In their geologic composition—the distinctive hue or texture of the local mud, or the distinctive means by which local laborers pack that mud into bricks—they can embody a characteristically local aesthetic, an architectural or geologic *parlante*. Those mud surfaces, when inscribed, carry messages to both residents and visitors, both friendly and hostile. And their competing, sometimes contested, messages make them targets of destruction, or attractive spoils of war. Recent threats to cultural heritage in the Middle East demonstrate just how volatile inscribed bricks and sculpted mud can be—and just how critical it is that we, as a global community, comprehend, document, and, if possible, conserve these records before their historical voices are erased.[24]

Writing on Stone Cliffs and Mud Bricks: Landscape and Architectural Inscription

From 500 BCE to 500 CE, the people of the Nazca Desert in southern Peru had inscribed massive fifteen- to twenty-mile-long line-drawings into the alluvial landscape by brushing away red pebbles and sand, exposing the lighter-colored ground underneath. These geoglyphs of flora, fauna, everyday objects, and geometric forms were once imagined to serve as gigantic astronomical calendars, yet the Nazca Lines are now believed to have been used as part of ritual procession routes or in religious rites.[25] Around the same time that the Nazca began marking the ground, Darius the Great, king of the Persian Empire, oversaw the carving of an illustrated autobiography—inscribed in three cuneiform languages: Old Persian, Elamite, and Babylonian—high on the limestone face of Mount Behistun in Iran.[26]

Later, in the first century CE, the Chinese began carving myriad texts—names of places, people, and deities; records of public-works projects; civic announcements; prayers, eulogies, and poetry—into granite

FIGURE 32A. A geoglyph figure of a parrot, found in the Nazca Desert in Peru. Photograph by Unukorno / CC-BY-3.0.

FIGURE 32B. Rock inscriptions found at Longyin Cave in Guilin, China. Photograph by Zhangzhugang / CC-BY-SA-3.0.

boulders and cliffs. Through these *moya*, or "polished-cliff carvings," art historian Robert Harrist proposes, "the Chinese have transformed geological formations into landscapes imbued with literary, ideological, and religious significance."[27] He argues that it's important to study these texts not only in terms of their content and style, but to regard them also as "environmental case studies," as "integral parts of their landscape settings," as texts addressed to a public readership engaged in "peripatetic reading."[28] The carving and the rock are, like cuneiform and clay, entangled materially and historiographically: the carvings themselves serve as historical records, they guide visitors' exploration of the landscape, and, as Harrist says, they "embed historical memory in the topography of China." Geoglyphs and *moya* thus also exemplify the muddily mixed genealogies of inscription, landscape, and what Henri Lefebvre calls "the production of space."[29]

City walls and building facades made of clay bricks, sticks, and stone have long served as substrates for inscription, too.[30] In the fifth or sixth century BCE (or perhaps even centuries earlier, according to some scholars), the Olmecs, Zapotecs, and Mayans in Mesoamerica began carving scripts into their monumental sculptures and buildings; these architectural inscriptions constitute some of the earliest-known examples of Mesoamerican writing.[31] Around the same time in Greece, Innis reports, "the laws of Draco and Solon were written on stelae of wood or stone and laws were regularly recorded on the walls of public buildings or on separate stelae in a public place."[32] Thus, "with the use of writing," and with the use of the city's surfaces themselves as a medium, "the judicial order became a public document, definite and ascertainable."[33] Yet other urban inscriptions called for a different ruling order. When, in the third century BCE, inscriptions began appearing on stone pillars positioned in or near cities in the Indian subcontinent (as well as on more geographically distributed live rocks), their texts served a spiritual purpose: to champion the nascent religion of Buddhism.[34]

The "epigraphic habit" captivated ancient Greece and the Roman empire.[35] "The Romans seemed to inscribe onto and into everything," according to classicist Christopher Johanson. Around the Forum an ancient inhabitant or visitor could find "the written word covering every surface of every major monument."[36] Rome's building facades and walls, doorways and courtyards were made of fired brick or terracotta, concrete (whose content of volcanic sand, pozzolana, has accounted for its longevity), tufa (a volcanic stone), limestone, or marble. These surfaces were not designed to be used as substrates for writing, but through the Romans' social practices, "the fabric of the city" ultimately served to record major laws, achievements, legal transactions, as well as jokes, jabs, and private confessions.[37]

Through the work of its official and amateur authors—who came from all parts of society, including slaves—the city was "informally archiving itself on its skin," Johanson says.[38] Archaeologist Louise Revell suggests that the writings were an integral part of political processes and religious services and thus were bound up in the social practice of "what it was to be Roman."[39] Such processes and rituals of course involved myriad forms of mediation—public address, sculpture, and other modes of pageantry. Thus, the scripts were, like Harrist's *moya*, embedded in their environments, cross-referenced with other messages relayed by other media formats, and read by moving, sensing, and often celebrating or mourning bodies.

The Islamic world has been similarly rich with epigraphy. "In a largely aniconic artist culture"—that is, one that forbids the creation of images of sentient beings—Yasser Tabbaa explains, "public inscriptions were by necessity one of the primary visual means of political and religious expression and one of the few ways for a dynasty to distinguish its reign from that of its predecessor."[40] In the tenth through the twelfth centuries CE, the Fatimids of Cairo, known for the splendor of their art and architecture, displayed official writing on the exteriors of their minarets and other public structures. As in Greece and Rome, architecture functioned here as an infrastructure for communicating territorial claims and codifying beliefs. While places like the mosque of al-Hakim also featured prominent Arabic writing *inside,* for the worshiping community, art historian Irene Bierman contends that "the act of putting writing in Arabic, in several places at pedestrian level, and in large-scale letters on the minarets of the mosque . . . itself located outside the royal city of Cairo, made that writing viewable by all who passed that public space."[41] These exterior Greek or Arabic scripts were occasionally placed on gateways and city thresholds, too, and were intended to publicly herald both territorial claims and allegiance to a particular linguistic culture and ideology.

The specific aesthetic properties of those "public texts"—their "color, materiality, and form," their floriated Kufic script, and their occasional use of gold or glass mosaic—also played a key role in how and what they communicated: power, opulence, and, as other scholars have argued, confused political goals.[42] Tabbaa notes that the ornate Fatimid script was "deliberately ambiguous. . . . This simultaneity of visibility and incomprehension, of inclusiveness and exclusiveness"—of making proclamations

FIGURE 33. Near the Qalawun complex, 2009, Cairo. Photograph by Christopher Rose / CC-BY-NC-2.0.

public, but incomprehensible—"underlies the intentions of a dynasty that always seemed divided between its messianic purposes and its encrypted messages."[43]

Writings on these landscapes and landforms, and on the mud and stone walls of these myriad cities, all carry public messages to their inhabitants and visitors. But in different contexts, they serve different purposes: directing ritual, marking territory, proclaiming power, echoing history, evoking spiritual values, announcing laws, accommodating dissent, perhaps even provoking disorientation and confusion—and in all cases negotiating, materially and textually, between local and global political concerns.

Writing Cities into Being: The Scripts of Urban Planning and Administration

Written charters and drawn plans have brought cities into being, and scrivened documents have kept them in order. Angel Rama, in his posthumously published *The Lettered City*, explains how Iberian colonialists employed a combined strategy—involving both writing and urbanization—to impose a new order on the New World. In his introduction to the book, John Charles Chasteen fleshes out the many ways in which inscription and city-building converged:

> [T]he Iberian monarchs created precocious urban networks, carefully planned with pen and paper, their geometrical layout standardized by detailed written instructions. New cities housed both the institutions of state power and the writers who dealt in edits, memoranda, reports, and all the official correspondence that held the empire together.[44]

These written documents, and the educated *letrados* who created and archived them, enabled the Spanish and Portuguese conquerors to impose an ambitious, rational, systematic plan on existing indigenous settlements and, more rarely, in brand new towns. While the conquerors and their subjects stripped the landscape of its gold and silver, they also (re-) molded its mud into grids of adobe-walled structures set around central plazas dominated by a church.

Rama focuses on the *letrados'* administrative authority—their ability to "manipulate writing in largely illiterate societies" in order to evangelize "and oversee the transculturation of an indigenous population numbering in the millions."[45] And part of that evangelizing, Rama argues, involved conveying an urban imaginary, marshaling "diagrams that translated the [political] will into graphic terms"—typically, orderly checkerboard grids—which were intended, in turn, to inspire a translation into *material* terms.[46] Conqueror and conquered alike were to imagine transforming those paper-based urban visions into stone and adobe realities. Again, politics were to take material form in the architectural and aesthetic.

Yet the grid plan already *was* a material reality in many indigenous Mesoamerican settlements. Not only was plaza-centered urban design present in pre-Columbian settlements, but the Spaniards, impressed by the grandeur and order of New World cities, may have even imported their urban-planning ideas back to the Old World and employed them in the re-design of Spanish cities under Philip II.[47] Anthropologists have also taken issue with Rama's claim that the conquerors were entering a New World devoid of its own literate culture. Anthropologist Frank Solomon and sociolinguist Mercedes Niño-Murcia argue that new colonial literacies, "sponsored by church and by state, were not expanding into a graphic void. For when Spaniards brought the alphabet, they brought it to a society which already had its own advanced resources for recording information."[48] As we discussed earlier, various ancient Mesoamerican civilizations had developed scripts. Some indigenous populations, like those that Solomon and Niño-Murcia studied in Peru, continued (and continue to this day) to use the ancient medium of the khipu, or knot-cord, to monitor taxes and military operations and to track census records, genealogies, and agricultural calendars; and many villages developed vibrant (and remarkably exhaustive) local cultures of handwritten record keeping.[49]

While the colonialists' grand urban plans may have duplicated forms that already existed in indigenous settlements, they did promise to refashion those existing structures, to reconstitute them within a new ideological framework. Cortes, for example, remade the sacred central plaza of the Great Temple of Tenochtitlán into a new Spanish American plaza and cathedral. In many existing settlements, an urban plan and orientation that once reflected cosmological principles now symbolized rational order and the power of a new God. Cathedrals were sited alongside, or atop, temples and other pre-Columbian structures. Sites and streets took on new names: names that once reflected local geographic features, architectonic forms, or agricultural concerns were re-Christened in Spanish, forcing

FIGURE 34. Frontispiece of the *Codex Mendoza*, circa 1542, depicting the founding of Tenochtitlán and the conquest of Colhuacan and Tenayucan. Via Bodleian Libraries. Public domain.

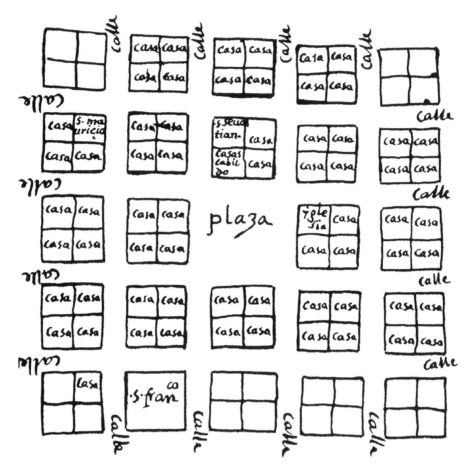

FIGURE 35. First known colonial map of Caracas, 1578, by Governor Juan de
Pimentel. Public domain.

indigenous readers "to pay more heed to the European-framed models
conveyed graphically in written documentation."[50] In some cases, colonial
influence was more subtle: as anthropologist Setha Low explains, colonial
power made itself palpable even in the *Kulturtechniken* of masonry and
building.[51] Ideology was made manifest in the way mud was shaped into
bricks. And indigenous laborers molded those bricks, and forcibly remod-
eled their own homes, through labor with profound symbolic significance.

Yet even if the New World was no tabula rasa, and those colonial urban
imaginaries couldn't be translated "verbatim" into brick, the written plan
still served its political function. The ideal city plan, Rama says, has the
"rhetorical capacity . . . to impose hierarchical order on spiraling em-
pires."[52] While, on the city's "physical plane," we might be lost amidst its

muddy "multiplicity and fragmentation," its juxtaposition of temples and cathedrals, its confusion of cosmic orientations and rational grids, we can rely on the *letrados* to provide signs to "organize and interpret" the mess, "rendering the city meaningful as an idealized order."[53] Those signs might take the form of handwritten documents or, later, printed guidebooks, street signs, or even curated routes on Google Maps. It is worth noting, though, that well into the age of print, indigenous writing—particularly writing *on* the landscape—continued to play a key role in rural villagers' territorial markings: "possession to territory was . . . inscribed on paper, on the land itself," through the digging of *zanjas*, or boundary ditches, or through census takers' chalk marks on building facades.[54]

Rama specifies that the written plans for the ideal city "transposed" not into a concrete construction, not into "the fabric of the living city," but merely into a compelling urban imaginary. Meanwhile, anthropologist Brinkley Messick argues that we can find concrete historical parallels

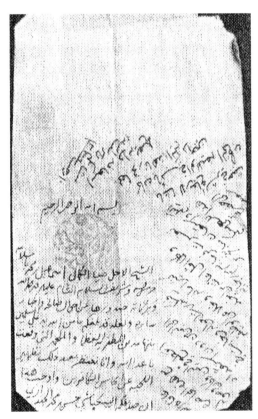 

FIGURE 36A. A spiral letter, 1917, Ibb, Yemen. Public domain.

FIGURE 36B. Contemporary satellite view of Ibb, Yemen. Via Apple Maps.

between writing and urban form: script made manifest in brick. He examines the history of Islamic architectural inscriptions and their formal parallels in the very "articulation" of urban space.[55] Messick discusses so-called Arabic "spiral texts," texts in which the writing rotates in a spiral shape, entwining form and content, and he argues that "this poetics of written space then can be extended to general domains of spatial organization: towns, architecture, and the space of the state."[56] He contrasts the "curvilinear urban script" of the Yemeni town of Ibb with the zoned, planned-out newer regions. While Ibb was "a labyrinth of closely packed multistoried houses on narrow and winding alleys and culs-de-sac," featuring lots of "residual, irregular spaces," the newer regions were characterized by "relatively straight-line, wide thoroughfares with some space left between the buildings."[57] This "new separation and precedence of urban form over urban content," and the parallel evolution in urban form, Messick argues, "is analogous to the changeover from spiral texts to their straightened successors." Whether we can claim a *causal* relationship is perhaps not the issue; what we see here is a morphological resonance between writing, an integral political-economic and cultural media infrastructure, and the shape of the city itself.

Many design historians have made similar claims about the media *of* design (from verbal instructions to blueprints to parametric tools) and the character of the architectural drawing or drawn urban plan, both of which are thought to shape the designer's proposed plans—and, eventually, the resulting concrete constructions. Scholars have researched the impact of graph paper and photography and 3D modeling on design practice; particular architects' penchants for sketching in charcoal or watercolor or on napkins; the history and epistemology of various projections in architectural drawing; and so forth.[58] Despite the prevalence of such research, Bernhard Siegert calls for an end to "expressions" about design "that do little more than reinscribe the ideology of the artist's [he uses 'artist' and 'architect' interchangeably] imaginary agency," that imagine architecture as "some ineffable act of creation." Siegert exhorts design theorists and historians to recognize "design as a cultural technique." Yet they already do, whether they use Siegert's particular terminology or not. They already attend to the "material cultures, practices, and workshop conditions" of design; they examine its historical "technologies, materialities, codes, and visualization strategies"—the means by which they make the material aesthetic and political.[59] Drawing, in particular—in graphite or ink on parchment or paper or screen—is widely recognized as a historical and political practice that is central to the identity of the architect: as Reyner Banham proclaimed, "being unable to think without drawing became the mark of one truly socialized into the profession of architecture."[60]

"The architects of the ancient world," architectural historian Mario Carpo suggests, "would have drawn up their actual project designs only at the building site and while the works were in full swing. The drawings that they made were working plans, often done at full scale"—in other words, written directly on the building site.[61] The earth was their substrate. Sometimes those plans were inscribed at smaller scale onto the lower walls of the under-construction buildings themselves, or onto clay tablets.[62] Thus, in many ancient cities, the writing of architectural and urban plans—if they were written out at all—and the realization of those plans most likely happened simultaneously, and in the same medium. Other genres of architectural thought—rules, theory, standards, etc.—likewise took form on different media substrates: manuscripts, printed books, oral address. These formats of communication shaped the advice authors dispensed, which in turn shaped the built environment their readers created.[63] Clay tablets and scrolls shaped architectural thought, which in turn informed the arrangement of bricks and stones. These texts thus mediated the translation of mud and stone into urban form—a form that both embodied an ideology and created a platform for a society to perform its politics.

Urban Writing Cultures: Circulating Texts

In Rama's lettered cities, colonial-era *letrados* generated and circulated texts to broadcast and legitimate the colonial order. Meanwhile, in Peruvian villages by the seventeenth century, "some kurakas (Andean nobles) and Andean commoners close to the scribal establishment could emulate the [colonialists'] ponderous legalistic prose that spoke to power."[64] Archaeologists have noted other examples of historical "subjects" who have learned their rulers' language and script as a means of empowerment or protection, or simply for purposes of self-education.[65] These are among the insights that the textual record alone cannot tell us; the archaeological context surrounding those texts helps us better understand who has the power to communicate within a colonial city—or any city, for that matter—and what power that privilege might confer.

The Andeans generated a vibrant culture of literacy—both through programs sanctioned by the state and the church, and informally, through their own kinship organizations and communities. Many of the

Spanish-language writings they produced were collaborative and palimp-sestic documents containing transcriptions of legal briefs interwoven from different periods of time, and translating not only one language into another, but also the spoken word into written form; native dictation or testimony was sometimes filtered through a mestizo interpreter and recorded by Spanish notaries.[66]

Today, Solomon and Niño-Murcia write, "modern *campesinos* (rural residents) bring to the bureaucratic-legalistic style of writing a devotion and enthusiasm that startle outsiders"; households "cherish their goatskin-wrapped packets of titles and lawsuits as vital endowments."[67] Information that is regarded as vital to the community is typically preserved in manuscript form, not in print; and "letters that matter often appear as art: as epigraphy, as embroidery, and as carvings."[68] The most critical texts thus materialize in stone, mud, and thread—contrary to the normative "hierarchy" of textual authority, and standard timelines of progressing "literacy," within the world of print capitalism. While record keeping was intended to keep social order in the Iberian colonies, the villagers of Tupicocha see their own self-directed record keeping "as the very linchpin of communal life," the "very heart of the social contract," as well as a means of determining what's "actually there" in the archive, in order to promote "equitable treatment by outside authorities" like state organizations and NGOs.[69]

Manuscripts have proven similarly central to the cultural identity of Timbuktu, in Mali.[70] These vellum and parchment documents—primarily in Arabic, but also in a few African languages—were created between the thirteenth and seventeenth centuries, when Timbuktu was an intellectual, spiritual, and cultural center and a hub for the trade of salt, gold, cattle, grain, . . . and manuscripts. The several-hundred-thousand-item local historical collection, containing both materials imported from elsewhere in the Islamic world and those copied locally, included texts on a wide variety of topics: poetry, music, African history, Islam, medicine, science and mathematics, and so forth. As the city developed its library, its leaders also commissioned mosques, including the magnificent Djingareyber, Sankoré and Sidi Yahia mosques, which served as centers for Islamic scholarship, and which, like much of the city's architecture, were constructed from banco, a mixture of mud and straw, on a timber frame.

When the Moroccan army invaded in 1591, its soldiers looted the libraries and carried their preeminent scholars off to Marrakesh. Yet many of Timbuktu's manuscripts survived, secreted away in private homes (many families later established their own private libraries), hidden in trunks or caves, or buried in the sand (over the years, some items have been carted or sold off to foreign museums or libraries, too). This literate history has also remained a popular secret: "Even most Malians have known nothing about the writings, believing that the sole repositories of the region's history and culture were itinerant musician-entertainers-oral historians known as *griots*," reported the *Smithsonian Magazine*'s Joshua Hammer in 2006. Musician Toumani Diabaté, who claims a griot heritage fifty-two generations long, told Hammer, "We have no written history."[71] That written history has been strategically concealed repeatedly throughout Mali's history, each time a city or village's written culture has been threatened by colonial invasion, flood, fire, or by tribal or radical insurgency.

Yet over the past several decades, archaeologists and archivists have begun to call attention to the documents and focus on their preservation. Much of this work has been centered at the Ahmad Baba Institute, which, in 1964, with support from UNESCO and several other Islamic countries, sent its staff across Mali in search of the diasporic manuscripts. In 2009, the Institute moved into a new home with proper climate control for preservation of the material documents, and equipment and funding for their digitization. Other private collections have used Western funding (from the Mellon and Ford Foundations, for instance) to construct their own private libraries—the Bibliothèque Mamma Haidara, Bibliothèque al-Wangari, and the Bibliothèque Allimam Ben Essayouti—and initiate their own digitization efforts. Here at these sites, again, local and global politics converge, as do "old" and "new" media regimes.

Yet digitization is no foolproof defense, as media archaeologists, forensic experts, and archivists know well.[72] Another attack—this time from Islamist insurgents—transpired in 2012, and the Malians' centuries-old preservation strategy—burying their written heritage in the earth—attracted global media attention. The Tuareg tribe allied with Islamic militants and seized Timbuktu. The jihadists, Hammer reports, ultimately abandoned the Tuareg, declared sharia law, and began attacking anything *haram*, or un-Islamic. "Eventually the militants set their sights on the city's ultimate symbols of open-mindedness and reasoned discourse: its manuscripts."[73] The dormant network of manuscript-activists sprang to action, smuggling over 350,000 manuscripts—by donkey, by boat, by night, often through jihadist checkpoints—to safety in Bamako. "The people here have long memories," said reporter Sidi Ahmed. "They are used to hiding their manuscripts. They go into the desert and bury them until it is safe."[74]

FIGURE 37. Still images from "Timbuktu Manuscripts Face an Uncertain Future" by AFP News Agency, and "Storm-Proofing the World's Biggest Mud Building" by BBC Earth's *Human Planet*. Fair use.

Early in 2013, French troops arrived in response to new threats from al-Qaeda.[75] Hammer reports that, at that time, the city was preparing for its Maouloud festival, which involves a public reading of some of their most revered manuscripts. The jihadists, faced both with impending French resistance *and* an impending *haram* ritual reading, threatened to destroy the manuscripts as a show of force against the French. The confiscation or destruction of archaeological and archival riches has long been a key strategy of war.[76] On January 25, the jihadists entered the restoration and digitization rooms at the Ahmed Baba Institute and burned 4,202 manuscripts. Despite this great loss, most of Timbuktu's written heritage was preserved—by digitization, yes; but also by mule and mud. The jihadists never ventured into the basement storage, where they would've found 10,603 restored manuscripts. Thousands of other written documents were shielded, too, behind mud walls or buried in sand, where they've hidden during so many times of trial.

Before we leave Timbuktu, I should note that mud has even more long-standing and widespread applications in preserving the city's cultural heritage. Not only have mud and sand helped to obscure Timbuktu's written artifacts and thereby prevent their destruction; but mud has also proven integral to the maintenance of its architecture, which embodies the city's spiritual and cultural heritage. Residents have used banco to rebuild, brick by brick, mausoleums destroyed in recent years by al-Qaeda. And since the fourteenth century, Timbuktu's residents have regarded it as their "religious and social obligation" to contribute to the maintenance of the city's mud mosques, which are constantly threatened by geological and climatic forces, particularly engulfment by sand (i.e., desertification).[77] UNESCO reports that, at least prior to the mosque's recent formal restoration (funded by the Aga Khan Trust), the community contributed to a restoration "ritual" at least biennially. After the banco is delivered and kneaded, the master mason, "well armed with magic spells, applies the first clods of banco while the others chant incantations." Then, both children and adults form "a chain to pass the banco from hand to hand to the sound of beating drums and flutes." By consulting ancient documents, the city's written heritage, they were able to refurbish the western facade of the Djingareyber Mosque's inner courtyard. Again, we see mud and text entwined in urban development and restoration, in the creation and maintenance of urban communities, in the cultivation of distinctive cultural identities, and in international development.

Standardization: Bricks and Concrete

Before bricks were uniformly manufactured, they featured a great deal of local variety, informed by local materials and local masonry customs and the idiosyncrasies of individual masons' work. Some of the oldest dried bricks, made around 7500 BCE from shaped mud, were found in present-day Turkey, and the earliest *fired* bricks, from around 3000 BCE, were found in the Indus Valley, in present-day Pakistan. Yet even in ancient Rome, the manufacture of bricks was standardized—they came in bessales, or 2/3-foot square modules; sesquipedales, 1.5-foot square; and bipedales, two-foot square—and they featured stamps identifying the name of the clay field or brickyard (*figlina*) where they originated, the name of its owner, the name of the brick-maker (*officinator*), and the consuls in office during its manufacture.[78] As Jean-Pierre Adam explains, "These bricks and their subdivisions are found at absolutely every level of the buildings as well as in walls, frames, arches and lintels, vaults, floors, or heating in-stallations."[79] By the nineteenth century, the introduction of wire cutters and dryers, brick-pressing machines and extruders, and other machinery dramatically routinized and standardized the production of bricks, which are today composed of clay-bearing soil, sand, and lime or concrete.

By the 1930s, a German architect named Ernst Neufert sought to fur-ther rationalize construction by publishing a set of architectural stan-dards, the *Bauentwurfslehre* (published in English as *Architects' Data*), which remains today a valuable resource. He drew heavily on his teenage experi-ence as a bricklayer. Inspired by the work of Die Brücke—Internationales Institut zur Organisierung der geistigen Arbeit, a Munich-based group dedicated to the organization of intellectual work and the development of standardized formats, he sought to build upon their efforts to normalize paper dimensions. He argued that "standard [paper] formats constitute the basis for the dimensions of furniture used for writing and record keeping. These are also constitutive of the dimensions of spaces."[80] Standardizing these various infrastructures would facilitate the circulation of ideas, pro-mote easy translation between disparate industries, save on storage space, and facilitate what he called "rapid design."[81]

Neufert discerned parallels between the proportions of standardized paper and Renaissance architecture, and he proposed that similar prin-ciples could reform the modern construction industry.[82] The A0 sheet of paper, one square meter in area, could be proportionally linked to a hypo-thetical "standard-format brick" via Neufert's "Octametric System," a set of norms based on an eight-part subdivision of the meter. The regularity of the Octametric System would purportedly increase the efficiency and cost-effectiveness of the construction process, and would allow builders to use the brick as a unit, an inscription, of measurement: one could count the number of standard-sized bricks to determine a room's dimensions, and then plan for its appointment with standard-sized furniture and ap-pliances. The bricks, architectural historian Nader Vossoughian says, "are thus media—that is, tools of communication—as well as materials, instruments of construction. They are intended as instruments for regulating—and not just building—buildings."[83]

In short, the forms of paper and brick are calibrated to one another and are scaled up to shape the furnishings in brick-built rooms. Those bricks could then be read as measurements of the room's dimensions. And according to Vossoughian, the standardization impulse that links those forms together also manufactures the need for more writing (and eventual codification in printed texts). "Over the course of the twentieth century," he writes, standardization "increased the designer's dependency on handbooks and manuals, which centralized and homogenized the production of architectural knowledge."

> It stimulated the spread of design systems, which regulated architectural decision-making across multiple scales. . . . It reimagined the "art of building" (Vitruvius [the first-century BCE Roman architect and engineer]) as a system for organizing and arranging dimensional norms, which interpolated the architect as a kind of "computer"—that is, as someone who calculates, computes, and organizes. Finally, it anticipated the phenomenon of digital design, which replaces the drafting table with the programmable "black box."[84]

Yet perhaps this "reimagining" wasn't so radical. Perhaps what we see here is a reiteration of the print-based design standardization, the "copy-book simulacra," that we discussed in our previous chapter. Another *topos* revisited.

Brick's ostensibly less regimented cousin, concrete, has also been credited with allowing designers to reimagine the "art of building." It's liquid, poured rather than installed in units, and chemically active. That liquid metamorphoses into solid form within mere hours of the pour. According to architect Francesca Hughes, concrete's material properties transformed construction and opened up new possibilities for conceivable designs.[85] Yet this material un-tamed-ness also made it a prime target for standards and specifications: "criteria for performance and written instruments of its own control."[86] "No other construction material's handling had ever, nor has ever, been so keenly determined," Hughes argues.

> [T]he quantification of every aspect of production, every small move of the laborer's body prescribed, the degree of vigorousness with

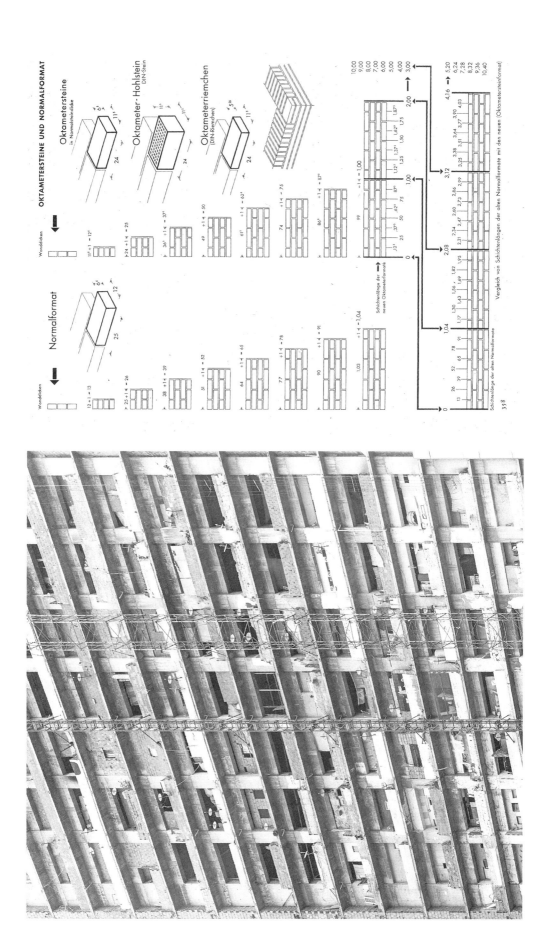

which a tester might knead a sample, the pressure with which a cement trowel might be applied to smooth over the top surface of a filled mold—all was set down, dictated *ad absurdam*.[87]

Traditionally, the "embedded knowledge" of laborers and foremen, about both material science and quality control, had proven sufficient on the construction job site. With the imposition of standards, however, "such knowledge was effectively lent both form and formality (extracted and written)."[88] Laborers' intuitive understanding of the material was thus externalized and formalized in writing (as we saw in our previous chapter with the codification of architectural knowledge in printed treatises). That externalization of knowledge paralleled a division of labor: as architectural historian Adrian Forty explains, chemists and engineers developed cements; industrialists sought to commercially exploit cement production; and "ordinary builders," originally aiming to improve on traditional rammed-earth construction, developed, often by trial and error, "the practical application of the material and subsequently the technique of reinforcing it with steel."[89]

Also, like brick, concrete is both modern and premodern, unnatural and natural, in its mix of primordial materials and new techniques and technologies. For millennia, civilizations have been mixing burnt limestone with sand, aggregates, and water and using it as a mortar—but cement, a binding component of concrete, has also occurred geologically for epochs. Natural deposits, where limestone has reacted with oil shale, have been found in Israel, and the excavation of Neolithic sites in Galilee and Serbia revealed buildings with concrete floors. As we discussed earlier, the Romans used pozzolana, volcanic sand, in their cement, too.

Yet this ancient material is also quintessentially modern. Concrete is an essential ingredient in Italian architect Antonio Sant'Elia's recipe for a Futurist architecture of calculation and "audacious temerity," and it has "contributed to the formation of modern architectural identities in an age of unprecedented urbanization" and monotonous suburbanization, with its ubiquitous office slabs, housing blocks, and parking lots.[90] Concrete

Opposite page:

FIGURE 38A. "Oktametersteine und Normalformat," 1943, from *Bauordnungslehre*. Courtesy Neufert-Stiftung.

FIGURE 38B. The Centro Financiero Confinanzas, also known as Torre de David, 2014, Caracas, Venezuela. CC-Zero.

found high-profile, progressive champions in the likes of Le Corbusier and Louis Kahn. It has also allowed for the creation of new, technically sophisticated forms: shells, extended spans, cantilevers. Still, its "crudeness" and the craft of its production, Forty argues, have also "provided a means of reconnecting with architecture's supposedly primitive origins in mud."[91] American architect Paul Rudolph, a noted brutalist (from *béton brut*, meaning "raw concrete"), reportedly complained that American concrete contractors' focus on precision gave their work a "thin metallic-like quality." "Concrete is mud," he said. "I work with concrete not against it. I like mud."[92]

Concrete also embodies an ambiguous politics. Cement production involves mixing limestone with clay, along with shells, chalk, shale, slate, sand, iron ore, and/or other materials and baking at high temperatures to produce lumps of "clinker," which is then ground up and mixed with gypsum and limestone. The process—from burning the lime, to powering the kilns, and ultimately to transporting the materials—is a source of significant carbon emissions.[93] In comparison, older building materials and techniques, like rammed earth and mud brick, require significantly less energy. Yet across a building's lifecycle, concrete, with its high thermal mass, requires relatively little energy for heating and cooling and thus proves quite efficient.[94] Still, as a global commodity like steel or oil, its component parts are extracted and distributed via an expansive logistical network.[95] And concrete is traded worldwide, often via the thousand-plus ships owned by massive companies like HeidelbergCement or LafargeHolcim.[96] Despite the standardization of this global product, however, there is still room for local variation: when we mix uniformly produced cement with local labor, steel, and aggregates, concrete can exhibit local variations, inspiring discussion of the material's potential regional characters, such as a Japanese or a Swiss concrete.

Perhaps place can thus be written in concrete. It can speak to class politics, as well. "In global terms," Forty argues,

> reinforced concrete is one of the new "technologies of poverty"—in overall quantity consumed, its use by self-builders in poor countries probably exceeds all other applications. In the shanty towns of the world, its use is characterized by ingenuity rather than innovation: new or even relatively old developments in concrete technology are irrelevant, what matters is the way small amounts of reinforced concrete are made to go a long way.[97]

Outside the "shanty towns," those new developments—including the creation of thin, elastic high-performance concrete, or the integration of optical fibers to generate a translucent material—have made possible new "forms of expression": decorative grainy surfaces, or the use of photo-engraving or digital etching to inscribe imagery or pattern into building skins, allowing, Cohen and Moeller suggest, "for a technologically based *architecture parlante*," an architecture that speaks its function or identity through form.[98]

Writing on Walls: Industrial Materials and Indigenous Inscriptions

Concrete has also historically been used—in unsanctioned practices, peripheral to the world of famous architects and international construction companies—to provide a platform for voices speaking in marginal languages. Concrete facades and walls, those ubiquitous urban partitions and screens, have given rise to their own epigraphic habit. Of course much has been written about the history of urban graffiti as a marker of territory or a means of individual or collective expression. Anthropologist Julie Peteet has studied graffiti on the concrete, cinder-block, brick, and stone walls of the occupied West Bank at the height of the intifada in the late 1980s and early 1990s. For Palestinians, she argues, that writing has served simultaneously to "affirm community and resistance, debate tradition, envision competing futures, index historical events and processes, . . . inscribe memory, . . . provide political commentary, . . . record events and commemorate martyrdom," and "issue directives both for confronting occupation and transforming oneself in the process."[99] Typically created by Palestinians and erased by Israelis, she says, these marks undoubtedly carried very different meanings for each. Yet both groups, as well as those foreign to the region and the conflict, could read the walls "much the way an archaeologist reads stratigraphy—layer by layer," with superimposed texts reflecting the temporality of an unfolding dialogue or the volatile "victory in an ongoing battle," or serving as a "barometer of discontent and resistance."[100] The flat, banal, brutal face of a concrete wall, whose act of dividing and denying served as a profound symbol of deep conflict, seemed to invite agonistic inscription. "The riot of signs on stones, and their erasure," Peteet argues, "signaled a contest over place and its definition. It made the stone walls into encoded tablets, public, didactic, archival, and interventionist spaces of riposte."[101]

Meanwhile, Calcutta hosted a different battle of public lettering—

FIGURE 39A. Graffiti on a portion of the Israeli/Palestinian separation wall, 2013, Bethlehem. Photograph by Gary Walsh, courtesy of Trocaire / CC-BY-NC-2.0.

FIGURE 39B. A child standing by wall writing, 1987, Calcutta. Photograph by Eric Parker / CC-BY-NC-2.

between official and commercial signage and informal wall writing. According to architectural and urban historian Swati Chattopadhyay, the early- and mid-twentieth-century city was clad in layers of text. Building facades—in plaster and brick, and more often by the early twentieth century, concrete—featured their owners' names and building names, dates of construction, street names and house numbers, all of which were embedded in the buildings' walls, "their permanency staking a claim in the city in the longue durée."[102] Businesses also painted semipermanent signboards on their facades, and an open strip of wall below the upper-story windows typically offered a long, unbroken space for commercial frame-mounted billboards.[103] Informal posters, which advertised films or introduced political candidates, added a fleeting surface-layer of applied text, "changing the materiality of the wall and its claim to obdurate permanence by showing up its susceptibility to reinscription and transformation."[104]

At the very top stratum of this palimpsest, an additional layer of informal wall writing by subaltern and marginalized groups manages to overpower the official and commercial scripts. In the process, Chattopadhyay says, it also challenges the permanence of state and corporate infrastructures.[105] Writers often first whitewash the walls to create a fresh space for their inscriptions, many of which then employ visual effects that mimic the shapes and materials of the facade; these writers and their scripts "appropriat[e] the wall by following its geometry of surfaces, solids, and voids," and "resonating" its "patchwork plaster and . . . exposed brickwork."[106] The wall is thus not simply a blank substrate; its mud and concrete give form to the writing it supports. At the same time, in "talking over" the facade's official scripts—house numbers and commercial billboards—this political wall-writing "express[es] the wall's impermanence and malleability, . . . bring[ing] forth new intentions and forg[ing] new readership and political agency."[107] The banality and brutality of concrete thus offer opportunities, again, for home-grown means of local inscription, for the subaltern to have a voice (we'll listen more closely to such voices in the next chapter).

The Mud and the Mark

Mud, that most humble of geological resources, and its material analogs clay, stone, brick, and concrete, have supplied the foundations for our human settlements and forms of symbolic communication. In mud-brick walls and clay tablets and concrete buildings we can observe the aggregated histories of communication and urbanization; we see the integration of *Kulturtechniken*'s dual lineages of cultivation—engineering the earth and training the mind. Written decrees and urban plans have proven instrumental in marshaling the resources to bring settlements and cities into existence, molding cities from clay and codes and cables, and in regulating and standardizing the use of those resources. The complexity of urban existence then necessitates the production of more and more written records. We sometimes observe formal parallels between a society's written texts, its building materials, and its urban morphology, as in Ibb and the colonial New World. And we often find that our cities and our media reflect one another in their operative logics and politics. Those bricks and stones can even speak their own "geologic *parlante*," reflecting the distinctive character of a place. And various writing cultures—like those etching lines into the Peruvian landscape, those carving on stones in China, those collecting manuscripts in the mud-and-timber city of Timbuktu, those generating household bureaucratic archives in postcolonial South America, or those protesting, in spray paint on concrete walls, in Calcutta and the West Bank—have used those bricks and stones as a platform for written expression. While their public inscriptions have held different meanings for different populations, those public writers have invariably, through their mark-making, reshaped the cities they lived in—and used their walls and written symbols to negotiate political forces at various scales.

Writing and urbanization are entangled materially, politically, economically, culturally, and historiographically. And as we've witnessed in the recent destruction of many treasures of the world's cultural heritage (as well as many non-monumental hospitals and homes) in the Middle East, those most humble geologic resources—when molded into bricks and texts, into monuments and manuals for living—are powerful emblems of, and lightning rods for, cultural politics. Wind, rain, and sand will continue to take their toll on these ancient monuments, cliff carvings, and other geologic media, thus gradually diminishing the archive from which we can write and experience our global cultural heritage. But an even more potent corrosive force, it seems, is the hubristic destruction inherent in a radical form of *Kulturtechniken*. The media of sledgehammers, bulldozers, dynamite, and Tomahawk missiles are equally powerful "symbolic operators," as Siegert might call them—not through their cultivation and inscription of meaning, but through their erasure.

4

Speaking Stones

VOICING THE CITY

A 2000 photograph by Richard Pare (see p. 116) depicts architect-engineer Vladimir Shukhov's Shabolovka radio tower, commissioned by Lenin, completed in 1922, hailed as a constructivist icon and now in dire need of restoration.[1] When I encountered this photo in the archives at the Canadian Centre for Architecture, where I was a visiting scholar in the summer of 2012, I wondered what, within this particular institutional context, this photograph was *about*—what it was documenting. I imagined we might use the photograph to tell the story of Russian constructivist design, or of photographer Richard Pare's numerous visits to the Soviet Union over the past twenty-plus years to document this and other neglected modernist structures. Yet what we might also discern in this photograph is the presence of something invisible, intangible—an immaterial spatial history that has echoed across the past century. This sturdy hyperboloid structure, now greatly weakened by extensive corrosion, has been the source of evanescent waves of sound that have roused revolutions.

Lenin regarded radio as an invention of tremendous political significance; he likened it to "a newspaper without paper and without wires," a tool for distributing propaganda far and wide without physical infrastructural encumbrances (and equally well suited to selectively disseminating untraceable messages among comrades).[2] It was the live voice, "the history-making event of its speech in present time," Susan Buck-Morss writes, "that carried mass-political charisma."[3] While the voice enchanted aurally, the infrastructure that carried it—the electrical grids and radio towers—appealed visually, exploiting a historical connection between the technological sublime and nationalism.

As we have seen, the attention paid to these modern communication architectures foreshadowed present-day fascinations with high-security data centers and the seaside shacks where transoceanic fiber-optic cables

FIGURE 40. "View of the Shabolovka Radio Tower (also known as Shukhov Tower), Moscow, Russia," 2000, by Richard Pare. Copyright Richard Pare.

come ashore. Yet the marvel of radio technology and its promise to collapse geographic distance didn't mean that there was no need for, or appeal to, old-fashioned orality: the live, present human voice embodied in its speaker. Buck-Morss acknowledges that, in the age of mass society,

> the voice as a medium for organizing the masses demanded a new technology. Megaphones magnified sound by directing its focus, but still required the visual presence of the speaker to reach a mass audience at all. Speakers' podiums recognized this fact, and they were a common design of revolutionary artists in the early years of the Bolshevik regime, even after electronic loudspeakers increased the audio range.[4]

One such podium is depicted in El Lissitzky's *Lenin Tribune*. In 1920, while the Shabolovka radio tower was under construction, Lissitzky invited his students in Vitebsk to design "a podium on which leaders of the revolution could speak to the people."[5] In 1924 Lissitzky took his student Ilia Chashnik's design and, for reasons that many scholars have speculated about, perched a Lenin figure at the top. A version of that figure—Lenin mid-proclamation, in jacket and tie, with outstretched arm and pointed finger—had first appeared in a 1920 poster proclaiming, "Prizrak brodit po Evrope, prizrak kommunizma" (A specter haunts Europe, the specter of communism).[6] Lissitzky later expressed his own satisfaction with the podium design: "It's just what I wanted, the sweep of the structure emphasizing the gesture," which is a pronounced forward lean rather than a dramatic gesture with the arm (see Figure 41).[7] What is also gestured toward here is the sound of the voice. What we see in these two images, Pare's and El Lissitzky's, are constructions that function as sonic *infra*structures, supports for vocality. In one instance, that voice is extracted from its body, electronically disseminated, audible across a vast geography. In the other, the voice is embodied, limited in reach, and dependent on a physical structure to lend it height, projective power, and prominence. These two images represent coterminous constructions.

The cities of the world have accommodated electronically amplified and broadcast sound, which we explored in chapter 1, for less than two hundred years. For millennia people relied on mechanical or architectural forms of amplification like the speaker's platform and even the city itself, its forums and facades functioning as a sounding medium. In this final chapter we'll listen closely to a particular medium, the voice, that

FIGURE 41. *Lenin Tribune,* 1920, by El Lissitzky. Public domain.

might stretch our contemporary understanding of the term *medium*, which presumes the presence of a technological intermediary. Yet the voice was indeed the primary means of communication in preliterate cultures, and is still a vital part of our communication repertoires today. It would seem that the only "infrastructure" we'd need for oral communication is all packaged within our resounding bodies, Jean-Luc Nancy's *corps sonore*, but we must acknowledge that all vocalizations happen *in* a setting, a space, either physical or virtual.[8]

Kittler regarded the city as a computational network encoded with location data and filled with "media [that] are at work replacing people with their addresses."[9] Yet "addressing" can also affirm and interpellate, rather than replace, the city's human inhabitants. And such humanist forms of address have informed—both intentionally and accidentally—the design, construction, and inhabitation of cities for millennia. In this chapter we'll consider how the city itself has functioned as a sounding board, resonance chamber, and transmission medium for vocality: for interpersonal communication, vocal expressions of affect, and public address.[10] While we do have recourse to audio recordings of the city and its broadcasts from the age of electrical sonification, we often have to turn to other methods, other sources of evidence, to replay the deep history of the sounding city for which there is no archive. To recapture those voices long since faded away—the signals that aren't "actually there" in the media archive—we often have to listen to the spaces and artifacts around them. By listening to mute prints and photographs, like Pare's and El Lissitzky's, and to the drawings and models and artifacts in collections and excavation sites around the world, and by listening for resonances among materials in disparate sites, we can continue to piece together the city and its architecture's history as sounding media.

Voice, Polis, Demos: Spaces and Sounds of Democratic Deliberation

Lewis Mumford reminds us,

> The city, as it develops, becomes the center of a network of communications: the gossip of the well or the town pump, the talk at the pub or the washboard, the proclamations of messenger and heralds, the confidences of friends, the rumors of the exchange and the market, the guarded intercourse of scholars . . . all these are central activities

of the city. In this respect the permissive size of the city partly varies with the velocity and the effective range of communication.[11]

A city's velocity and effective range depends in part on the material environment in which communication happens. Mumford's anecdotes paint a picture of an early modern city, but his acknowledgment that the city is a space of vocality is timelessly pertinent. A city's resonance has implications for civic representation (i.e., whose voices are heard, both in public and private realms), the strength of social ties and community identity, the vibrancy of the city's economy and cultural life, and the quality of its public health.

In recent years, archaeologists, drawing inspiration from sensory history, have begun to pay more attention to sensory experience, and particularly to acoustics: from the sounds produced in ancient sites by historical musical instruments or tools to the acoustic properties of various locations and how they informed drama, everyday speech, and a variety of other performative and communicative activities. Archaeologists working in the field of *archaeoacoustics* have studied the sonic architectures of ancient sites, from Stonehenge to Peruvian temples to American petroglyph sites, wondering how their acoustics might have shaped ritual performance and vocality, as well as inhabitants' experiences.[12] Much conjecture is involved in piecing together ancient multisensory experiences and ancient builders' intentionality, and the speculative nature of such archaeoacoustics research has generated debate.[13]

Mathematician and archaeologist Iegor Reznikoff, who has studied Paleolithic art in caves throughout Europe, has identified a correlation between a cave site's acoustic resonance and its concentration of wall markings; he suggests that densely decorated sites were likely the location of rituals using instruments and chant.[14] At Chichen Itza in Mexico, the Mayans built a pyramid along the narrow end of their Great Ball Court, which was surrounded by vertical stone walls that created reverberations and resonances, augmenting "the perceived mass and size of the leader's voice, raising his stature and perceived power."[15] And in Peru, in a network of tunnels beneath the city of Chavín, archaeologists found a set of marine-shell trumpets, *pututus*, corroborating their theory that somewhere between 1500 and 400 BCE the tunnels functioned as a series of resonance and sound-transmission tubes. "Tones in the same frequency range as both human voices and the shell trumpets produced consistent resonances in the alcoves."[16] City complexes of the period typically featured a U-shaped urban plan, which created an acoustic shell that amplified projected speech, but later settlements, like Caylán (800–1 BCE) on Peru's north coast, were typically composed of rooms clustered around an enclosed, sunken central plaza. The urban plan here created an acoustically isolated environment that could accommodate a variety of sonic activities—from panpipe performances to intimate conversations.[17]

Archaeologists have also examined sound-amplifying wall niches like the curved, carved projection known as the Oracular Chamber in the Hal Saflieni Hypogeum, an underground cemetery used in Malta from 4000 to 2500 BCE.[18] In what is now southwest Iran, sometime between the eighth and sixth century BCE, the Elamites situated their Kūl-e Farah open sanctuary near the opening of a gorge; the site seems geologically predisposed to function as a "giant sound box."[19] And informed by Vedic Hinduism, which places great importance on acoustics, particularly speech and music, archaeologists have been exploring the sonic properties of stone in ancient Indian architecture (stone, you'll recall from our previous chapter, also served in this region as a substrate for early Buddhist writings).

The ancient Greeks' appreciation of acoustics was also informed by spiritual and metaphysical beliefs: they made use of oracular sites, where the gods could speak to mortals, and Pythagoras's "harmony of the spheres" proposed the existence of a harmonious natural order.[20] "Given their strong interest in all forms of aural activities, including music, oration, rhetoric, and religion," Barry Blesser and Linda-Ruth Salter write, "the ancient Greeks were likely to have been aware of how these activities were influenced by spatial acoustics."[21] The diversity of activities in the open agora, or marketplace, for instance, invited walking and casual conversation, and generated a cacophony of citizens' voices. In their amphitheaters, meanwhile, the stepped seats of rough-hewn limestone—whether by design or by accident—acted as an acoustic filter, suppressing low-frequency background noise and isolating the higher-frequency performer's voices.[22] The theaters' locations, often among rolling hills, also provided favorable acoustic conditions.

While renowned for its theatrical innovations, ancient Greece is also the quintessential example of a civilization founded upon a particular structural form of rational communication: the linking of meeting places, debate, and democracy. Architectural historian Anthony Vidler argues that Plato's ideal city—of which we find six versions throughout his oeuvre—is primarily "a city of discourse," which "exists first and foremost for the dialogues themselves."[23] Aristotle, too, prescribed a city that would contain no more people than could hear a herald's voice.[24] Aristotle's *Poetics*, philosopher Mladen Dolar notes, establishes the "political dimension of the voice, [and] its deep involvement in the constitution of the political"; this is a voice capable of not just general vocality, but of speech, of intelligibility.[25]

Classicist Christopher Lyle Johnstone, noting in 1997 that "physical setting has been virtually ignored in rhetorical scholarship," draws on archaeological research to explore how the architecture of Athens' agora, where most civic functions were carried out until the early sixth century, and the architecture of its civic buildings—including the law courts, stoa, and various auditoria—shaped both an orator's delivery and his audience's engagement, and even limited the size of the audience (it's important to note that juries usually numbered at least two hundred, and sometimes close to five hundred).[26] He, like others practicing archaeoacoustics, acknowledges the speculative and conjectural nature of his work. Yet he proposes that the stoa—a long, narrow structure with walls (typically made of stone) along both short ends and one long side, and an open colonnade along the other long side—probably had a "pronounced reverberation effect," which would have distorted speakers' voices.[27] Experienced speakers, however, "might have selected [their] cadences so as to take advantage of the building's acoustical properties"; if they found the structure's acoustic "sweet spot," the rhetorical effect could be "mesmerizing and engrossing."[28] Meanwhile, in the bouleuterion, the square or rectangular council house, tiered seating, high ceilings, and internal columns allowed speakers and auditors to see one another, cultivating a sense of intimacy, and permitted some degree of acoustic subtlety. "Thus could a speaker employ an ordinary speaking voice in addressing a fairly large audience, and thus could he make the sorts of asides and *sotto voce* comments that would be ineffective in a less intimate setting."[29]

In the fifth century BCE, the political assembly moved to the Pnyx hill. While only a short walk from the agora, it was far removed from the agora's mobility and cacophony. The Pnyx's layout "emphasized the seriousness of attending to words," Richard Sennett argues; it "made political use of . . . sitting, spectator bodies."[30] Yet the physical setting also had affective power; the scenery cultivated pathos and ethos. From this site,

> one could look toward the Acropolis and see the Nike Temple nestled neatly inside the larger Parthenon behind it, as though the arrangement of these two temples was deliberately designed for the speaker (from among an all-male assembly) with this orientation in mind:

FIGURE 42. Panorama of Athens, from the Pnyx. Photograph by Tomisti / CC-BY-SA-3.0.

> winged victory nested within the temple of the city's patron goddess, declaring hegemony held by her citizens. . . . The ancients understood the importance of the view offered by the assembly place.[31]

The broader topography was also part of the scene. The rolling hills and mild climate of many ancient Greek cities permitted the *demos* to meet out-of-doors or in open buildings and appreciate the surrounding scenery. This setting "contributed to the success not only of the amphitheaters but also of Greek democracy, which might not have flourished without the frequent, publicly shared experiences" that these meeting places made possible.[32]

For the Romans, too, cities were predicated on rhetoric: "Never in my opinion," Quintilian writes, "would the founders of cities have induced their unsettled multitudes to form communities had they not moved them by the magic of their eloquence."[33] "The eloquence of Cicero," who rhetorically situated his arguments in relation to particular sites in the urban environment, "made the stones speak," argues classicist Catharine Edwards.[34] The Roman architect Vitruvius tells of ancient builders who sought to cultivate acoustics that maximized the "clearness and sweetness" of orators' voices.[35] Inspired by the principles of harmonics, the Romans placed bronze vessels beneath the seats of their auditoria, which would supposedly resonate with and amplify the voice. The technique, while inventive, was likely ineffectual.

Despite their attempts to discipline urban sound through the imposition of mathematical order, ancient Rome was "constant chaos and constant hubbub," a city that grew up helter-skelter, without a plan, across a varied topography of hills and marshes; with craftsmen and vendors and entertainers in the streets and some of its noisiest trades—coppersmiths, hammerers, money changers—concentrated in the city center.[36] Multiple languages—Syriac, Coptic, Punic, Celtic, Hebrew, Latin—mingled here with animal sounds, and those street noises permeated the apartment blocks stacked four or five stories high.[37]

In 1872 archaeologists found in the Roman forum a marble relief representing an emperor, either Trajan or Hadrian, standing on the forum's Rostra Augusti (a speaker's platform), delivering a public address or *adlocutio* (an address to the army). In Julio-Claudian times, the emperor often delivered speeches from across the forum, on a platform at the Temple of Divus Iulius, while his heir occupied the Rostra Augusti. Inspired by such finds, architectural historian Diane Favro and classicist Christopher Johanson have created digital models of the forum to understand how the space accommodated funeral processions, multisensorial affairs choreographed to appeal to multiple audiences. They've attempted to model and understand, in part, how the forum functioned acoustically as a space for speech and pageantry: "How did accompanying sounds reinforce the activities? . . . Where did spectators stand? . . . What route to the forum was taken by participants?"[38] Such models could help to reveal how the material urban landscape functioned as an "infrastructure" for the sights and sounds of these public events—how various architectures "dictated the choreography" and "created a formal tableau" that assigned status to particular sensory experiences.[39]

Johanson explained to me the particular challenges of modeling the sounds of ancient sites. With so many variables, including the dimensions and materials of the buildings surrounding the plazas, each of which is a "tightly controlled sonic environment," and the numerous waterworks throughout Roman cities, it's hard to piece together a recreation of what they would've sounded like, how they functioned as infrastructures for mediation.[40] Sound was competing with other media, too. As we saw in chapter 3, these same spaces were plastered with public writings and ornamented with various plastic arts; "all of these are part of the competitive elements when someone's giving a eulogy." Johanson and his colleagues have thus focused their work mainly on visual interactions in ancient spaces, because "it's the one element that can be tied to some kind of evidence and reproduced with a deliberate representational strategy." Yet he and his partners at the Experiential Technologies Center at UCLA,

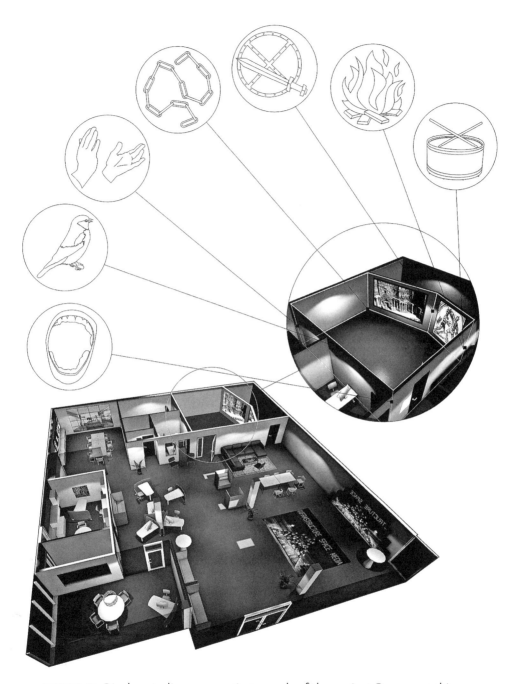

FIGURE 43. Display studio representing sounds of the ancient Roman amphi-theater. Originally published in Anna Foka and Viktor Arvidsson, "Experiential Analogies: A Sonic Digital Ekphrasis as a Digital Humanities Project," *Digital Humanities Quarterly* 10:2, 2016. Figure by Anna Misharina, 3D model by Mattis Lindmark. Courtesy of Anna Foka.

along with researchers in other archaeology labs, see potential in integrating acoustical programs with their digital models.[41]

Favro argues that new research in this area needs to attend more closely to *non-elites'* participation in and responses to public events. Gregory Aldrete's work represents one contribution toward this end. He has chronicled the various gestures and acclamations through which everyday people could interact with the Roman emperor and other elite presenters. To express their support or discontent, the "urban plebs" chanted or sang phrases in response, they buzzed and trilled, they snapped their fingers and waved their togas, and they employed different techniques of applause—obviously, a form of bodily sound-making that doesn't involve the voice at all.[42] Emperors coveted applause as an indicator of their subjects' loyalty and approval. Nero was particularly impressed by the Alexandrians' noise-making repertoire—which included "the roof-tiles," a cupped-hand clap; "the bricks," a flat-hand clap; and "the bees," a collective humming and trilling—and he appointed assistants to coach his own subjects in the art of clapping.[43] These nonverbal expressions were then performed en masse, in Rome's public spaces, whose acoustic conditions dramatically impacted the sonic effect. As Megan Garber writes in the *Atlantic*,

> One reason Roman leaders so systematically built amphitheaters and racetracks throughout the lands they conquered was to, on the one hand, foster a sense of "Romanness" among their subjects. But it was also, on the other, to offer a place where the public could become, publicly, "the governed." The amphitheater was a place of conversion. "To be a legitimate emperor," Aldrete says, "you have to appear in public and receive the applause of the people."[44]

Media historian Carolyn Birdsall describes how German National Socialist leaders employed similar mass acoustic events—thousands of voices joined in singing or chanting, feet marching rhythmically, often amplified by loudspeaker-equipped vans—to reverberate throughout and occupy urban space.[45] By cultivating an "affirmative resonance," these sonic events interpellated Nazi subjects, united them as a group, and resoundingly affirmed the Nazi regime's ability to effect acoustic and political control over the city (in Birdsall's case, Düsseldorf) and its inhabitants.

While political regimes have certainly exploited acoustics as a disciplinary technology, other governments and assemblages have continued

FIGURE 44. Stereoscopic view of an old German meeting house in Waldoboro, Maine, date unknown, by Asa H. Lane. Via the New York Public Library digital collections. Public domain.

to create spaces where both elites and everyday citizens can be seen and heard—and validated in various forms of representative government. Lewis Mumford explains that population growth in New England in the seventeenth century incited forms of urban management that harken back to Plato's and Aristotle's ideas about the optimally sized city, one defined by a range of audibility. The New England town, Mumford writes, "ceased to grow beyond the possibility of socializing and assimilating its members: when near crowding, a new congregation would move off under a special pastor, erect a new meeting house, form a new village, lay out fresh fields."[46] The visibility and audibility of the town meeting were central to the town's *demos*: "the citizens met face to face in a special building, the town hall: they saw and heard their fellow citizens, and they discussed problems relating to a unit immediately within their grasp and vision."[47]

Those towns were commonly laid out in six-mile squares, with large meeting houses located at their centers, in the heart of acoustic activity. Simple, boxy, wood-frame structures, the houses had hipped roofs and, often, wood plank floors, and a high pulpit and pulpit window along one wall. As the towns grew, they commonly added seating galleries (or simple raised platforms) along the other three walls. Because the houses were used for both religious services and political functions, some towns, in an effort to preserve the separation of church and state, created a separate floor at the balcony level and used the first floor for state business, the upper floor for church. Given their interior volume and material composition, the houses were likely quite reverberant spaces, but the bodies that packed them dampened the echo. And as historian Richard Cullen Rath argues, these spaces prioritized democratic acoustics, allowing all to hear and be heard.[48] The "town hall" principle held sway for leaders of the French Revolution, too. In response to corrupt legal practices of the *ancien régime*, revolutionaries embraced the principles of the "living voice" and the "public nature of court proceedings," Mladen Dolar argues.[49] They recognized that "democracy is a matter of immediacy, it is of the voice; the ideal democracy would be the one where everybody could hear everybody else's voice."

Even the horizontally and vertically expanded and unmanageably populous cities of the nineteenth century sought out sites and opportunity for congregation and audition. As Mumford again reminds us, "In every . . . [early nineteenth-century industrial] center the political auditorium became the chief civic institution: Exeter Hall, Albert Hall, Madison Square Garden, the endless Mechanics' Halls."[50] Like their ancestors, the orators in these venues had to be attuned to their acoustics.

> Schooled or unschooled, people were veteran auditors of hours-long sermons, stump speeches, wedding toasts, union exhortations, lyceum lectures, revival harangues. Connoisseurs of such holdings forth, they appreciated delivery and style and listening for sound as well as soundness of argument.[51]

The venues may have changed and the audiences may have diversified over the millennia, but many of our cities have continued to provide spaces where a *demos*, an urban community and its individual urban subjects, constitute themselves (or divide themselves) through sound. However, as neoliberalism translates social values into economic terms and strongly impacts the way cities are built and governed, we might wonder if contemporary urban spaces still provide sites for a political public sphere to thrive—or if, in the words of political scientist Wendy Brown, we might be "undoing the *demos*."[52] We'll return to this question later on.

Voicing Economy and Territory: Drawing Urban Sonic Boundaries

Sound has always been an index of economic activity. "Sound is not apart from the economic order," writes Eric Wilson, "but one of its fundamental, if less frequently recognized components."[53] Particularly in the early modern age, when urban streets were sites of commerce (as was often the case in the ancient world, too), we can discern among the sights and sounds of the city a gradual shift into a new age of print capitalism, and, at the same time, the persistence of vocality as a vital means of communication. Print proliferated, yet the voice still resounded. It's important to note that, contrary to claims that the "Gutenberg revolution" effected an abrupt shift to visual culture and away from "orality," aural and visual forms of communication were coterminous and mutually influential during this period. The spread of the printing press did bring new published forms to cities across Europe, yet the voice often duplicated the messages those new publications carried and continued to provide its own, unparalleled broadcast services. In this age before newspapers, Hillel Schwartz writes, "town criers cried the news, advertisements, and official proclamations at each crossing, preceded by wooden clappers, drums, trumpets, horns, bells, fifes. The illiterate dictated letters to street scribes, and public notaries reread contracts back to wary customers."[54] Shopkeepers might have conveyed their goods and services on signage, but they also "uttered" their merchandise—as vendors still do (often to city officials' chagrin) in the alleyways of Beijing and on the streets of many other contemporary cities. " 'What do you lack?': uttered over and over, it would be the aural equivalent of a flashing neon sign."[55] And during exceptional occurrences, both disastrous and wondrous—like city-wide epidemics or festivals—groans, shrieks, and bells cut through the consistent din.

The material urban environment of course informed how those cries and calls resounded. Most buildings in early modern London, for instance, were five or six stories high and made of wood and plaster, and those owned by the wealthy often included glass windows. These materials would've created a fairly reverberant environment. Yet the streets—mostly mud, with a few rough-hewn stones or cobbles embedded—could've dampened the din a bit.[56] The design of that urban architecture was profoundly informed by the voice, too, as we noted briefly in chapter 2. Through the medieval period, before the spread of printed architectural treatises and plans, designers relied on the "oral transmission of [their] disciplinary corpus."[57] Particularly during the Gothic period, from the twelfth through the sixteenth century, architectural theory was captured in "lodge secrets" and "the esoteric geometry of medieval master masons." Design focused on a set of geometric rules that lent themselves to verbal description. Yet even with the rise of print-schooled designers, their work still accommodated, and civilized, the voice. Sixteenth-century Italian architect Andrea Palladio, author of *The Four Books of Architecture*, envisioned cities of broad streets with porticoes and paved sidewalks that would facilitate the circulation of goods and people while still serving as an orderly public scene, in keeping with his conception of the city as a theatrical space. In the enlightenment city, Anthony Vidler writes, "the order was total—no disturbance, and . . . supremely silent. People, crowds, their cries, smells, and movement" would ideally be "absorbed into the stable equilibrium of the rational street."[58]

The new printed architectural treatises like Palladio's advanced a new architectural order—one whose success depended upon the ability of a rational plan to discipline and muffle its human inhabitants—both out-of-doors and indoors.[59] In medieval homes, walls were thin, often hung with tapestries to retain heat and keep out the din; floors were made of earth, stone, or rough planks; and ceilings were typically low.[60] Leon Battista Alberti, in his 1452 *On the Art of Building*, advocated that new homes have public, semiprivate, and private rooms; that husbands and wives have separate rooms, with separate doors, so that the groans of an ill or birthing wife wouldn't disturb her husband; and that the grandmother have a separate room "well away from all the din coming from the family and outside."[61] While new homes of the elite aimed to separate the masters from their servants and to divide them into separate acoustic zones, the house's highly reverberant volumes and surfaces—their long, whisper-amplifying hallways and uninsulated windows—undoubtedly magnified sound within and permitted the infiltration of noise from without.[62]

Some early modern civic or religious buildings were even themselves regarded as having a voice—particularly as mediated through their bells, which were "part of the ordinary and usual sounds of city life" since at least the seventh century CE.[63] "Bells shaped the habitus of a community," Alain Corbin argues in his study of French village bells.[64] Bells served a similar function in colonial cities and towns of the northern and central Andes. Superimposed on the colonialists' secular grid was "the space and practice of the church"—a space delimited by the peal of church bells. "The territory within which such a sound carried was constituted as a legal community, mapped onto provincial space—the *resguardos*, or indigenous communities, of the New Kingdom of Granada were built around this concept, with all native people living 'a son de campana,' within the sound of the church bell."[65] Meanwhile, in the plaza, a *pregonero*, or town crier, translated the colonial administration's orders and announcements into indigenous languages.

Urban bells were used to raise alarm, call people together, provide a sonic signature for particular acoustic territories, and, through their marking of time, regulate a shared temporality for the community, too. By the late nineteenth century, however, bells came to be heard as "unmodern"; stripped of their former spiritual significance, they were simply another contributor to the urban cacophony. Schwartz wonders: "Was it that modern citizens were unprepared for reverberations off the steep canyons of dense urban avenues where the ringing of bells could be felt as well as heard?"[66] Given media scholars' and technologists' occasional tendency toward teleological models of media history and their presumption that new technologies improve upon and phase out their predecessors, they might surmise that the bells were simply rendered obsolete—that some new technology emerged to perform their cultural and political-economic functions more efficiently. Yet we need to recognize that the bells were merely one element in a richly mediated environment. The Andean plaza, for instance, wasn't merely an *aural* space; it was—as were Corbin's villages and Favro's forum—"filled by a multiplicity of practices that were simultaneously inscribed aurally and ritually into urban space, as well as pictographically and alphabetically in paintings, murals, and written documentation."[67] Ethnomusicologist Ana Maria Ochoa Gautier agrees, citing a "long Latin American lineage of interrelating oral and written texts."[68] Archaeologists and classicists, as well as many early modern and Renaissance scholars, have also emphasized the widespread coexistence and intermingling of "orality" and "literacy," rather than the supplanting of the former by the latter.

This is an important reminder: although in this chapter we are training our ears specifically on the voice, that auditory instrument has always been merely one in a larger sonic, visual, textural, and performative symphony of urban mediation. The way we hear urban voices is informed by this broader urban "sensory economy," by our cultural and historical and spatial contexts, by our own situational or generational "audile techniques," as sound scholar Jonathan Sterne calls them.[69] "Each generation," Schwartz acknowledges,

> inhabits a different acoustic universe, constituted by different musics and memories of sound, by different thicknesses of walls and densities

of traffic, by different means of manufacture and broadcast, by different diets and ear-damaging diseases, by different proportions and preponderances of metal rattling in kitchens, clanging on the streets, or ringing in the (differently polluted) air above.[70]

Those urban streets and airspaces also play a significant role in how sound resounds, and in how listeners hear it. The lesson applies equally well to bells and human voices, to written and printed texts, to the myriad media that have inhabited and enriched our cities across time.

The Amplified Voice of Reverence and Revolt: Spaces of Faith and Protest

Just as the meetinghouse sat at the geographic and social center of its New England town, the grand mosque has traditionally sat at the center of the Arab city, serving as both its religious and cultural hub. Its minaret has provided a visual and acoustic center to the urban landscape. It is from here where the *muezzin*, facing Mecca, broadcasts the *adhān*, or call to prayer, five times a day. The call unifies the community of faith within its acoustic reach, and synchronizes their daily rhythms in accordance with spiritual time. And the minaret, like the belfry, has also historically incited debates over spatial and sonic politics. In 1311, the Council of Vienne prohibited the call to prayer in Christian territory, where the *adhān* was regarded as not only a nuisance, but also an offense in its declaration that Mohammed is a messenger of God.[71] Other sonic infringements raised Christians' ire: they complained of Muslims' nighttime celebrations during the month of Ramadan, and their preaching and prayer in public places.[72] In 1347, the bishop of Osca decreed that the height of all mosques and minarets be reduced; in 1461, King John II proposed that the call to prayer be performed—by voice, trumpet, or another instrument—from the mosque doors rather than from the minaret, presumably because the lower altitude would delimit the call's acoustic range; and in 1477, he called for much more extreme measures: the destruction of all the minarets in Valencia.[73]

These restrictive measures remind us that not only are listening practices *culturally* and *historically* informed, as we heard in chapter 1, but, in this case, they're liturgical, epistemological, and ontological, too. Sound, particularly sound-in-space, is an integral part of Islam's "system of belief." As art historian Oleg Grabar has noted, "Islamic culture finds its means of self-expression in hearing and acting rather than in seeing," for "it is not forms which identify Islamic culture . . . but sounds, history, and a mode of life."[74] Yet forms—medial, architectural, urban—shape and construct a *habitus* for those sounds and actions. Fellow art historian Nina Ergin believes that, despite the centrality of sound in Muslims' religious practice, and despite the fact that some builders of mosques have placed acoustic concerns at the center of their architectural practice, historians studying the Islamic built environment have paid too little attention to sound, particularly to Qur'anic recitation—that is, the devout voice.[75] What's more, she argues, that voice isn't heard in isolation, either inside or outside the mosque. Outside, it mingles with the sounds of the city, and inside it is but one instrument in a synesthetic *Gesamtkunstwerk*—a total artwork composed of

> the sounds of the call to prayer, Qur'an recitations, eulogies, sermons, prayers, and the clicking of prayer beads; the physical building and its furnishings, such as the pulpit, rugs, tiles, lamps, Qur'an copies and Qur'an stands; the movements of the worshippers prostrating, Qur'an reciters rocking back and forth in rhythm with their chanting; and even the smell of the incense.[76]

In recent decades, the Islamic voice has extended into the multisensorial urban environment not only from the minaret, but also through an increasing array of mediated forms. Anthropologist Charles Hirschkind has studied cassette tape recordings of Qur'an recitations and sermons, which since the 1970s have been played everywhere from private bedrooms to taxicabs to cafes, thereby "reconfigur[ing] the urban soundscape, imbuing it with an aural consciousness."[77] Just as the call to prayer sonically gathers a community of faith, the cassette tape has the potential to transform a more delimited, quotidian urban environment into "a space of moral action." Anthropologist Brian Larkin reports that, in Nigeria, "Sufi followers tie speakers across the narrow alleyways of urban districts"—highly reverberant, contained environments—"and perform impromptu '*yabo*' (praise) sessions. . . . Muslim movements sponsor cars with large loudspeakers fixed to the top, relaying their *wa'azi* (preaching) as they drive slowly from street to street."[78] And in spiritually mixed cities, Christian churches, too, "make great use of loudspeakers, amplifying their services to the surrounding neighborhood," sometimes even for all-night prayer vigils. The mediation of the *adhān* through the loudspeaker (the *n'urar magana*, the "talking machine")—much more indiscriminate and distributive in its reach than the personal cassette player—extends not only the (often distorted) call's acoustic reach, but also its potential for political discord. In the Nigerian city of Jos, Larkin writes, "one can hear several mosques all emitting their sounds at the same time and often in direct 're-taliation' to other mosques," as well as Christian churches playing hymns in competition.[79] Sound artist and scholar Lawrence Abu Hamdan explores the heated spatial politics of similar "loudspeaker libertarianism" in Cairo in his 2014 video, *The All-Hearing*.[80]

When the loudspeaker became an extension of the minaret, the amplified call to prayer stirred long-simmering controversy over the politics of sound (or noise, depending upon the listener's perspective), "rights to the city," and religious freedom.[81] Such discord was particularly pronounced in cities in which the community surrounding the mosque was religiously diverse. The loudspeaker itself often became a subject of legislation or a material target in uprisings of ügious violence. Continuing in the tradition of King John II, some city officials have imposed decibel limits on the amplified call or ordered mosques to redirect their speakers inward, restricting the material spaces in which the call can resound. Some mosques in Singapore (and elsewhere) even agreed, as a compromise, to broadcast a live call over the radio five times a day. The public, inclusive, *broadly-*

FIGURE 45. Still from *The All-Hearing*, 2014, by Lawrence Abu Hamdan. Fair use.

cast call thus became an individualized, "miniaturized," privatized experience. The muezzin's voice was still live, but his resonance chamber had shifted from the city to a network of shops and family apartments, whose inhabitants listened simultaneously to the same call from their distributed locations. As the relationship between physical and acoustic space shifted, the ontology of sacred space changed dramatically, too. Lee explains:

> Through the use of radio, the extended and separated profiles of Muslims in the urban environment now form uninterrupted acoustic space, and resultantly, a unified social and religious space. It is the radio, rather than the physical proximity of a mosque, that facilitates the cohesion of the Islamic community and maintains its identity within the larger, urban context of Singapore.[82]

Newer networked forms of media—sermons on YouTube and religious communities on Facebook and Twitter, for example—have the potential to bring even more widely distributed Muslims together into an "imagined community," but they also facilitate the fracturing of Islam into niche communities free to listen to the particular voices that appeal to their sensibilities. We see and hear this with Islamic State and their savvy use of social media to incite a global following. Larkin argues that even in the material city, such subjective, selective listening practices, which he calls "techniques of inattention," are necessary for "attuning" oneself to urban living. "The endemic, repetitive nature of religious conflict"—fed by loudspeakers as well as religious pamphlets, public preachers, and radio and television broadcasts—"means that in order to operate in the urban arena one has to cultivate inattention, the ability not to hear" certain messages, the messages that don't interpellate one as a listening subject.[83]

In some cases, that proximity of sounding and listening bodies, and the exceptional and confrontational rise of discordant voices, are essential to the expression of particular political "modes of life," to quote Grabar. In other words, some urban practices depend upon compression and cacophony. Voices of demonstration and collective dissent have long punctuated urban soundscapes, transforming streets and squares into resonance chambers for protest. Urban parks—"public" secular spaces— have commonly served as venues for such uprisings, despite their often unpredictable acoustics. The United States' first purpose-built urban public parks, for instance, were intended to serve as acoustic spaces of exception, oases within the urban din.[84] If we consider what it must've sounded like to have a conversation within the chaos of the nineteenth-century urban street, we need to consider the city's material properties as an acoustic environment. The voice would have interacted, or competed, with a host of sounds: traffic, whose clatter was tuned by the materials of road construction (pavement, shells, stones, wood); the noises made by a great mass of people (and their horses); and reverberations throughout those steep canyons of rising skyscrapers.[85] What's more, Schwartz says, is that the nineteenth-century city was "a heat sink, its large brick or stone buildings and pavement retaining heat, raising the local temperature and speeding sound along."[86] Parks, with their sound-dampening earth and foliage and their occasional walls and elevation changes, often provided a reprieve from the din.

By the mid-nineteenth century print was widely available—in fact, as Henkin reminded us in chapter 2, it was plastered and littered all over the city—and the mechanically reproduced image was gaining in popularity.[87] From the clandestine circulation of books to the underground press, print had, for centuries, provided opportunities for the dissemination of dissenting voices. Yet even then, with plenty of other platforms for proclamation, the city was still a place of public address, offering myriad material platforms for voicing calls for reform. One such place was New York City's Union Square Park. Its design was repeatedly modified over the years to either accommodate or contain voices of protest. As architectural historian Joanna Merwood-Salisbury explains, the square was "deliberately designed to support participatory democracy. The triangular parcels of land left over by the imposition of the [elliptical park] on the grid were expressly made for 'the assemblage of large masses of our citizens in public meetings.'" The gathering of huge rallies in support of the Union showed the square to be a "theater adequate to the utterance of the national voice," proclaimed Samuel Ruggles, one of Union Square's developers, in 1864.[88] Through its continual renovation, planners aimed to use the square as an infrastructure to create "active and informed citizens as well as foster social harmony," yet it remained, and *remains*, a site for radical meetings and rallies (including many that integrate a variety of media: locative technologies, text messages, cloth banners, and, still, the bull-horned or naked human voice).[89]

The loud speaker, again, transformed the voice's spatial politics. "By the 1930s," Schwartz writes, "loudspeakers were touted as capable of commanding audiences of half a million"—far larger than any Athenian agora could accommodate.[90] And in more recent decades demonstrators

FIGURE 46. Federica Montseny speaks at the historical meeting of the Confederación Nacional del Trabajo in Barcelona in 1977. Photograph by Manel Armengol / CC-BY-SA-2.0.

have employed entire *sound systems* that reverberate off stone and glass walls—and which, as Israel Rodríguez-Giralt, Daniel López Gómez, and Noel García López argue, serve not only to broadcast a common, unifying sound among an assembled group, but also to "catalyze" the creation of new spatialities and collectivities.[91] In other words, the amplified voice, through its acoustic reach, creates or claims space and constitutes the listening and sounding publics who can then occupy it. The parks in many Chinese cities, for instance, commonly provide spaces for collective activity. Chengdu's People's Park, renowned for its clamor, frequently draws dance troupes, choirs, bands, karaoke competitors, and exercise groups toting amplifiers.[92]

The particular material properties of those urban gathering spaces and their codes of operation also inform how collectives form and how voices resound there.[93] In his discussion of the "spatiality of discontents," sociologist Asef Bayat explains how "particular spatial forms"—sites that are central, accessible, and maneuverable—"shape, galvanize, and accommodate insurgent sentiments and solidarities."[94] Consider Tehran's Enqelab Street: its proximity to transport hubs and its various cultural and commercial institutions—including theaters, cafes, printing houses, a book bazaar, and universities (where students commonly circulate revolutionary publications and audio cassettes)—have long drawn together a socioeconomically and culturally diverse population. These spatial conditions, and the convergence of various media forms hosted there, are, Azam Khatam argues, among the reasons why Enqelab Street "has been a recurrent site of struggle between Iranians and their government and has played a central role in the country's contemporary political transformations," from the 1979 Iranian Revolution to the 2009 election protests.[95] Perhaps its acoustic conditions have played some role in its conduciveness to congregation, too? In some cities, general urban conditions like deteriorating infrastructure and increasing securitization and socioeconomic fragmentation, along with urban development projects like population-displacing "urban renewal" initiatives (which are often accompanied by the crashes and rumblings of demolition and construction) have incited protest; in such cases, the material city as a whole often prompts citizens to raise their voices.[96]

Consider, also, Cairo's Tahrir Square, which in 2011 gave rise to an intense uproar not because it was *planned* to serve, as its name translates, as *Liberation* Square. In fact, Tahrir Square wasn't planned at all, according to Nasser Rabbat; it's more of a trapezoidal assemblage of leftover spaces, the product of an "urban-planning failure."[97] In this it resembles the broken infrastructure of pirate radio, as Matthew Fuller described it in chapter 1: "botched," "broke-up." The square's "unwieldy open span and its hodgepodge of built edges" are in part what constitute its appeal as a site of demonstration. It's what *circles* that square, Rabbat argues, that serves as a centripetal force, fomenting debate. Around Tahrir Square's perimeter are

> architectural reminders of all the forces that want to lay claim to [Egyptians'] identity and garner their loyalty—a fantastic ancient heritage and a graceful belle époque, a powerful yet convoluted government, a dream of regional unity, multiple markers of religion, education, and resistance, and unaffordable temptations of luxurious American consumerism.[98]

The square itself is bounded by such a cacophony of ideologies that it becomes an echo chamber where these competing discourses converge—and where Cairenes add their own raised voices to the mix. The square's architectural *parlante* of neo-Classicism, neo-Mamlukism, historicism,

FIGURE 47A. Protesters in Tahrir Square, 2012, Cairo. Via Voice of America. Public domain.

FIGURE 47B. Tahrir Square, 2011, Cairo. Photograph by Jonathan Rashad / CC-BY-2.0.

modernism, totalitarianism, and bureaucracy, Rabbat suggests, provided a historical base to which protesters were compelled to add their own antici-patory *parlante* of revolution (we should note that this language manifested not only through raised voices, but also through posters and banners—print and writing on various substrates—and in intense social media activity).[99]

We might debate the efficacy of the Arab Spring and later demonstra-tions in inciting widespread, enduring social change. And we must lament the lack of inclusivity and civility of the events: women's voices, in particu-lar, were suppressed, their bodies assaulted.[100] Yet Vishaan Chakrabarti ar-gues that the gatherings in Liberation Square—and, I'll add, those in New York's Zuccotti Park and Istanbul's "rough around the edges" Taksim Gezi Park, too—at least gave us "faith not only in humanity's common right to as-semble but our common expectation that cities, by definition, must provide ever-restless places of assembly."[101] It was at Gezi, after all, where a threat to urban public space invigorated a mass public movement: the government had proposed to replace one of the city's few green spaces with a shopping mall and a replica of Ottoman-era military barracks. That movement cued the "sound of the revival of urban Istanbul," and prompted citizens to build temporary structures that functioned as scaffoldings for their raised voices and handwritten demands.[102] As Istanbul-based architecture critic Gökhan Karakuş declared in 2013, "It took the citizens of Istanbul declaring the park and square public space, a civic space, a democratic space, for this to happen. This spatial performance of utopia is, I believe, the first step in the momentous [though now seemingly failed] realization of a truly democratic nation with primarily an Islamic population."[103] "Performing utopia" would also require making those public spaces inclusive and safe for all the voices and bodies that gather there—or, as Saskia Sassen proposes, making it pos-sible for threatened or "invisible" groups to co-opt the city's underutilized or abandoned spaces, its *terrains vagues*, to "become present" to themselves and to others unlike them.[104] Can (un)planning and design aid in these pur-suits? Our archaeological investigations—which involve understanding the intertwined layers of history that enable a site to "work," or not, as a public space—have the potential to inform future design and planning practices for our urban public spaces.

Scripting Spaces for Urban Voices: Urban Sound Design

It's often the accidental, unplanned, "broke-up" sites and structures of urbanity—the serendipitous encounters at the well; the casual, peripatetic conversations in the agora; the kludged together infrastructures of grass-roots broadcast; the gathering spaces left over by capitalist development—that provide ideal resonance chambers for vocality. But what happens to discourse, to the public sphere, when those urban sites of speech are all hyper-planned—when we have dedicated "speaker's platforms" and means of measuring and regulating acts of vocalization? Consider office furniture manufacturer Herman Miller's now-defunct Sonare Technologies unit, founded in 2005 to research, design, and manufacture "sound and acoustics solutions for speech privacy, facility sound management, and interior design" in the workplace. In their inaugural year they attempted to bring to market Babble, a unit containing a sound processer and speakers, which would "provide true voice confidentiality by rearranging the phonemes of your voice and transmitting, in real time, with your spoken voice."[105] Nearby coworkers—a common phenomenon in increasingly "open" workspaces—would hear only what sounds like an "indiscernible, low-volume group conversation." "Babbled" employees would ostensibly maintain vocal privacy *and* benefit from greater productivity, by being freed to transform any area of the workplace into a "cone of silence" (well, not really; it's more a "morass of gobbledygook"). The device never took off, and Sonare faded away. Yet employers and architects are still creating open workplaces, and acoustic engineers are using insulated drywall, acoustic door seals, and other techniques of sound-masking to maintain workers' "vocal privacy" and minimize distraction.

As we look toward the future, there's increasing potential to engineer *in* or *out* particular sounds not only in the office, but also at the urban scale. We face opportunities to design soundscapes for entire cities and shape their functionality as communicative spaces. Arup, a global firm of "designers, planners, engineers, consultants, and technical specialists," has a team specializing in acoustics.[106] I visited Arup Acoustics' SoundLab, where engineers can listen to the sounds of simulated buildings, recreate the acoustic conditions of spaces past, or sonically "experience major infrastructure projects"—from trains to wind farms to airports—during the design process.[107] Arup is even occasionally asked to sound-design entire cities, as they were with Dongtan, China (an eco-city project that eventually fell through). Dongtan's automotive fleet was to be entirely electric, which would have created space within the soundscape for city-dwellers to hear sounds—birds, voices, wind in the trees—that would've otherwise been masked by combustion engines.[108] Arup's Neill Woodger suggests that "people haven't really known that they can change the sounds of a city—they can change the road surface, for example, and that has a huge effect."[109] Raj Patel, global leader of Arup's Acoustics group, told me that sound isn't considered separately from the master plan; Arup uses an integrated model that takes into consideration such things as the movement of wind and rain, sun angles, street traffic, and aircraft to design a space that balances the needs for light and sound, openness and intimacy, optimal siting for different functional units, and so forth.

In various projects around the world, sound has been a major consideration in the design of public places, at least in part so that these spaces can better facilitate socialization and interpersonal communication and cultivate a sense of security. As Anne Kockelkorn and Doris Kleilein wonder, however, "Is this approach just about acoustical cosmetics," about "sonic branding," "or does it mark the beginning of a broader understanding of planning?"[110] Sound has indeed become an ingredient in "place-making" projects, and acoustics have factored more commonly into restaurant, retail, and even hospital design. Yet sound has also played a role in the planning of technologized surveillance and discipline. Consider the use of long-range acoustic devices, or sound cannons, for crowd-control at various demonstrations over the past several years, and the use of ShotSpotter sensors that enable police forces to sonically geo-locate the origin of gunshots.[111] Architect Olivier Balaÿ, along with his colleagues at the CRESSON research center for sound, space, and the urban environment, advocate that sound is much more than a disciplinary tool, however. Sound should instead be an integral part of conversations about urban quality of life, public health, urban character, and sustainability. The CRESSON group aims to integrate sound more fully into urban-planning decisions, encouraging urban officials, engineers, and designers to consider particular communities' signature, place-defining "soundmarks": the mix of voices in public spaces; the sounds of industry and transportation; and even how building heights and building materials impact local acoustics.[112]

Arup has also worked with the city of Pittsburgh on its Smart Streets project, which was intended to "reactivate" the streetscape between two dissociated neighborhoods. Using MassMotion, software that can simulate mass human behavior, they investigated how people might want to use the space, where they'd likely congregate and converse, then considered what infrastructure they'd need to support those activities. That infrastructure would incorporate wayfinding, ambient lighting, and information distribution, including information kiosks and signage, some of which could have sonic dimensions. Echoing Favro and Johanson, who investigated the pageantry of ancient Rome, Patel emphasized that there's an "artistic" or speculative dimension to their engineering work, too. His team frequently collaborates with sound artists and works with performing arts venues, and they bring insights from those projects into their urban infrastructural projects. One of those projects was a dark, inhospitable tunnel in Leeds, U.K., on top of which run several transit lines. The designers relocated bus stops, added acoustic panels, and worked with sound-and-light artist Hans Peter Kuhn to create a light and sound installation that registers the vibrations of the transit lines overhead. Just as there has been much research into the use of lighting to reinvigorate and increase a sense of safety in declining neighborhoods, there is great, as-yet untapped potential to use sound in similar ways.[113]

Sound—particularly vocal intelligibility—can also increase the efficiency and safety of transit systems. In 1987, thirty-one people died in a fire at Kings Cross, a major interchange of the London Underground, in part, Raj Patel says, because they couldn't hear evacuation instructions.[114] Today, many metropolitan transit systems are prioritizing acoustics—including New York City's Metropolitan Transit Authority, with whom Arup has worked on the new Second Avenue subway. They've focused on using sound-absorbing finishes, minimizing the noise of mechanical systems, supporting rails with rubber-encased ties, and improving the whole infrastructure behind the public address system, from the speaker's booth to the microphone, cabling, and loudspeakers.[115]

Public address and public safety are global concerns, but in speaking with Patel about Arup's work, I wondered if there are cultural differences around the world in what is regarded as an optimal acoustic condition, an optimal soundscape. Patel said that, while cultural tolerance for noise (and the very definition of noise) varies in different parts of the world, we do "seem to be moving toward a slightly more uniform expectation" of what cities should sound like. Overzealous engineers and designers in the early days of modern acoustics embraced such a uniform expectation—what Emily Thompson calls the "one best sound," a universal "modern sound," tamed, sanitized, unshaped by the space in which it's created.[116] Yet "postmodern acoustical technologies," she suggests, "summon forth the sound of space so easily and in so many varieties, we hardly know what to listen to first." We have the technology to program in tremendous sonic variety, but Patel claims we're using that technical know-how instead to generate consonance, or perhaps conformity.

The forces of globalization tend to homogenize local character and taste, including the qualities of and desires for our soundscapes. And some contemporary approaches to urban design—smart cities, responsive environments, the urban Gesamtkunstwerken of the Google age—represent holistic, and often hubristic, approaches to city-building. The builders of these networked developments often design out opportunities for unplanned (and seemingly "unmodern") modes of communication: streets seem intended primarily to shuttle people from one charging station to another, rather than to foster face-to-face interactions, and the city's surfaces are screens displaying programmed content rather than substrates or sounding boards for public texts and voices.[117] It seems that, in such places, there is little "residual" media infrastructure to dig into.

Yet there has already arisen a large contingent of critics who argue that such developments, by contradicting millennia of urban design experience, are misguided.[118] These over-zoned, over-rationalized cities, devoid of any historical sensibility and resonance, defy "the fact that real development in cities is often haphazard, or in between the cracks of what's allowed."[119] "The danger now," according to Richard Sennett, is that our new "information-rich" cities "may do nothing to help people think for themselves or communicate well with one another." A media city that makes no provisions for a layering of communicative infrastructures, that wipes away the deep time of urban mediation and mutes its echoes, is more stupefying than smart, more akin to Kittler's info-processing machine than to a vibrant metropolis.

While the archaeoacoustic case studies we examined earlier in this chapter, and the lessons from ancient architects like Vitruvius, show that city-builders have long recognized the importance of acoustics in fostering urban communication and communion, sonic sensitivity is still relatively rare in the design professions. Few design degree programs require any training in acoustics. Yet a small, specialized group of designers and engineers has been advocating for sound as a critical design concern. While some employ ethnographic methods, inspired by R. Murray Schafer's soundscape studies, to better understand cities' acoustic ecologies, others have at their disposal sophisticated labs and computer models, acoustic building materials and masking technologies, to engineer an "ideal" sonic urban environment—one minimizing the sounds of traffic and other stress-inducing noises, while potentially enhancing opportunities for communication and conversation.[120] Of course that "ideal" depends on context. We can only imagine what kind of soundscapes of "control, discipline, and terror" Lenin or Hitler would've architected, had they had their own teams of acoustic engineers."[121]

Yet what we often hear in the echoes from cities past is that however conscientiously designers design our plazas and meetinghouses; however meticulously planners and urban administrators aim to "zone" and regulate particular urban sounds and sounding behaviors; however carefully engineers insulate our office towers and apartment blocks, our urban voices often resist containment. Those voices exploit the entire city itself— its forums and facades—as their sounding medium, resounding within its volumes and ricocheting off its surfaces. An array of philosophers, historians, and critics have proposed that vocality—and particularly its application in "eloquent" address, deliberation, and demonstration—has historically played a critical role in constituting not only the demos, but also the physical polis in which that public resides. As so many of our physical cities are rationalized and data-fied and commercialized around us, threatening the demos, we can only hope that our public voices, and the diverse resonating bodies from which they emanate, will continue to resist containment and social engineering. While there is indeed much harmful machinic and mediated cacophony that can be helpfully contained in our future-cities (we can certainly do more to protect disenfranchised populations from harmful industrial and traffic noise, for instance), that dampening will ideally open up space on the sonic spectrum for more meaningful vocality. Those master-planned, technologized future-cities might be somebody's ideal of sentience and sustainability, but they're unlikely to be regarded as socially sound without offering sites and opportunities for serendipitous soundings, for messy interminglings of myriad mediations.

Conclusion

CODING URBAN PASTS AND FUTURES

For three days in April 2016 the Palmyra Arch made a showing in London's Trafalgar Square. It was a resurrection of sorts. The original Arch of Triumph, a richly ornamented tripartite structure, was built in present-day Syria in the third century CE under Septimius Severus. It had been largely destroyed by Islamic State (IS) in October of 2015, just months after the rebels had also executed Khaled al-Asaad, Palmyra's 83-year-old head of antiquities. The arch's proxy, roughly two-thirds the size of the original, was made of Egyptian marble quarried in Carrara, Italy. Its masons were not Roman craftsmen or slaves, but robots. A production of the Institute for Digital Archaeology (IDA), the new arch was computationally fabricated, 3D-printed from a model generated by compositing dozens of photographs taken by archaeologists, amateur researchers, and tourists. It wasn't a perfect replica: the London arch represented only the central of three conjoined arches at Palmyra, and the printers couldn't quite handle the detail on the Corinthian capitals. "Of course, a reproduction is only a reproduction," the IDA's director of technology admitted, but, in some cases, that reproduction might be "all that we have."[1]

Digital archaeology, the organization's leaders proclaim, "puts . . . crucially important repositories of our cultural identity and shared history forever beyond the reach of those who would destroy them." Palmyra, we are to infer, represents the *world's* shared history, and its thorough documentation will ensure its immortality, allow for its continual rebirth in the face of conflict and natural disaster. The Institute, a collaboration between researchers at Oxford and Harvard universities and Dubai's Museum of the Future, is building an open-source Million Image Database, which it likens to a "Google Earth for heritage": a UNESCO-backed collection of crowd-sourced photographs of ancient sites and artifacts.[2]

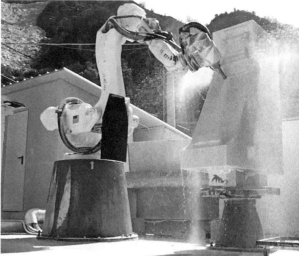

FIGURE 48. Still images from *Palmyra Arch of Triumph Unveiling* by Garry Knight and *Triumphal Arch of Palmyra Under Construction* by TorArt. Fair use.

In addition to culling those photos from social media, inviting photographers to submit their own material, and digitizing images from print archives, the Institute has also equipped an army of volunteer photographers with roughly five thousand "discreet" and user-friendly 3D cameras to create high-quality scans of "important sites in conflict zones throughout the Middle East and North Africa" (and thereby, some critics worried, potentially putting their own mortal bodies at risk).[3]

That repository offers to archaeologists a rich archive through which they can look more deeply into the world's artifacts, seeing more of "what's actually there," in Ernst's terms, but simply imperceptible to the naked eye: "hidden inscriptions, invisible paint lines, the faintest palimpsests," fissures and cracks.[4] The Institute has scanned ancient pottery and gemstones, epigraphy, and Latin and Ptolemaic inscriptions and carried out reflectance transformation imaging, polynomial texture mapping, and multispectral imaging (all advanced imaging techniques) in southwestern France's Marsoulas Cave, home to many Paleolithic cave paintings. The repository can then also serve as regenerative source material, an architectural plan for repairing and rebuilding and keeping "what's actually there" *there*—or somewhere, like a busy tourist destination in some other Western city—indefinitely.

The Institute isn't the first to undertake such a documentation project; others, like CyArk, whose "key partners" come mostly from the tech industry; the New Palmyra project, which is supported in part by the MIT Media Lab; and Rekrei, another crowd-sourced photogrammetry platform founded by two archaeology graduate students, have also been creating 3D archives of cultural heritage sites.[5] Yet the IDA is certainly the most vocal; their executive director, Roger Michel, has a knack for commanding the virtual rostrum, or speaker's platform, along with millions in private funding from various U.S. sources.[6] And they've got the flash of the Museum of the Future—an entrepreneurially oriented, sheikh-funded "incubator for ideas" and "driver for innovation" whose *own* building will be 3D-printed—to shrewdly position themselves as mediators between the past and the future.[7]

Archaeologists have long been sophisticated users of technical media: satellite imagery, lidar, muography (which, to put it reductively, records the effects of cosmic rays!), binaural microphones, geographic information systems, huge databases of archaeological data, CT scans, modeling software, and, from their earliest days, photography and film.[8] As Kittler noted, the military has spawned many of these and other advanced media technologies. Yet armies and rebel forces have also long recognized the cultural, political, and strategic value of "old" media, like cultural artifacts, too. For millennia, conquerors have ransacked libraries and burned archives (as in Timbuktu), and "sites and items of archaeological interest have always been collateral damage," or spoils of war, in times of conflict.[9] Still, some regard Islamic State's recent "targeted destruction" of world heritage sites—sites in which the entire global community has a vested interest, because, we believe, this is where so many of our fundamental human practices and customs (agriculture, writing, urbanization) took root—as unprecedented in its scale and intention.[10] IS even has its own "Ministry of Antiquities" with subdivisions for excavation, exploration, research, marketing, and administration.[11] In March of 2015 Irina Bokova, director-general of UNESCO, condemned IS's "cultural cleansing" of antiquities as a war crime: "The systematic destruction of cultural symbols embodying Syrian cultural diversity reveals the true intent of such attacks, which is to deprive the Syrian people of its knowledge, its identity and history."[12] Bokova repeats a common explanatory narrative: IS's destructive behavior is attributable, in part, to their desire to obliterate diverse ethnic and religious histories within the region. Other critics cite their iconoclasm and extremist jihadi Salafism, and their attempt to cultivate a mediated image of ruthlessness that will appeal to angry young potential recruits.

Yet Chiara De Cesari, a scholar of cultural memory and former archaeologist, suggests that archaeology itself is partly to blame for this destruction to its own domain. Of course IS can exploit archaeology for material gain; the group, known for its media savvy, recognizes that its raids will receive global media coverage (they even have their own documentarians) and will be particularly galling to the preservation-oriented West, while its loot will simultaneously feed the global antiquities market and generate income.[13] But archaeology is also deeply embedded in the cultural strata of the Levant, the region encompassing those countries in the eastern Mediterranean. Here, De Cesari says, we find a long history of "politically mobilized antiquities" and deep-seated connections between archaeology and nationalism—themes we addressed in the introduction, and which reappeared in our discussion of print, writing, and the voice.[14] De Cesari cites Saddam Hussein's obsession with ancient Mesopotamian antiquities, his well-funded archaeological projects (e.g., excavations, museums, publications, festivals), his efforts to reconstruct the city of Babylon (and even inscribe his own name on the bricks), and his Baath party's Project for the Rewriting of History from the 1970s and 1980s, which presented Iraqis as the most "civilized" descendants of a continuous Semito-Arab lineage. Hussein fashioned himself into a modern-day Nebuchadnezzar. Islamic State later absorbed not only many former Baath officials, but also the party's tactics for nationalist archaeological spectacle.

Meanwhile, De Cesari argues, Near Eastern and biblical archaeologists in the region, most of them Euro-American, continue colonial patterns of practice by devaluing Islamic layers of material culture (instead privileging pre-Islamic artifacts), and by enforcing a strict hierarchy in the field, wherein local laborers are sometimes subjected to exploitative labor conditions.[15] Archaeological sites in the Levant, De Cesari writes, are thus "imbued with the presence of colonialism and its persisting legacy in the oppressive nationalisms that followed: they are a sign of the ultimate failure of the emancipatory project of the post-colonial nation-state. Their destruction thus emerges as an act of spatio-political production," one that produces (ironically, through acts of destruction) Islamic State "as a radically new political agent unmoored from the fraught legacy of the past and in fact born out of its annihilation."[16] Again we witness that destructive *Kulturtechniken* we encountered at the end of chapter 3. The "media" of sledgehammers, bulldozers, and dynamite "erase" a tainted landscape and an alienating cultural heritage, and thereby clean the slate for new cultural forms: violent YouTube videos, propaganda magazines, and inflammatory Twitter accounts that constitute their own cultural "rewriting" project.[17] By creating their own sophisticated, self-mythologizing media universe, Islamic State aims to script the future.

Local archaeologists, curators, and preservationists in Syria and Iraq have adopted comparatively rudimentary, and very much analog, defense strategies.[18] In anticipation of Islamic State's approach, some museum staff have buried their treasures or smuggled them to safety, as we saw with the manuscripts of Mali. In fact, al-Asaad was allegedly executed because he refused to divulge the location of his secret store to IS. Some curators have stocked their galleries with replicas; consequently, when rebels rampaged through the Mosul Museum with pickaxes and sledgehammers in early 2015, some of the targeted statues were believed to be plaster copies rather than originals. Other precious artifacts were, ironically, rendered safe from harm because they had been confiscated decades ago in colonialist archaeological expeditions. Those objects now rest in locked vitrines within a network of Western museums. Some institutions that have benefited from this colonialist archaeological heritage have, perhaps in an act of atonement, recently offered to add their own Near Eastern antiquities to the global digitization effort. Markus Hilgert of Berlin's Pergamon Museum proposed that the items in their collection could be 3D-scanned and combined with other institutions' digital models to "create a physical walk-through exhibition combining every stage of the ancient city."[19]

As we discussed in the previous chapter, archaeologists are already creating such simulations to better understand the multisensorial and kinesthetic dimensions of ancient cities, and how those contexts shaped their inhabitants' experiences. The Institute for Digital Archaeology's Palmyra arch, meanwhile, claims to reflect nothing of its original context, yet it still implies a cultural connection to its ancestral home. In Palmyra, the original arch was linked by a colonnaded street to the Temple of Bel. The tripartite double-faced arch served to mask a sharp bend in the street, maintaining the illusion of ordered connections within the urban form and framing urban views. At Trafalgar Square, on the other hand, the single arch sat on a dark, reflective plinth circumscribed by a cautionary yellow-and-black "do not cross" boundary line, which visitors circumnavigated amidst the clamor of traffic and the snaps of cell-phone cameras. Yet even here, far from its original home, the arch's siting was significant: positioned on an axis between London's National Gallery and Nelson's Column, the proxy arch was meant to bridge the ancient and contemporary cities, to symbolically suggest that London and Palmyra are linked through their shared cultural heritage. Perhaps this made then–prime minister David Cameron a modern-day Septimius Severus.

The proxy arch was never intended to be *of the city*—nor was it *of* Dubai or New York, where it traveled later in 2016. Its most fitting temporary home, it seemed, was in Venice, where a segment of the arch resided in the World of Fragile Parts exhibition at the 2016 Architecture Biennale: a fitting context for a pricy, elaborate aesthetic creation whose value is hinged to its controlled circulation within the global market.[20] But eventually, ideally, the proxy arch would go back to its ancestral home. Using the Institute's printing technology to recreate the arch in Palmyra, director Michel proposed, would not only undo Islamic State's destruction, but it would also fulfill another lack: the project would "provide jobs for local people," including residents of the adjacent city of Tadmor, many of whom had fled in recent years.[21]

Some critics argue that those local people—and other threatened groups throughout the Middle East and around the world—would've been much more deserving recipients of the time, effort, expertise, and money expended on the arch. UNESCO's Bokova rejects the notion that one must choose between protecting people and protecting their heritage, because culture is ultimately about human identity and belonging. She might say that safeguarding antiquities represents a form of "deep time," long-view humanitarianism. Yet others wonder what, exactly, the Institute thought it was protecting. Those critics lament not only the apparent artificiality of the reproduction, but also its naïve motivations—its creators' failure to ask the political questions that, as we discussed in the introduction, critical archaeologists have long been asking about the nature of their enterprise. What does it mean to have Western universities, tech companies, and capital transform the culture of a non-Western city into a mediated artifact, and then dictate its circulation? Whose interests are served when the technological, intellectual, and financial elite marshal their resources to resuscitate, to promise immortality to, a particular instantiation of a city that has already weathered multiple cycles of history across its multimillennial existence (even the arch itself was restored in 1930)? What are the historiographical and political consequences of grafting over wounds in the urban landscape?

As Michel explained in an open letter on the Institute's website in May 2016, "I am not suggesting that anyone erase the evidence of terroristic violence. What I *am* talking about is refusing to privilege the beliefs of those who engage in cultural cleansing above the righteous desires of local stakeholders to retain visible links to their ancient past."[22] But how are those local stakeholders served by a robot-routed arch sitting amidst the tourists of Trafalgar Square? And if that arch were to come home to, or to be reprinted in, Palmyra, what are the ontological implications of such a re-materialization of the past?[23] What is being rebuilt, what past is being made present? What are the politics of using state-of-the-art scanning technology, computational fabricators, and luxury materials sourced from thousands of miles away to simulate a structure crafted thousands of years before, likely by skilled laborers and slaves, from a mix of locally quarried sandy-colored granite and limestone and Egyptian red granite?[24] What do we learn from this reenactment? What labor practices and geopolitics are embodied and erased in this re-mediation?

It seems that, to some degree, the Institute has fetishized both the Arch, by removing it from its context and conditions of production, as well as their own cutting-edge tools and methods of re-creation. It's this fetishization of "the new" that media archaeology is intended to counter, in part by encouraging consideration of the epistemologies materialized in different historical media formats. In the Palmyra project, those formats include archival images, sophisticated scans, modeling software, and the stone structures themselves—both the original and the re-creation. Yet the broader political questions we posed above—about the inclusiveness of the media archives we make and exploit, about the power dynamics of particular methodologies, about the broader social implications of research, for instance—are not, as we discussed in the introduction, always media archaeology's forte. We have to consider, for instance, the limitations of engaging with the past through a solely visual archive—an archive composed of a mix of colonial records, tourist photos, and scans laboriously collected by activist documentarians.[25] The Million Image Database, and others like it, are archives of entangled politics—and the research and design work those archives generate enters a landscape politicized by layers of history, including fraught engagements with earlier archaeological efforts. These are among the questions that self-reflexive archaeologists-as-such have been asking themselves about the ethics and cultural politics of their practice.

Palmyra has been a media-city for thousands of years: its caravan traders and wealthy merchants likely recorded exchanges between East and West, its Roman builders created theaters and public fora for speech and pageantry, and its rulers wrote decrees. Its artisans applied Greek and Aramaic (and even some Hebrew) inscriptions to the city's mud-brick walls and stone statuary to textually (and texturally) honor the dead and commemorate important figures; and those commemorations often revealed details about business, religion, and everyday life in the ancient city. Over the past century alone, Palmyra has served as a much-photographed cultural heritage site; a backdrop for Islamic State's spectacular media events; a 3D archive for digital archaeologists; and an urban imaginary that is transportable, in souvenir form, to city squares and fairs around the world.

And when its reconstructed Arch of Triumph made a brief appearance in New York's City Hall Park in September 2016, it entered a realm likewise featuring layers of mediation. Surrounded by grand, Beaux-Arts courts and municipal buildings and the remnants of Newspaper Row, shadowed by the massive antennae crown of nearby One World Trade Center, the arch framed the columned entrance portico and Palladian windows of City Hall. While a few hundred years of history converge here, New York's palimpsest is more immediately visual and visceral than deeply historical; its sheer proliferation of texts and images is a product of capitalism, rather than one of deep time's accumulation.[26]

Both the proxy arch and another major urban insertion just three miles northwest of City Hall, Hudson Yards, embody the entangled temporalities and materialities of the mediated city. Both represent the "solutionist," even fetishistic, use of technological tools to tidy up an awkward mix of presents and pasts, a messy mélange of urban, environmental, cultural, and media histories. While the recreated arch was meant to demonstrate the potential for new technologies to rescue the archaeological past from human destruction, it ultimately embodied a much more ontologically and politically confused gesture. It began by translating ancient building techniques through vanguard visualization and fabrication tools; delivering, via sophisticated global logistical systems, millennia-old metamorphic rock to an electrified, commercialized public square that, a mere quarter-millennium earlier, had sat adjacent to ponds and meadows. Once on-site, that robot-sculpted rock was hoisted into place with mechanical lifts, under the careful watch of hard-hatted supervisors, (a few) news photographers, and me. Quite a messy entanglement of labor practices, building techniques, and technologies—a knot of temporalities, materialities, and geographies.

The cranes over in Hudson Yards, meanwhile, are building massive platforms that conceal equally massive infrastructural gashes in the landscape—train lines and tunnels—and thus elevate the new urban district above worries of rising sea levels. Here, vanguard technologies—sensors, monitoring software, and regulating algorithms—are embedded into streets, smartphones, and operating systems in order to predict and redirect the urban future, rather than revive its past. Just a couple years earlier, back in Palmyra, Islamic State intended to use the media of front loaders and Facebook to erase the urban past and all its ideological baggage, and thereby script and simulate a new (post-urban?) future.

Palmyra, old New York's Civic Center, and new New York's Hudson Yards—all serving dual roles as both material urban sites and ethereal urban imaginaries—represent the perpetual condition of our media cities: always-already both data and dirt, both new and old (even if developers and data-driven designers sometimes make every effort to bury the messy past). Among these three examples, we behold a collection of seeming contradictions: the city as an ancient logistical center for caravans, and the city as a test-bed info-processing center; a reliance on infrastructural path dependencies, and a simultaneous rejection of those antiquated systems that paved the way for millennia of urban evolution; a commitment to the preservation of material cultural heritage, local character, and environment, and, at the same time, a feverish pursuit of innovation and clean-slate development; an appreciation for the slow processes by which geologic and environmental forces and living creatures reshape their landscapes, and, meanwhile, a preference for faux patinas and manufactured heritage.

We encounter sites of similar confusion and entanglement, both monumental and mundane, in all of our cities—including, I imagine, yours. You might have observed, with bemused curiosity, technicians installing cell-phone towers, unconvincingly camouflaged in the dress of spindly evergreens, along the highway. And despite such half-hearted efforts of "green-washing," you might still worry about the potential health effects of all those electromagnetic waves coursing through the ether and penetrating your apartment walls. Perhaps you've marked the closure of mega-chain bookstores in your prime urban shopping areas and skimmed countless articles on the "death of the book"—yet you've also noted the recent opening of yet another independent bookshop. Maybe you've seen your phone booths supplanted by public WiFi hotspots or pop-up libraries. Maybe you've peered down open manholes and watched utility workers swap out copper wires for fiber optics. Maybe you've observed, or even joined, demonstrators from Black Lives Matter or Occupy—or representatives from Ukraine's Euromaidan movement or Taiwan's Sunflower

Movement, or those mourning the kidnapping of forty-three students from Iguala, Mexico—as they've raised their voices, their hand-scrivened placards, and their glowing cell phones in your streets and public squares.

Even in this age of privatized screens and earbud acoustics, you might have witnessed the mysterious appearance of new forms of public address and inscription, as Brazil's pichação script and WRDSMTH's typewriter-inspired wheatpastes pop up on your facades and billboards. Perhaps your old art deco telephone buildings have meanwhile metamorphosed into data centers and luxury condos, and micro-radio antennae have popped up on your rooftops. Maybe your city has even launched a new radio network—a LoRaWAN (Long Range Wide Area Network) to accommodate the chatter from its residents' intelligent devices, eager to join the Internet of Things.[27] And perhaps your local public library has launched a tech incubator while also initiating a community archiving program, where families can share their ancestral papers and senior citizens their oral histories. Libraries, which are another of my central research interests, are microcosms of our entangled urban mediations: they're public sites where metropolitan populations can preserve and produce various forms of urban intelligence, old and new, and gather them together into an intellectual "commons."

These are scenes of media cities in perpetual transition—cities poised between the noisy, scribbled-on, messily wired, palimpsestic cities of yesterday, and the sensor-embedded, data-driven, efficiency-minded "smart" cities of tomorrow. Or so we are led to believe by simplified, sanitized, and stratified tales of urban development and technological "progress." In reality, however, as I've attempted to demonstrate throughout this book, urban environments everywhere are characterized by a lot of messy materiality, "residual" media, and different notions of ambient intelligence, sometimes even reflecting competing epistemologies and clashing politics. Cities themselves serve to mediate between these various manifestations of intelligence—legal codes and copper cables, inscriptions and imaginaries, algorithms and antennae, public proclamations and system protocols—and to bring the "old" and the "new," the ore and the ether, together into close contact. Clay and code, dirt and data, pasts and presents intermingle here. And—provided that our future cities are designed to accommodate these untidy, productively "confused" materialities and temporalities, to amplify the echoes of the past—they always will.

Acknowledgments

In the nearly fifteen years that have passed since the idea for this book was born in a class syllabus, I've encountered innumerable people and resources, in scattered cities, that have inspired and informed the project's development. I will undoubtedly fail to dig all those moments of generosity and illumination out from the recesses of my memory, so I hope to be able to thank in person (or via some other means: posted letter, telegram, stela, public proclamation) those whom I might inadvertently forget to acknowledge here.

First, I must thank my students at New York University, the University of Pennsylvania, and, for the past dozen years, The New School. Those of you who, since 2002, have enrolled in my Media and Architecture, Urban Media Archaeology, Media and Materiality, Sound and Space, and Maps as Media classes have inspired me with your curiosity, creativity, and criticality. You've shaped the ideas in this book, and I've written it in part to honor our work together—as well as to provoke discussions and inspire projects among my future students and in other classrooms around the world. I am particularly grateful to my past and present research assistants: Tanya Toft, Steve Taylor, Yeong Ran Kim, Josie Holzman, Rory Solomon, and Joshua McWhirter. Josh served as "image editor" *extraordinaire* for *Code and Clay, Data and Dirt*, choosing artwork and overseeing image rights clearances. I am greatly indebted to him for his keen eye and conscientious oversight of a complicated process. Rory not only aided me in teaching the mapping studio where I was able to sketch out the boundaries of the present project, but he has also shared with me years of brainstorms, laughs, and friendship. Simon Ganahl, a former postdoctoral advisee, has also been a valued interlocutor and friend.

I am also grateful for the various institutions and organizations that have granted me space, time, and support to dig into the archives, survey the field, and write up my notes. I benefitted greatly from the generosity of the Canadian Centre for Architecture, where I enjoyed a visiting scholar-ship in 2012; the Korea Foundation, which granted me a field research fel-lowship in 2012; the Digital Cultures Research Lab at Leuphana University, where I was a visiting fellow in 2015; and the Internationales Kolleg für Kul-turtechnikforschung und Medienphilosophie at the Bauhaus-Universität Weimar, which invited me to visit as a Senior Scholar in 2016. I was at the IKKM when I finished this manuscript and submitted it to the publisher. Thanks, too, to all the brilliant librarians and archivists who have sup-ported my work at dozens of institutions.

I also owe a special debt of gratitude to The New School, which has, over the years, awarded me two semesters of academic leave and several research and teaching grants, as well as the opportunity to work with some wonderful colleagues in our Emergent Infrastructures research group and in the Graduate Institute for Design, Ethnography, and Social Thought. Not only has The New School provided a stimulating, creative environment in which to work, but it has also brought me many brilliant colleagues and friends, many of whom have shaped this work and my own intellectual development. I thank Carol Wilder, Peter Haratonik, Barry Salmon, and Anne Balsamo, all former department chairs and deans who have championed my work. I am grateful, too, to Deidre Boyle, Sumita Chakravarty, Doris Chang, Kate Eichhorn, Elizabeth Ellsworth, Melissa Grey, Lisa Grocott, Joseph Heathcott, Jessica Irish, Robert Kirkbride, Jamie Kruse, Carin Kuoni, Laura Liu, Brian McGrath, Miodrag Mitrasi-novic, Dominic Pettman, Jane Pirone, Trebor Scholz, Rachel Sherman, Radhika Subramaniam, Miriam Ticktin, Jilly Traganou, and Susan Yelav-ich. Special thanks are due to Julia Foulkes, Orit Halpern, and Aleksandra Wagner, with whom I've shared many long conversations and works in progress.

Those drafts have circulated at other institutions, too. I am grateful to my hosts and audiences at Cornell University, the Helsinki Collegium for Advanced Studies, the Humlab at Umeå University, the Institut für Wis-senschaft und Kunst in Vienna, Korea University, the Maryland Institute for Technology in the Humanities at the University of Maryland, and the University of Amsterdam (and others I'm undoubtedly forgetting). Years ago my NYU colleagues Tom Augst, Finn Brunton, Gabriella Coleman, and Lisa Gitelman read a draft prospectus for this book and helped me to envision it in chapter form. I also owe many thanks to Carolyn Birdsall, Anne Burdick, Matthew Kirschenbaum, Malcolm McCullough, Trevor Muñoz, Jussi Parikka, Lisa Parks, Carrie Rentschler, Jonathan Sterne, and Patrik Svensson for giving me opportunities to share portions of this work, and for offering their own invaluable critique and encouragement. In particular, the extraordinarily talented and generous Nicole Starosielski has been an astute reader and trusted friend.

Over the past several years, *Places Journal* has granted me a virtual *rostra augusti* (that reference should resonate from the preceding chapters) to experiment with some of the ideas and case studies explored in this book. I've had the pleasure and honor of working with two outstanding editors, Nancy Levinson and Josh Wallaert, who've welcomed me as a regular long-form columnist and helped to shape my thinking and my voice. I've also been privileged to work with the esteemed University of Minnesota Press on three projects over the past decade. I am indebted to Danielle Kasprzak, Pieter Martin, Anne Carter, and copyeditor Mary Russell, project manager Wendy Holdman, and indexer Roberta Engleman for investing in me, and for their expert guidance and support.

Finally, I reserve special thanks for Andy and my family, all of whom have been unwavering sources of love and support. I dedicate this book to them—and to three recently departed, dearly loved ones: Rudy, Roxy, and Dugan, who always provided welcome respite from the stresses of writing, and whom I now imagine in eternal pursuit of countless Frisbees tossed on some expansive, ethereal field.

Notes

Introduction

1. http://www.hudsonyardsnewyork.com/the-story/building-hudson-yards.
2. For more on Hudson Yards, the High Line, and the development of Manhattan's Far West Side, see my "Instrumental City: The View from Hudson Yards, circa 2019," *Places*, April 2016, https://placesjournal.org/article/instrumental-city-new-york-hudson-yards/, and David Halle and Elisabeth Tiso, *New York's New Edge: Contemporary Art, the High Line, and Urban Megaprojects on the Far West Side* (Chicago: University of Chicago Press, 2014).
3. Center for Urban Science and Progress, "NYU CUSP, Related Companies, and Oxford Properties Group Team Up to Create 'First Quantified Community' in the United States at Hudson Yards," press release, April 14, 2014, http://cusp.nyu.edu/press-release/nyu-cusp-related-companies-oxford-properties-group-team-create-first-quantified-community-united-states-hudson-yards/. For more on pneumatic infrastructures, see Juliette Spertus, "Fast Trash!" *Urban Omnibus*, May 12, 2010, http://urbanomnibus.net/2010/05/fast-trash/, and Shannon Mattern, "Puffs of Air," in *Air: Alphabet City 15*, ed. John Knechtel (Cambridge, Mass.: MIT Press, 2010), 42–56.
4. CUSP; Orit Halpern, Jesse LeCavalier, Nerea Cavillo, and Wolfgang Pietsch, "Test-Bed Urbanism," *Public Culture* 25:2 (2013): 272–306.
5. Jessica Leber, "Beyond the Quantified Self: The World's Largest Quantified Community," *Fast Company*, April 22, 2014, http://www.fastcoexist.com/3029255/beyond-the-quantified-self-the-worlds-largest-quantified-community.
6. See, for instance, the work of Kate Crawford, Adam Greenfield, Gökçe Günel, Orit Halpern, Rob Kitchin, and Anthony Townsend.
7. Shannon Mattern, "Methodolatry and the Art of Measure," *Places*, November 2013, https://placesjournal.org/article/methodolatry-and-the-art-of-measure/; "Interfacing Urban Intelligence," *Places*, April 2014, https://placesjournal.org/article/interfacing-urban-intelligence/; "History of the Urban Dashboard," *Places*, March 2015, https://placesjournal.org/article/mission-control-a-history-of-the-urban-dashboard/; "Instrumental City: The View from Hudson Yards, circa 2019," *Places*, April 2016, https://placesjournal.org/article/instrumental-city-new-york-hudson-yards/;

"The City Is Not a Computer," *Places*, February 2017, https://placesjournal.org/article/a-city-is-not-a-computer/; "City by the Numbers: Big Data and the Urban Future," Pratt Institute, Brooklyn, N.Y., October 11, 2014, https://www.pratt.edu/events/single/?id=15793; "Smart Cities? Impossible Objects, Political Objects, and Measuring Objects" conference, The New School and Storefront for Art and Architecture, New York, April 23, 2017, http://www.wordsinspace.net/urbanintel/2017/04/09/urban-intel-storefront-event/.

8. Quoted in Brian Libby, "Quantifying the Livable City," *Atlantic City Lab*, October 21, 2014, http://www.citylab.com/tech/2014/10/quantifying-the-livable-city/381657/.

9. Some of the following passages are adapted from my *Deep Mapping the Media City* (Minneapolis: University of Minnesota Press, 2015).

10. Malcolm McCullough, *Ambient Commons: Attention in the Age of Embodied Information* (Cambridge, Mass.: MIT Press, 2013). See also Malcolm McCullough, "Must Media Mean Remoteness?" *Harvard Design Magazine* 38 (2014): 13–19.

11. Orit Halpern traces the twentieth-century history of responsive environments and intelligent architectures in her brilliant *Beautiful Data: A History of Vision and Reason Since 1945* (Durham, N.C.: Duke University Press, 2015).

12. See my Media and Architecture course syllabi, available in the Teaching section of wordsinspace.net.

13. James Ackerman, *Origins, Imitations, Conventions: Representation in the Visual Arts* (Cambridge, Mass.: MIT Press, 2002); Beatriz Colomina, *Privacy and Publicity: Architecture as Mass Media* (Cambridge, Mass.: MIT Press, 1994); Peter Bacon Hales, *Silver Cities: Photographing American Urbanization, 1839–1915* (Philadelphia: Temple University Press, 1983); Neil Levine, "'The Significance of Facts': Mies's Collages Up Close and Personal," *Assemblage* 37 (December 1998): 70–101; Richard Pare, *Photography and Architecture: 1839–1939* (Montreal: Canadian Center for Architecture, 1982); Shelley Rice, *Parisian Views* (Cambridge, Mass.: MIT Press, 1999).

14. Walter Benjamin, *Illuminations*, Trans. Harry Zohn (New York: Schocken Books, 1969); David B. Clarke, ed., *The Cinematic City* (New York: Routledge, 1997); Colomina, *Privacy and Publicity*; Edward Dimendberg, *Film Noir and the Spaces of Modernity* (Cambridge, Mass.: Harvard University Press, 2004); Sergei Eisenstein, "Montage and Architecture," Trans. Michael Glenny, *Assemblage* 10 (1989 [1938]): 111–31; Erkki Huhtamo, *Illusions in Motion: Media Archaeology of the Moving Panorama and Related Spectacles* (Cambridge, Mass.: MIT Press, 2013); Richard Koszarski, *Hollywood on the Hudson: Film and Television in New York from Griffith to Sarnoff* (New Brunswick, N.J.: Rutgers University Press, 2010); Ranjani Mazumdar, *Bombay Cinema: An Archive of the City* (Minneapolis: University of Minnesota Press, 2007); Scott McQuire, *The Media City: Media, Architecture, and Urban Space* (Thousand Oaks, Calif.: Sage, 2008); Francois Penz and Andong Lu, eds., *Urban Cinematics: Understanding Urban Phenomena through the Moving Image* (London: Intellect, 2011);

John David Rhodes and Elena Gorfinkel, eds., *Taking Place: Location and the Moving Image* (Minneapolis: University of Minnesota Press, 2011); Allen J. Scott, *On Hollywood: The Place, the Industry* (Princeton, N.J.: Princeton University Press, 2005); see also Charlotte Brundson, "The Attractions of the Cinematic City," *Screen* 53 (Autumn 2012): 209–27, for a literature review of "cinematic city" texts.

15. M. Christine Boyer, *Cybercities* (New York: Princeton Architectural Press, 1996); Paul Ceruzzi, *Internet Alley: High Technology in Tysons Corner, 1945–2005* (Cambridge, Mass.: MIT Press, 2008); Stephen Graham and Simon Marvin, *Telecommunications and the City: Electronic Spaces, Urban Places* (New York: Routledge, 1996); Malcolm McCullough, *Digital Ground: Architecture, Pervasive Computing, and Environmental Knowing* (Cambridge, Mass.: MIT Press, 2004); William J. Mitchell, *City of Bits: Space, Place, and the Infobahn* (Cambridge, Mass.: MIT Press, 1996); Mark Shepard, ed., *Sentient City: Ubiquitous Computing, Architecture, and the Future of Urban Space* (Cambridge, Mass.: MIT Press, 2011); Anthony Townsend, *Smart Cities: Big Data, Civic Hackers, and the Quest for a New Utopia* (New York: W. W. Norton, 2013); Mark Wigley, "Network Fever," *Grey Room* 4 (2001): 82–122.

16. See my "Ear to the Wire: Listening to Historic Urban Infrastructures," *Amodern* 2 (2013), http://amodern.net/article/ear-to-the-wire/. See also Karin Bijsterveld, *Mechanical Sound: Technology, Culture, and Public Problems of Noise in the Twentieth Century* (Cambridge, Mass.: MIT Press, 2008); Steve Goodman, *Sonic Warfare: Sound, Affect, and the Ecology of Fear* (Cambridge, Mass.: MIT Press, 2010); Brian Larkin, *Signal and Noise: Media, Infrastructure, and Urban Culture in Nigeria* (Durham, N.C.: Duke University Press, 2008); Emily Thompson, *The Soundscape of Modernity: Architectural Acoustics and the Culture of Listening in America, 1900–1933* (Cambridge, Mass.: MIT Press, 2002); Mark Wigley, *Buckminster Fuller Inc.: Architecture in the Age of Radio* (Zurich: Lars Müller Publishers, 2015).

17. Eric Gordon, *The Urban Spectator: American Concept-Cities from Kodak to Google* (Hanover, N.H.: Dartmouth University Press, 2010), 2.

18. Scott McQuire, *The Media City: Media, Architecture, and Urban Space* (Thousand Oaks, Calif.: Sage, 2008), vii.

19. Lisa Gitelman, *Always Already New: Media History and the Data of Culture* (Cambridge, Mass.: MIT Press, 2006); *Scripts, Grooves, and Writing Machines: Representing Technology in the Edison Era* (Stanford, Calif.: Stanford University Press, 1999); Carolyn Marvin, *When Old Technologies Were New* (New York: Oxford University Press, 1990).

20. Nooney has presented a feminist critique of media archaeology, and she highlights—as does Parikka—its indebtedness to feminist materialist thinkers (e.g., Sarah Ahmed, Karen Barad, Jane Bennett, Rosi Braidotti). See Laine Nooney, "Materialist Methods for Mystery House(s): A Feminist Media Archaeology of Early Video Games," Society for Cinema and Media Studies conference, Chicago, March 2013, http://www.lainenooney.com/research-blog/scms-2013; and Nooney, "Sierra On-Line and the Archaeology

of Video Game History" (Ph.D. diss., Stony Brook University, 2014). Among the women most frequently cited by and included among media archaeologists (whether they *want* to be included or not) are Avital Ronell, N. Katherine Hayles, Cornelia Vismann, Lori Emerson, Marvin, and Gitelman.

21. See my "Theoretical Humility," *Words in Space*, May 7, 2012, http://www .wordsinspace.net/wordpress/2012/05/07/theoretical-humility/ and "The Cultural Techniques (+ Political Economy) of Theory-Making," *Words in Space*, October 16, 2013, http://www.wordsinspace.net/wordpress/2013/10/16/the -cultural-techniques-political-economy-of-theory-making/. See also Berenice A. Carroll, "The Politics of 'Originality': Women and the Class System of the Intellect," *Journal of Women's History* 2 (1990): 136–63; Margaret W. Conkey, "Questioning Theory: Is There a Theory of Gender in Archaeology?" *Journal of Archaeological Method and Theory* 14 (2007): 285–310; Donna Haraway, "Situated Knowledges: The Science Question in Feminism as a Site of Discourse on the Privilege of the Partial Perspective," *Feminist Studies* 14 (1988): 575–99.

22. Jussi Parikka, *What Is Media Archaeology?* (Malden, Mass.: Polity Press, 2012), 15.

23. Nooney, "Sierra On-Line," 49–50. See also, in addition to Parikka (ibid.), Wendy Hui Kyong Chun and Thomas Keenan, eds., *New Media, Old Media: A History and Theory Reader* (New York: Routledge, 2005); Erkki Huhtamo and Jussi Parikka, eds., *Media Archaeology: Approaches, Applications, and Implications* (Los Angeles: University of California Press, 2011); Geert Lovink, "Archive Rumblings: Interview with German Media Archaeologist Wolfgang Ernst," *nettime* (2003), http://www.nightacademy.net/texte/wolfgang_ernst.htm.

24. Thomas Elsaesser, "Media Archaeology as Symptom," *New Review of Film and Television Studies* 14 (2016), 181–215; Nooney, "Sierra On-Line," 49–50.

25. Michel Foucault, *The Archaeology of Knowledge and the Discourse on Language*, trans. A. M. Sheridan Smith (New York: Pantheon Books, 1972 [1969]), 16.

26. John Durham Peters, "Introduction: Friedrich Kittler's Light Shows," in Friedrich Kittler, *Optical Media: Berlin Lectures 1999*, trans. Anthony Enns (Malden, Mass.: Polity, 2010), 5.

27. Wolfgang Ernst, "Media Archaeography: Method and Machine versus History and Narrative of Media," in *Media Archaeology: Approaches, Applications, and Implications*, eds. Erkki Huhtamo and Jussi Parikka (Los Angeles: University of California Press, 2011), 239. See also Wolfgang Ernst, *Digital Memory and the Archive*, ed. Jussi Parikka (Minnesota: University of Minnesota Press, 2012).

28. Friedrich A. Kittler, "The City Is a Medium," *New Literary History* 27 (1996): 717–29. See also Kittler, *Gramophone, Film, Typewriter*, trans. Geoffrey Winthrop-Young and Michael Wutz (Stanford, Calif.: Stanford University Press, 1999).

29. Kittler's work presaged Benjamin Bratton's similar work on "scaled-up," spatialized computation; Bratton writes of "planetary scale" computation in *The Stack: On Software and Sovereignty* (Cambridge, Mass.: MIT Press, 2015).

30. Panoramas are immersive, inhabitable, circular visual installations. Erkki Huhtamo, *Illusions in Motion: Media Archaeology of the Moving Panorama and Related Spectacles* (Cambridge, Mass.: MIT Press, 2013). Architectural historians offer their own history of the panorama, which digs a bit deeper historically, than Huhtamo's. See Nigel Westbrook, Kenneth Rainsbury Dark, and Rene Van Meeuwen, "Constructing Melchior Lorich's Panorama of Constantinople," *Journal of the Society of Architectural Historians* 69 (2010): 62–87.

31. Siegfried Zielinski, *Deep Time of the Media: Toward an Archaeology of Seeing and Hearing by Technical Means* (Cambridge, Mass.: MIT Press, 2006).

32. Writer John McPhee is credited with coining the phrase "deep time" in his *Basin and Range* (New York: Farrar, Straus and Giroux, 1981). Rosalind Williams, in her study of subterranean technologies (mines, subways, sewers, etc.), links the notion of "deep time" to Marx's "subsurface history," Freud's subconscious, and structuralism's "deep structures." *Notes on the Underground: An Essay on Technology, Society, and the Imagination*, new ed. (Cambridge, Mass.: MIT Press, 2008).

33. Zielinski, *Deep Time of the Media*, 31. Zielinski's work offers additional historiographic insights that are useful for my work. In his 1999 *Audiovisions*, for instance, he traces the lineage of audiovisual *dispositifs* that allowed for the cinema and television to develop simultaneously, rather than sequentially, as the dominant narrative has it. Siegfried Zielinski, *Audiovisions: Cinema and Television as Entr'acts in History* (Amsterdam: Amsterdam University Press, 1999). This notion of entwined paths of evolution will reappear throughout this book.

34. Zielinski, *Deep Time of the Media*.

35. Ibid., 3.

36. Jussi Parikka, *Geology of Media* (Minnesota: University of Minnesota Press, 2015).

37. Ernst thus incidentally reminds us to recognize the material and temporal specificity of the city's media—its mud bricks, stone carvings, wheat-pasted billboards, and media-facades—which inform how the material environment archives its own heritage and, as McCullough might put it, its environmental intelligence.

38. Ernst, "Media Archaeography," 241. I'm grateful to Laine Nooney for reminding me of this quotation.

39. Wolfgang Ernst, "Radically De-Historicizing the Archive. Decolonizing Archival Memory from the Supremacy of Historical Discourse," in *Decolonizing Archives*, eds. L'Internationale Online and Radio Ištok (L'Internationale Books, 2016), 12, http://www.internationaleonline.org/bookshelves/decolonising_archives.

40. Erkki Huhtamo, "From Kaleidoscomaniac to Cybernerd: Notes toward an Archaeology of the Media," *Leonardo* 30 (1997): 221–24; "Dismantling the Fairy Engine: Media Archaeology as Topos-Study," in *Media Archaeology: Approaches, Applications, and Implications*, eds. Erkki Huhtamo and Jussi Parikka (Los Angeles: University of California Press, 2011).

41. Erkki Huhtamo and Jussi Parikka, "Introduction: An Archaeology of Media Archaeology," in *Media Archaeology: Approaches, Applications, and Implications,* eds. Erkki Huhtamo and Jussi Parikka (Los Angeles: University of California Press, 2011), 3.

42. In 2014, media archaeologists did join forces with archaeologists-proper at a site in New Mexico, where, in the early 1980s, video game maker Atari dumped thousands of commercially unsuccessful games. See Andrew Reinhard, "The Video Game Graveyard," *Archaeology,* June 9, 2014, http://www .archaeology.org/issues/139–1407/trenches/2189-new-mexico-atari-dump -site-excavation. See also Bill Morrison's 2017 film *Dawson City: Frozen Time,* about the excavation of silent film reels in a gold rush town in the Yukon Territory.

43. Angela Piccini reminds us that archaeologists' methods extend beyond the iconic excavation: "Archaeologists-as-such practice landscape archaeology, field archaeology, field walking, rescue archaeology, desk-based assessment. They focus on stratigraphic superimposition and conduct meta-archaeologies of historiographic narratives" (Angela Piccini, "Media-Archaeologies: An Invitation," *Journal of Contemporary Archaeology* 2 (2015): 6). Several years ago I began offering graduate studios that incorporate more hands-on fieldwork, and that integrate insights from anthropology, material culture, and archaeology; see, for instance, my "Urban Media Archaeology" and "Media and Materiality" courses, both available in the Teaching section of my website, wordsinspace.net. This turn to archaeology-proper also began to inform my own research; see my "Silent, Invisible City: Mediating Urban Experience for the *Other* Senses," in *Mediacity: Situations, Practices, and Encounters,* eds. Frank Eckardt et al. (Berlin: Frank & Timme, 2009): 155–76; "Digging through Archives and Dirt: Entangling Media Archaeology, Archaeology Proper, and Architectural History," Network Archaeology Conference, Miami University, Ohio, April 19–21, 2012, https://networkarchaeology.wordpress.com/2012/ 01/20/digging-through-archives-and-dirt-entangling-media-archaeology -archaeology-proper-and-architectural-history/; and "Methodolatry and the Art of Measure."

44. Parikka, *Geology of Media*; Lisa Parks, *Cultures in Orbit: Satellites in the Televisual* (Durham, N.C.: Duke University Press, 2005); John Durham Peters, *The Marvelous Clouds: Toward a Philosophy of Elemental Media* (Chicago: University of Chicago Press, 2015); Nicole Starosielski, *The Undersea Network* (Durham, N.C.: Duke University Press, 2015); Janet Vertesi, *Seeing Like a Rover: How Robots, Teams, and Images Craft Knowledge of Mars* (Chicago: University of Chicago Press, 2015). In 2003 Peters also elucidated the values of considering parallels between media studies and geology, whose methodologies bear some resemblance to archaeology-proper. The methodological concerns he addresses—e.g., that geological "texts cannot be interpreted apart from an interpretation of the processes that produced them"; that geologists "study not only content [of those texts], but signal and channel properties as well"; that geologists face the "problem of belated reception,

interpreting messages that come posthumously"; that geologists must "draw inferences from an incomplete record of deep time"—are concerns that shovel-wielding media archaeologists must face as well. Peters, "Space, Time, and Communication Theory," *Canadian Journal of Communication* 28 (2003), http://www.cjc-online.ca/index.php/journal/article/view/1389/1467.

45. See the extensive 2015 "Media Archaeologies" forum in the *Journal of Contemporary Archaeology*, with contributions from Jussi Parikka, Wolfgang Ernst, Grant Wythoff, and archaeologists Angela Piccini, Ruth Tringham, and Michael Ashley, among others (*Journal of Contemporary Archaeology* 2 (2015): 1–147). I wrote about Tringham, Ashley, and Steve Mills' use of various media in practicing and documenting multisensorial fieldwork in my "Silent, Invisible City," 155–76. See also Sara Perry, "What Archaeologists Do," *Savage Minds*, September 3, 2014, http://savageminds.org/2014/09/03/what-archaeologists-do/; Sara Perry, "What Archaeologists Do: Between Archaeology and Media Archaeology," *Savage Minds*, September 13, 2014, http://savageminds.org/2014/09/13/what-archaeologists-do-between-archaeology-and-media-archaeology/; and Sara Perry's and Colleen Morgan's subsequent posts about their own digital media-archaeological project: http://savageminds.org/author/saraperry/. See, too, the April 2016 Insuetude conference, organized by media scholar Grant Wythoff and archaeologists Zoe Crossland and Brian Boyd at Columbia University, where participants "reflected on methodological and philosophical overlaps between the cultures of the two disciplines: media archaeology and archaeology-proper," http://societyoffellows.columbia.edu/events/insuetude/.

46. For theoretical surveys and intellectual histories of archaeology, see Barry Cunliffe, Wendy Davies, and Colin Renfrew, eds., *Archaeology: The Widening Debate* (Oxford: Oxford University Press, 2002); Ian Hodder, ed., *Archaeological Theory Today*, 2nd ed. (Malden Mass.: Polity, 2012); Matthew Johnson, *Archaeological Theory: An Introduction*, 2nd ed. (New York: Wiley-Blackwell, 2010); William L. Rathje, Michael Shanks, and Christopher Witmore, *Archaeology in the Making: Conversations through a Discipline* (New York: Routledge, 2013); William H. Stiebing Jr., *Uncovering the Past: A History of Archaeology* (New York: Oxford University Press, 1993).

47. See, for instance, the work of Margaret Conkey, Joan Gero, Stephanie Moser, Marie Louise Stig Sørensen, Janet Spector, and Ruth Tringham.

48. Among the many books addressing these issues are: Nadia Abu El-Haj, *Facts on the Ground: Archaeological Practice and Territorial Self-Fashioning in Israeli Society* (Chicago: University of Chicago Press, 2001); Margarita Díaz-Andreu García, *A World History of Nineteenth-Century Archaeology: Nationalism, Colonialism, and the Past* (New York: Oxford University Press, 2007); Yannis Hamilakis, *The Nation and Its Ruins: Antiquity, Archaeology, and National Imagination in Greece* (New York: Oxford University Press, 2007); Philip L. Kohl and Clare Fawcett, eds., *Nationalism, Politics, and the Practice of Archaeology* (New York: Cambridge University Press, 1995); Randall H. McGuire, *Archaeology as Political Action* (Berkeley: University of California Press, 2008).

49. See, for instance, Ian Hodder, *Entangled: An Archaeology of the Relationships between Humans and Things* (Malden, Mass.: Wiley-Blackwell, 2012); Bjørnar Olsen, *In Defense of Things: Archaeology and the Ontology of Objects* (New York: AltaMira, 2010); and Bjørnar Olsen, Michael Shanks, Timothy Webmoor, and Christopher Witmore, *Archaeology: A Discipline of Things* (Berkeley: University of California Press, 2012). And if archaeologist Julian Thomas's 2015 prediction is correct, the future of archaeological theory means even more object-oriented ontologies (including especially the "branded," neologism-laden varieties put forward by various entrepreneurial philosophers) and "vibrant" matter. Julian Thomas, "The Future of Archaeological Theory," *Antiquity* 89 (2015): 1287–96.

50. For more on early-twenty-first-century British archaeological Romanticism, see Matthew Johnson, "On the Nature of Theoretical Archaeology and Archaeological Theory," *Archaeological Dialogues* 13 (2006): 125–30.

51. Jussi Parikka, "Operative Media Archaeology: Wolfgang Ernst's Materialist Media Diagrammatics," *Theory, Culture & Society* 28 (2011): 52–74. We have seen similar cycles of evolution in the humanities, some social sciences like geography, and higher education at large: the rise of neopositivism, scientification (through, for example, the infusion of GIS into geography, or the rise of the digital humanities), and neoliberalism; and a vehement, perhaps romantic, defense of the arts and humanities as an exception to instrumental rationality and commercially "useful" knowledge.

52. Parag Khanna, *Connectography: Mapping the Future of Global Civilization* (New York: Random House, 2016); Saskia Sassen, *The Global City: New York, London, Tokyo* (Princeton, N.J.: Princeton University Press, 1991).

53. See Brian Larkin, *Signal and Noise: Media, Infrastructure, and Urban Culture in Nigeria* (Durham, N.C.: Duke University Press, 2008); Lisa Parks, *Mixed Signals: Media Infrastructures and Cultural Geographies* (forthcoming); Anja Schwarz and Lars Eckstein, *Postcolonial Piracy: Media Distribution and Cultural Production in the Global South* (London: Bloomsbury, 2014); Nicole Starosielski, *The Undersea Network* (Durham, N.C.: Duke University Press, 2015); Ravi Sundaram, *Pirate Modernity: Delhi's Media Urbanism* (New York: Routledge, 2010); and Helga Tawil-Souri's work on media infrastructures in Israel and Palestine.

54. Ernst, "Media Archaeography," 249.

55. Ibid., 240.

56. Nooney, "Sierra On-Line," 71–72.

57. Clifford Geertz, *Negara: The Theatre State in Nineteenth-Century Bali* (Princeton, N.J.: Princeton University Press, 1980); Peter Hall, *Cities in Civilization* (New York: Pantheon, 1998); Paul Wheatley, *The Pivot of the Four Quarters: A Preliminary Enquiry into the Origins and Character of the Ancient Chinese City* (Chicago: Aldine, 1971).

58. Lewis Mumford, *The Culture of Cities* (New York: Harcourt Brace Jovanovich, 1938 [1966]), 6.

59. In regard to cities as "infrastructures" for communication, and in looking

at media infrastructures (e.g., cables and antennae and data centers) themselves, I draw on recent work in critical infrastructure studies. In my own work in this field I've explored the long history of media infrastructures and argued for the productivity of thinking about historical media *as* infrastructures. See my *Deep Mapping the Media City* (Minneapolis: University of Minnesota Press, 2015) and "Deep Time of Media Infrastructure," in *Signal Traffic: Critical Studies of Media Infrastructures*, eds. Lisa Parks and Nicole Starosielski (Urbana-Champaign: University of Illinois Press, 2015): 94–112.

60. Zielinski, *Deep Time of the Media*, 3.
61. Christopher L. Witmore, "Symmetrical Archaeology: Excerpts of a Manifesto," *World Archaeology* 39 (2007): 555–56.
62. Ibid., 556.
63. Ibid., 558.
64. Raymond Williams, *Marxism and Literature* (New York: Oxford University Press, 1977), 122.
65. My work thus responds to Alan Liu's call, in his keynote at the "Network Archaeology" conference at Miami University in spring 2012, for a "media-archaeological method . . . for capturing such networks of combined past and present—oral, written, print, analog, and/or digital" ("Remembering Networks: Agrippa, RoSE, and Network Archaeology," Network Archaeology Conference, Miami University, Oxford, Ohio, April 21, 2012). See OPSYS/Alexandra Gauzza's "Infrastructure Lifespans" timeline for the Harvard Graduate School of Design "Landscape Futures" event; the graphic is far too intricate to reproduce in print: http://m.ammoth.us/blog/wp-content/uploads/2012/03/Harvard-GSD_Landscape-Infrastructure-Symposium_March-23–24–2012_Poster-Program-s-2.jpg.
66. Richard R. John, "Recasting the Information Infrastructure for the Industrial Age," in *A Nation Transformed: How Information Has Shaped the United States from Colonial Times to the Present*, Alfred D. Chandler Jr. and James W. Cortada, eds. (New York: Oxford University Press, 2000), 56. See Derek Watkins' animated visualization of the spread of U.S. post offices: http://vimeo.com/27376376.
67. Graham and Marvin, *Telecommunications and the City*, 329.
68. For more on Wythoff's work-in-progress, see his website and github: http://wythoff.net/ and https://github.com/gwijthoff/paleoarchaeology.
69. I am not merely tracing the evolution of one media form, or one urban form, from another (genealogy). Nor am I drawing some object or settlement from the past into the present in order to shed light on both (archaeology). Nor am I searching for historical ruptures or variants (Foucauldian archaeology). Nor am I digging back through strata of media and urban evolution (geology).
70. Mumford, *Culture of Cities*, 4.
71. For more on ether, which we'll consider again in chapter 1, see G. N. Cantor and M. J. S. Hodge, eds., *Conceptions of Ether: Studies in the History of Ether Theories, 1740–1900* (New York: Cambridge University Press, 1981), and Joe

Milutis, *Ether: The Nothing That Connects Everything* (Minneapolis: University of Minnesota Press, 2005).

72. I discuss this ocularcentrism and provide an overview of texts and creative projects that redress this visual emphasis in Mattern, "Silent, Invisible City," 155–76.

73. Thompson, *Soundscape of Modernity*, 205.

74. Bruce R. Smith, "How Sound Is Sound History? A Response to Mark Smith," *Journal of the Historical Society* 2 (2002): 306–7.

75. Diane Favro and Christopher Johanson, "Death in Motion: Funeral Processions in the Roman Forum," *Journal of the Society of Architectural Historians* 69 (2010): 12–13. See RomeLab at the UCLA Experiential Technologies Center: http://etc.ucla.edu/research/projects/romelab/.

76. Olsen, Shanks, Webmoor, and Witmore, *Archaeology: A Discipline of Things*, 93.

77. Christopher L. Witmore, "Symmetrical Archaeology: Excerpts of a Manifesto," *World Archaeology* 39 (2007): 554.

78. Graeme Gilloch, *Myth and Metropolis: Walter Benjamin and the City* (Malden, Mass.: Polity Press, 1997).

79. See Jeremy W. Crampton and John Krygier, "An Introduction to Critical Cartography," *ACME: An International e-Journal for Critical Geographies* 4 (2006), 11–33; John Pickles, *A History of Spaces: Cartographic Reason, Mapping, and the Geo-Coded World* (New York: Routledge, 2004); Nancy Peluso, "Whose Woods Are These? Counter-Mapping Forest Territories in Kalimantan, Indonesia," *Antipode* 4 (1995): 383–406; David Pinder, "Subverting Cartography: The Situationists and Maps of the City," *Environment and Planning A* 28 (1996): 405–27; Bill Rankin, "Radical Cartography": http://www.radicalcartography.net/; Denis Wood, *The Power of Maps* (New York: Guilford Press, 1992). We've explored many of these critical cartographic approaches, as well as many examples of cartographic art, in my "Urban Media Archaeology" graduate studio course, which I taught at The New School from 2010 to 2014, and in my "Maps as Media" studio, which I inaugurated in 2015. Both courses are available in the Teaching section of my website, wordsinspace.net.

80. Mike Pearson and Michael Shanks, *Theatre/Archaeology* (New York: Routledge, 2001), 64–65. See also Todd Presner, David Shepard, and Yoh Kawano, *HyperCities: Thick Mapping in the Digital Humanities* (Cambridge, Mass.: Harvard University Press, 2014), and David Bodenhamer, John Corrigan, and Trevor M. Harris, eds., *Deep Maps and Spatial Narratives* (Bloomington: Indiana University Press, 2015).

81. See David J. Bodenhamer, "The Potential of the Spatial Humanities," in *The Spatial Humanities: GIS and the Future of Humanities Scholarship*, David J. Bodenhamer, John Corrigan, and Trevor M. Harris, eds. (Bloomington: Indiana University Press, 2010), 14–30.

82. Cliff McLucas, "Deep Mapping," Michael Shanks, https://web.archive.org/

web/20160318132926/http://metamedia.stanford.edu/~mshanks/projects/deep-mapping.html.

83. See my "Infrastructural Tourism," *Places* (July 2013), https://placesjournal.org/article/infrastructural-tourism/.

84. Graeme Gilloch, *Myth and the Metropolis: Walter Benjamin and the City* (Malden, Mass.: Polity Press, 1996), 4.

85. Rodney Harrison and John Schofield, *After Modernity: Archaeological Approaches to the Contemporary Past* (New York: Oxford University Press, 2010), 79.

86. Raymond Williams, *Marxism and Literature* (New York: Oxford University Press, 1977), 122.

87. Siegfried Giedion, *Mechanization Takes Command: A Contribution to an Anonymous History* (New York: Oxford University Press, 1948), 3.

88. Milutis, *Ether*.

1. Waves and Wires

1. "Marvelous clouds" is a reference to John Durham Peters's book on the "elemental" nature of media, *The Marvelous Clouds: Toward a Philosophy of Elemental Media* (Chicago: University of Chicago Press, 2015).

2. See Shannon Mattern, "Infrastructural Tourism," *Places*, July 2013, https://placesjournal.org/article/infrastructural-tourism/; and "Cloud and Field," *Places*, August 2016, https://placesjournal.org/article/cloud-and-field/.

3. Touch, "Immaterials: Light Painting WiFi," *Nearfield*, February 27, 2011, https://web.archive.org/web/20161107200802/http://www.nearfield.org/2011/02/wifi-light-painting.

4. Christina Kubisch, "Electrical Walks: Electromagnetic Investigations in the City," http://www.christinakubisch.de/en/works/electrical_walks.

5. Consider these alternatives: in eastern West Virginia, where 13,000 acres belong to the National Radio Quiet Zone, there exists a realm devoid of cell phone or radio reception that would interfere with the work of the area's most famous resident: the Robert C. Byrd Green Bank Telescope, a radio telescope tracking minute electromagnetic waves from space. See Joseph Stromberg, "Refuges of the Modern World," *Slate,* April 2013, http://www.slate.com/articles/technology/future_tense/2013/04/green_bank_w_v_where_the_electrosensitive_can_escape_the_modern_world.single.html. Its antipode—a geography dedicated to transmission—resides in northeastern Maine, where the U.S. Navy has installed a hexagonal geometry of antennas and cables to communicate at low frequency with submarines up to 40 meters beneath sea level. The Navy had even proposed installing 6,000 miles of antennae through the bedrock of the Laurentian Plateau, transforming this igneous rock into an "extremely-low frequency" transmitter for deeply submerged submarines. See Rob Holmes, "Very Long Radio Waves," *Mammoth*, July 25, 2012, http://m.ammoth.us/blog/2012/07/very-long-radio-waves/; Walter Sullivan, "How Huge Antenna Can Broadcast

into the Silence of the Sea," *New York Times*, October 13, 1981, http://www
.nytimes.com/1981/10/13/science/how-huge-antenna-can-broadcast-into
-the-silence-of-the-sea.html?pagewanted=all.

6. Michelle Hilmes, *Only Connect: A Cultural History of Broadcasting in the United States*, 4th ed. (Boston: Wadsworth, 2014), 58.

7. Joe Milutis, in conversation with Eugene Thacker, "CTheory Interview:
This Mysterious 'This.'" *CTheory*, October 19, 2011, http://www.ctheory.net/
articles.aspx?id=691. See also Jennifer Gabrys, "Atmospheres of Communication" in *The Wireless Spectrum: The Politics, Practices, and Poetics of Mobile
Technologies*, eds. Barbara Crow, Michael Longford, and Kim Sawchuk (Toronto: University of Toronto Press, 2010), 46–59.

8. James Carey, "Technology and Ideology: The Case of the Telegraph," in
Communication as Culture: Essays on Media and Society (New York: Routledge,
1992), 201–30.

9. Joe Milutis, *Ether: The Nothing That Connects Everything* (Minneapolis: University of Minnesota Press, 2005), xii.

10. Wayne D. Cocroft, "The Archaeology of Military Communications," *Industrial Archaeology Review* 35 (2013), 65–79; Michael Stratton and Barrie Trind-
er, *Twentieth Century Industrial Archaeology* (London: E & FN Spon, 2000),
89–90.

11. Mattern, "Infrastructural Tourism."

12. Jesse Westbrook, "High-Frequency Traders Find Microwaves Suit Their
Need for Speed," *Bloomberg Business*, July 24, 2014, http://www.bloomberg
.com/bw/articles/2014–07–24/high-frequency-traders-find-microwaves
-suit-their-need-for-speed.

13. University of Salford, "Archaeology of Communications Conference," Salford, U.K., March 3, 2012, http://www.cntr.salford.ac.uk/comms/archaeolo-
gyconference.php.html.

14. The British telephone kiosk, in contrast, has been saved "by public senti-
ment," and thus presents many sites for archaeological examination (John
Liffen, "Telegraphy and Telephones," *Industrial Archaeology Review* 35, May
2013, 32).

15. Ibid., 38.

16. Nigel Linge, "The Archaeology of Communications' Digital Age," *Industrial
Archaeology Review* 35, May 2013, 62.

17. Much of the following discussion about "radio cities" is drawn from my "Ear
to the Wire: Listening to Historic Urban Infrastructures," *Amodern* 2 (2013),
http://amodern.net/article/ear-to-the-wire/.

18. Quoted in Seymour N. Siegel, "Cities on Air," *Air Law Review* 8 (1937), 301.
Jean-Paul Thibaud also comments on the interaction between the built environment and radio-listening: "A transduction occurs between the material
urban forms and the perceived sonic forms, the visible becomes audible. . . .
The position of the listener in regards to the built environment is significant
in terms of the conditions of radiophonic reception. We are referring in this
case to a topophonic knot, in other words, the interference point between

media listening and architectural space." Jean-Paul Thibaud, "The Sonic Composition of the City," in *The Auditory Culture Reader*, eds. Michael Bull and Les Back (New York: Berg, 2003), 336.

19. James Hay, "The Birth of the 'Neoliberal' City and Its Media," in *Communication Matters: Materialist Approaches to Media, Mobility, and Networks*, eds. Jeremy Packer and Stephen B. Crofts Wiley (New York: Routledge, 2012), 121–40.

20. Mark Wigley, *Buckminster Fuller Inc.: Architecture in the Age of Radio* (Zurich: Lars Müller Publishers, 2015), 41.

21. Ibid., 32, 33, 36.

22. David Sarnoff, founder of RKO, spent nearly a decade of his early working life at the Marconi Wireless Telegraph Company.

23. Hay, "Birth of the 'Neoliberal' City and Its Media," 131.

24. Le Corbusier, *The City of Tomorrow and Its Planning* [originally *Urbanisme*], trans. Frederick Etchells (New York: Dover, 1987 [1925]), 187.

25. Eric Gordon, *The Urban Spectator: American Concept-Cities from Kodak to Google* (Hanover, N.H.: Dartmouth College Press, 2010), 105.

26. Ibid., 95, 101, 102.

27. Frank Lloyd Wright, "Broadacre City: A New Community Plan," *Architectural Record* (1935).

28. Sam Jacob, "Dot Dot Dot," *Perspecta* 44 (2011), 137.

29. Wigley, *Buckminster Fuller Inc.*, 30.

30. Karin Bijsterveld, *Mechanical Sound: Technology, Culture, and Public Problems of Noise in the Twentieth Century* (Cambridge, Mass.: MIT Press, 2008), 68; Mike Goldsmith, *Discord: The Story of Noise* (New York: Oxford, 2013), 22. Goldsmith reports that "the council of the province of Sybaris, a Greek colony in the Aegean, ruled that potters, tinsmiths, and other tradesmen must live outside the city walls because of the noise they made. And while they were at it, they banned roosters too. This is the first known noise ordinance and the first known example of officially organized noise zoning too" (38). For more on the history of noise abatement, see Karin Bijsterveld, "'The City of Din': Decibels, Noise, and Neighbors in the Netherlands, 1920–80," *Osiris* 18 (2008), 173–93; Karin Bijsterveld, "The Diabolical Symphony of the Mechanical Age: Technology and Symbolism of Sound in European and North American Noise Abatement Campaigns, 1900–1940," *Social Studies of Science* 31 (2001), 37–70; John M. Picker, "The Soundproof Study: Victorian Professionals, Work Space, and Urban Noise," *Victorian Studies* 42 (1999–2000), 427–53; Raymond W. Smilor, "American Noise, 1900–1930," in *Hearing History: A Reader*, ed. Mark M. Smith (Athens: University of Georgia Press, 2004), 319–30; Raymond Smilor, "Cacophony at 34th Street and 6th: The Noise Problem in America, 1900–1930," *American Studies* 18 (1977), 23–38; and Emily Thompson, *The Soundscape of Modernity: Architectural Acoustics and the Culture of Listening in America, 1900–1933* (Cambridge, Mass.: MIT Press, 2002).

31. Hillel Schwartz, *Making Noise: From Babel to the Big Bang and Beyond* (New York: Zone Books, 2011), 530.

32. The decibel, while seeming to systematize the measurement of sonic strength, fails to account for the various situational, temporal, and psycho-physiological factors that determine intensity. As one critic describes it, the decibel is "not a unit qua unity at all," but a "bastard, dubious . . . tool of quantification" [quoted in Michel Chion, *Sound: An Acoulogical Treatise*, trans. James A. Steintrager (Durham, N.C.: Duke University Press, 2016), 23].

33. Cited in Bijsterveld, Mechanical Sound, 115.

34. Ibid., 162.

35. Lilian Radovac, "'The War on Noise': Sound and Space in La Guardia's New York," *American Quarterly* 63 (2011), 733–60.

36. Schwartz, *Making Noise*, 671.

37. Alexander Eisenschmidt, review of "Walter Benjamin: Aufklärung für Kinder (und Erwachsene); Radio Broadcasts by Walter Benjamin, 1929–32" by Harald Wieser, *Journal of the Society of Architectural Historians* 69 (2010), 262; see also Lecia Rosenthal, ed., *Radio Benjamin*, trans. Jonathan Lutes (New York: Verso, 2014).

38. Shundana Yusaf, *Broadcasting Buildings: Architecture on the Wireless, 1927–1945* (Cambridge, Mass.: MIT Press, 2014).

39. Ibid., 2.

40. For examples of ambient urban sound and radio art, see Anna Friz, "Someplaces: Radio Art, Transmission Ecology, and Chicago's Radius," *Sounding Out*, November 16, 2014, http://soundstudiesblog.com/2014/11/06/someplaces-radio-art-transmission-ecology-and-chicagos-radius/; Tate, Britain, "RadioCity," November 29, 2014–February 15, 2015, London, U.K., http://www.tate.org.uk/whats-on/tate-britain/eventseries/radiocity; Tuned City, http://www.tunedcity.net/.

41. John Harwood, "Wires, Walls, and Wireless: Notes Toward an Investigation of Radio Architecture," *Media-N* 10 (2014),http://median.newmediacaucus .org/art-infrastructures-hardware/wires-walls-and-wireless-notes-toward -an-investigation-of-radio-architecture/.

42. Yusaf, *Broadcasting Buildings*, 20.

43. Ibid., 22.

44. Ibid., 20.

45. Ibid., 20.

46. Ibid., 27.

47. Ibid., 27. For more on Broadcasting House, see Staffan Ericson, "The Interior of the Ubiquitous: Broadcasting House, London," in *Media Houses: Architecture, Media, and the Production of Centrality*, eds. Staffan Ericson and Kristina Riegert (New York: Peter Lang, 2010), 19–58.

48. Thompson, *The Soundscape of Modernity*, 296.

49. W. Karp, *The Center: A History and Guide to Rockefeller Center* (New York: American Heritage, 1982), 85.

50. Danielle Shapiro, *John Vassos: Industrial Design for Modern Life* (Minneapolis: University of Minnesota Press, 2016), 157. As Shapiro explains, Vassos's redesign of both the radio unit and its public architecture was essential to over-

hauling the medium's "image as a rough military technology" and making it more palatable to a new audience (140).

51. Thompson, *The Soundscape of Modernity*, 301.
52. Ibid.
53. Ibid., 312.
54. Ibid., 2. See also Charles M. Salter Associates, Inc., *Acoustics: Architecture | Engineering| The Environment* (San Francisco: William Stout Publishers, 1998).
55. Steen Eiler Rasmussen, "Hearing Architecture," in *Experiencing Architecture* (Cambridge, Mass.: MIT Press, 1962), 235.
56. See Hale J. Sabine, *Less Noise, Better Hearing: An Outline of the Essential Architectural Acoustics for the Practicing Architect and Engineer* (Chicago: Celotex Corporation, 1950).
57. Thompson, *The Soundscape of Modernity*, 171.
58. See also Applied Minds' Babble, a unit containing a sound processor and speakers that could scramble voices within its range. As reported in the *New York Times*, it was "intended to function as a substitute for walls and acoustic tiling" (John Markoff, "No Privacy in Your Cubicle? Try an Electronic Silencer," *New York Times*, May 30, 2005,http://www.nytimes.com/2005/05/30/technology/no-privacy-in-your-cubicle-try-an-electronic-silencer.html. Herman Miller was to bring the device to market via its Sonare Technologies unit, which has since dissolved.
59. Brian Larkin, *Signal and Noise: Media, Infrastructure, and Urban Culture in Nigeria* (Durham, N.C.: Duke University Press, 2008), 48.
60. Ibid., 50.
61. Ibid., 49.
62. Beatriz Sarlo, "Cultural Landscapes: Buenos Aires from Integration to Fracture," in *Other Cities, Other Worlds: Urban Imaginaries in a Globalizing Age*, ed. Andreas Huyssen (Durham, N.C.: Duke University Press, 2008), 37, 41.
63. Martjin Oosterban, "Spiritual Attunement: Pentecostal Radio in the Soundscape of a Favela in Rio de Janeiro," *Social Text* 2 (2008): 123–45; Thomas Blom Hansen, "Sounds of Freedom: Music, Taxis, and Racial Imagination in Urban South Africa," *Public Culture* 18 (2006): 185–208.
64. Olivia Remie Constable, "Regulating Religious Noise: The Council of Vienne, the Mosque Call, and Muslim Pilgrimage in the Late Medieval Mediterranean World," *Medieval Encounters* 16 (2010): 64–95; Charles Hirschkind, *The Ethical Soundscape: Cassette Sermons and Islamic Counterpublics* (New York: Columbia University Press, 2006); Tong Soon Lee, "Technology and the Production of Islamic Space: The Call to Prayer in Singapore," *Ethnomusicology* 43 (1999): 86–100.
65. Laura Kunreuther, "Technologies of the Voice: FM Radio, Telephone, and the Nepali Diaspora in Kathmandu," *Cultural Anthropology* 21 (2006): 328.
66. Ibid., 327.
67. Moni Basu, "Good Morning, Mosul: Pirate Radio Risks Death to Fight ISIS on Airwaves," CNN, October 22, 2016, http://www.cnn.com/2016/10/22/middleeast/mosul-offensive-pirate-radio-iraq/; Jack Moore, "Iraqi PM Tells

Mosul Citizens of 'Big Victory' Soon in First Radio Message to ISIS-held City," *Newsweek*, October 5, 2016, http://www.newsweek.com/iraqi-pm-tells -mosul-citizens-big-victory-soon-first-radio-message-isis-held-506224 ?rx=us.

68. Keiko Morris, "One World Trade Center Is Key to Durst's Broadcast Push," *Wall Street Journal*, March 4, 2016, http://www.wsj.com/articles/ one-world-trade-center-is-key-to-dursts-broadcast-push-1457138456.

69. See Carlotta Daro, "Networked Cities: Infrastructures of Telecommunica- tion and Modern Urban Theories," Canadian Communication Association Conference, Montreal, Canada, June 2010. Of course there existed both wireless telegraphy and telephony, too, but these technologies fall under the category of "radio." Long-distance telephony employed microwave towers for "wireless" transmission in the 1950s, but most of those microwave instal- lations have since been replaced by fiber-optic cables or satellites.

70. Liffen, "Telegraphy and Telephones," 29.

71. Kafka wrote: "The telephone and telegraph wires in Warsaw are, through bribes, supplemented so that they form a complete circle, which turns a city into an enclosed area in the sense of the Talmud, like a courtyard, so that even the most pious can move within this circle on Saturday carrying odds and ends like handkerchiefs." Franz Kafka, *Tagebücher*, quoted in Margaret Olin, "The Materiality of the Imperceptible," in *Sensational Religion: Sensory Cultures in Material Practice*, ed. Sally M. Promey (New Haven, Conn.: Yale University Press, 2014), 183. Orthodox Jewish communities still use phone and power lines to demarcate eruvin, although their construction has of- ten incited protests from those who object to public infrastructure being repurposed as religious symbols. See Tiny Kelley, "Town Votes for Marker Used by Jews," *New York Times*, January 25, 2006, http://www.nytimes.com/ 2006/01/25/nyregion/25tenafly.html; Matt A. V. Chaban, "Hamptons Town Nears a Deal on a Jewish Ritual Boundary," *New York Times*, May 29, 2016, http://www.nytimes.com/2016/05/30/nyregion/hamptons-town-nears-a -deal-on-a-jewish-ritual-boundary.html.

72. Quoted in Schwartz, *Making Noise*, 428. See also Robert MacDougall, "The Telephone on Main Street: Utility Regulation in the United States and Canada before 1900," *Business and Economic History On-Line* 4 (2006), http://www .thebhc.org/sites/default/files/macdougall.pdf.

73. Schwartz, *Making Noise*, 429.

74. *The American Architect and Building News* 10, October 28, 1881, 202.

75. William Orton, "A Review of the 'Opinions of Experts,' as to the Necessity for the Poles Now Erected in Tenth Street, in the City of Philadelphia, by the Western Union Telegraph Company" (New York: Russell Brothers, 1876).

76. Aminur Rahman Rasel, "Two Years Needed to Remove Overhead Cables," *Dhaka Tribune*, November 10, 2014, http://www.dhakatribune.com/ bangladesh/2014/nov/10/two-years-needed-remove-overhead-cables; Dan Ashley, "Efforts to Bury All Utility Wires in SF Nearly Impossible," *ABC 7 News*, January 22, 2015, http://abc7news.com/news/efforts-to-bury-all

-utility-wires-in-sf-nearly-impossible-/486804/. Today, aside from the obvious aesthetic and pragmatic concerns, wires (and the satellite dishes and other equipment they're connected to) still sometimes represent something sinister and corporeally threatening. See Justin Ascott, "City of Wires," https://vimeo.com/11270158.

77. Henry David Thoreau, journal entries, September 3 and September 22, 1851, *The Heart of Thoreau's Journals*, ed. Odell Shepard (New York: Dover, 1961), 57, 60.

78. Douglas Kahn, "Electrical Atmospheres," in *Invisible Fields: Geographies of Radio Waves*, eds. Jose Luis de Vicente, Honor Harger, Josep Perello (Barcelona: Actar, 2002), 25. See also Kahn's *Earth Sound Earth Signal: Energies and Earth Magnitude in the Arts* (Berkeley: University of California Press, 2013), and iconic sound artist Alvin Lucier's *Sferics*: http://www.alvin-lucier-film.com/sferics.html.

79. Shannon Mattern, "Puffs of Air," *AIR*, Alphabet City 15, ed. John Knechtel (Cambridge, Mass.: MIT Press, 2010), 42–56; Tom Standage, *The Victorian Internet: The Remarkable Story of the Telegraph and the Nineteenth Century's Online Pioneers* (London: Weidenfeld & Nicholson, 1998).

80. "The Long Distance Building of the American Telephone and Telegraph Company," Landmarks Preservation Commission, October 1, 1991, Designation List 239, LP-1747, http://www.neighborhoodpreservationcenter.org/db/bb_files/1991LongDistanceBuilding.pdf. There are multiple amateur historian websites chronicling the old small-town and small-city central exchange buildings (e.g., http://www.co-buildings.com/, http://www.thecentraloffice.com/).

81. Paul Ford, "Rotary Dial," *ftrain.com*, August 21, 2012, http://www.ftrain.com/rotary-dial.html.

82. Addison Godel, "When Windows Were Wires: The Projection of Network Invulnerability and the Architecture of AT&T Long Lines," *Grey Room* 61 (2015): 39–40.

83. New England Telephone and Telegraph Company, *Planning for Home Telephone Conveniences: For the Use of Architects, Engineers, Builders, Owners* (American Telephone and Telegraph Company, 1928). See also Emily Bills, "Hooking Up a Home," in "The Telephone Shapes Los Angeles: Communications and Built Space, 1880–1950." PhD diss., New York University, 2006, 255–326.

84. General Post Office, *Facilities for Telephones in New Buildings* (London: General Post Office, 1931).

85. James E. Katz, *Magic in the Air: Mobile Communication and the Transformation of Social Life* (New Brunswick, N.J.: Transaction Publishers, 2006), 53; Ariana Kelly, *Phone Booth* (New York: Bloomsbury, 2015). Hacker magazine *2600* has, since 1988, been collecting photos of payphones from around the world, http://www.2600.com/phones/.

86. Much of this discussion of the telegraph's urban development is drawn from James Carey, "Technology and Ideology: The Case of the Telegraph," in

Communication as Culture: Essays on Media and Society (New York: Routledge, 1992), 201–30; Gregory J. Downey, Telegraph Messenger Boys: Labor, Technology, and Geography, 1850–1950 (New York: Routledge, 2002); Richard R. John, "Recasting the Information Infrastructure for the Industrial Age" in A Nation Transformed: How Information Has Shaped the United States from Colonial Times to the Present, eds. Alfred D. Chandler Jr. and James W. Cortada (New York: Oxford University Press, 2000), 55–105; Joel A. Tarr, Thomas Finholt, and David Goodman, "The City and the Telegraph: Urban Telecommunications in the Pre-Telephone Era," Journal of Urban History 14 (1987): 38–80; and Kazys Varnelis, "The Centripetal City: Telecommunications, the Internet, and the Shaping of the Modern Urban Environment," Cabinet 17 (2004/2005): 27–33.

87. Tarr, Finholt, and Goodman, "The City and the Telegraph," 47, 48.

88. Much of the following discussion of the telephone's urban evolution is drawn from Ronald Abler, "The Telephone and the Evolution of the American Metropolitan System," in The Social Impact of the Telephone, ed. Ithiel de Sola Pool (Cambridge, Mass.: MIT Press, 1977), 318–41; Stephen Graham and Simon Marvin, eds., Splintering Urbanism: Networked Infrastructures, Technological Mobilities and the Urban Condition (New York: Routledge, 2001); Richard R. John, Network Nation: Inventing American Telecommunications (Cambridge, Mass.: The Belknap Press of Harvard University Press, 2010); and Varnelis, "The Centripetal City," 27–33.

89. Stephen Graham and Simon Marvin, Telecommunications and the City: Electronic Spaces, Urban Places (New York: Routledge, 1996), 317. Angel Calvo argues that in Europe, too, telephone networks were initially restricted to the town or city limits, largely in an effort to protect the state-owned telegraph network, in "The Shaping of Urban Telephone Networks in Europe, 1877–1926," Urban History 33 (2006): 411–34.

90. John, Network Nation; Robert MacDougall, "The People's Telephone; The Politics of Telephony in the United States and Canada, 1876–1926," Enterprise & Society 6 (2005): 581–7.

91. Jean Gottman, "Megalopolis and Antipolis: The Telephone and the Structure of the City," in The Social Impact of the Telephone, ed. Ithiel de Sola Pool (Cambridge, Mass.: MIT Press, 1977), 303–17; J. Alan Moyer, "Urban Growth and the Development of the Telephone: Some Relationships at the Turn of the Century," in The Social Impact of the Telephone, ed. Ithiel de Sola Pool (Cambridge, Mass.: MIT Press, 1977), 342–69; Ithiel de Sola Pool, Craig Decker, Stephen Dizard, Kay Israel, Pamela Rubin, and Barry Weinstein, "Foresight and Hindsight: The Case of the Telephone," in The Social Impact of the Telephone, ed. Ithiel de Sola Pool (Cambridge, Mass.: MIT Press, 1977), 127–57; Gerald Sussman, "Urban Congregations of Capital and Communications: Redesigning Social and Spatial Boundaries," Social Text 17 (1999): 35–51.

92. J. Alan Moyer, "Urban Growth and the Development of the Telephone: Some Relationships at the Turn of the Century," in The Social Impact of the Telephone, ed. Ithiel de Sola Pool (Cambridge, Mass.: MIT Press, 1977), 342–69.

93. Ammon Shea, *The Phone Book: A Curious History of the Book that Everyone Uses but No One Reads* (New York: Perigree, 2010); Philip Sutton, "A Look at 'The Book': The Fall and Rise of the Telephone Directory," *New York Public Library Blog*, December 14, 2010, http://www.nypl.org/blog/2010/12/14/look-book-city-directory. New York was publishing city directories as early as 1665.

94. Ford, "Rotary Dial."

95. Claude S. Fischer, *America Calling: A Social History of the Telephone to 1940* (Berkeley: University of California Press, 1992), 24, 27.

96. Lewis Mumford, "What Is a City?" *Architectural Record*, November 1937. Mumford acknowledged that Peter Kropotkin and Patrick Geddes had earlier "seized upon the implications" of the electric grid, car, telephone, and radio both for the possibility of urban decentralization and "for our civilization as a whole," in Lewis Mumford, *The Culture of Cities* (New York: Harcourt Brace Jovanovich, 1938 [1966]), 398.

97. Emily Bills, "Connecting Lines: L.A.'s Telephone History and the Binding of the Region," *Southern California Quarterly* (2009): 28.

98. Ibid., 34.

99. Merlyna Lim, "From Walking City to Telematic Metropolis: Changing Urban Form in Bandung, Indonesia," in *Critical Reflections on Cities in Southeast Asia*, eds. Tim Bunnell, Lisa B. W. Drummond, and K. C. Ho (Boston: Brill Academic Publishers, 2002), 83–84.

100. Ibid., 96.

101. Varnelis, "The Centripetal City," 27–28. Stephen Graham and Simon Marvin agree: "Because of the costs of developing new telecommunications networks, all efforts are made to string optic fibres through water, gas, and sewage ducts; between cities existing railway, road, and waterway routes are often used" (Graham and Marvin, *Telecommunications and the City*, 329).

102. Varnelis, "The Centripetal City," 33.

103. Australia's expansive Western Desert region represents an exception. See Lilly Hibberd and Curtis Taylor's "The Phone Booth Project," which documents the Martu people's continued reliance on phone booths: http://www.lilyhibberd.com/The_Phone_Booth_Project_new.html.

104. Ian Frazier, "Connected," *New Yorker*, January 25, 2016, http://www.newyorker.com/magazine/2016/01/25/connected.

105. See my "Instrumental City: The View from Hudson Yards, circa 2019," *Places*, April 2016, https://placesjournal.org/article/instrumental-city-new-york-hudson-yards/.

106. Kazys Varnelis, "Invisible City: Telecommunication," in *The Infrastructural City: Networked Ecologies in LA*, ed. Kazys Varnelis (New York: Actar, the Los Angeles Forum for Architecture and Urban Design, and the Network Architecture Lab at Columbia University, 2009), 128. See also Ingrid Burrington's series on Internet infrastructure, dating from August 2015 through January 2016, for *The Atlantic*: http://www.theatlantic.com/author/ingrid-burrington/.

107. Josh Barbanel, "Old Phone Buildings Are Being Converted into Condos," *Wall Street Journal*, December 5, 2013, http://www.wsj.com/news/articles/SB10001424052702304096104579240533401022924.

108. Jim Dwyer, "National Security Agency Said to Use Manhattan Tower as Listening Post," *New York Times*, November 17, 2016, https://www.nytimes.com/2016/11/18/nyregion/national-security-agency-said-to-use-manhattan-tower-as-listening-post.html?_r=1; Ryan Gallagher and Henrik Moltke, "Titanpointe: The NSA's Spy Hub in New York, Hidden in Plain Sight," *The Intercept*, November 16, 2016, https://theintercept.com/2016/11/16/the-nsas-spy-hub-in-new-york-hidden-in-plain-sight/.

109. Godel, "When Windows Were Wires," 58.

110. Telx, "Telx NYC1, NYC2 & NYC3," https://www.digitalrealty.com/storage/docs/resources/Telx_NYC_Trifecta.pdf.

111. Thomas Fuller, "As Myanmar Modernizes, Old Trades Are Outpaced by New Competitors," *New York Times*, November 19, 2013, http://www.nytimes.com/2013/11/20/world/asia/as-myanmar-modernizes-old-professions-go-the-way-of-the-typewriter.html?_r=0.

112. Lisa Gitelman, "Holding Electronic Networks by the Wrong End," *Amodern* 2 (2013), http://amodern.net/article/holding-electronic-networks-by-the-wrong-end/.

113. Lisa Parks, "Around the Antenna Tree: The Politics of Infrastructural Visibility," *Flow*, March 2009, http://flowtv.org/2009/03/around-the-antenna-tree-the-politics-of-infrastructural-visibilitylisa-parks-uc-santa-barbara/.

114. Nancy Owano, "Spray-on Antenna Gets Great Reception at Google Event," PhysOrg.com, February 14, 2012, https://phys.org/news/2012-02-spray-on-antenna-great-reception-google.html.

115. Peter Sloterdijk, *Foams*, Spheres Vol. III, trans. Wieland Hoban (Cambridge, Mass.: MIT Press, 2016).

116. Michael Chen, "Signal Space," *Urban Omnibus*, July 6, 2011, http://urbanomnibus.net/2011/07/signal-space/. See also Michael Chen, "Signal Space: New York's Soft Frequency Terrains," in *Bracket: Goes Soft*, eds. Neeraj Bhatia and Lola Sheppard (2012): 57–62; and Ted Kane and Rick Miller, "Cell Structure: Mobile Phones," in *The Infrastructural City: Networked Ecologies in LA*, ed. Kazys Varnelis (New York: Actar, the Los Angeles Forum for Architecture and Urban Design, and the Network Architecture Lab at Columbia University, 2009), 148–55.

117. Susan Crawford, "Blame Your Lousy Internet on Poles," *Backchannel*, August 31, 2016, https://backchannel.com/blame-your-lousy-internet-on-poles-1998a85c3ed9; "The Surprising Backbone of the Internet of Things," *Backchannel*, October 12, 2016, https://backchannel.com/the-surprising-backbone-of-the-internet-of-things-4330301084b0.

118. Chen, "Signal Space: New York's Soft Frequency Terrains," 58.

119. Diana Budds, "How Google Is Turning Cities Into R&D Labs," *Fast Company*, Feb 22, 2016, http://www.fastcodesign.com/3056964/design-moves/how-google-is-turning-cities-into-rd-labs; see also Doctoroff's 2015 presen-

tation at the Municipal Art Society Summit: "The Shared City: How Technology Will Improve Urban Living," *MAS Summit*, New York, N.Y., October 22–23, 2015, http://www.summit.mas.org/a-city-by-design-1/; and my "Instrumental City."

120. Adrian Mackenzie, *Wirelessness: Radical Empiricism in Network Cultures* (Cambridge, Mass.: MIT Press, 2010), 64–65.

121. Gillian Fuller and Ross Harley, "The Protocological Surround: Reconceptualizing Radio and Architecture in the Wireless City," in *From Social Butterfly to Engaged Citizen: Urban Informatics, Social Media, Ubiquitous Computing, and Mobile Technology to Support Citizen Engagement*, ed. Marcus Foth, Laura Forlano, Christine Satchell, and Martin Gibbs (Cambridge, Mass.: MIT Press, 2011), 39–54.

122. Steve Goodman, *Sonic Warfare: Sound, Affect, and the Ecology of Fear* (Cambridge, Mass.: MIT Press, 2010), xx.

123. Ibid., 28, 172

124. Christina Dunbar-Hester, *Low Power to the People: Pirates, Protest, and Politics in FM Radio Activism* (Cambridge, Mass.: MIT Press, 2014). See also the microradio work of Tetsuo Kogawa, who was a key figure in the "free radio" movement in Japan.

125. See RootIO: http://rootio.org/ and Luke Yoquinto, "New Ugandan Radio Stations Run on Sun, Smartphones, and Buckets," *New Scientist*, May 27, 2015, https://www.newscientist.com/article/mg22630232.100-new-ugandan-radio-stations-run-on-sun-smartphones-and-buckets/.

126. Goodman, *Sonic Warfare*, 173. See also Vice Media, "Pirate Radio," *Vice*, https://www.vice.com/en_uk/video/pirate-radio, and Faith Millin's *Drowned City* (2014), http://www.drownedcity.com/.

127. Sam Wolfson, "The New Pirate Radio Crackdown: 400 Stations Closed in the Past Two Years," *The Guardian*, July 26, 2015, http://www.theguardian.com/tv-and-radio/shortcuts/2015/jul/26/outlaw-sound-pirate-radio-defined-british-popular-music.

128. Last Moyo, "Participation, Citizenship, and Pirate Radio as Empowerment: The Case of Radio Dialogue in Zimbabwe," in *Piracy Cultures: How a Growing Portion of the Global Population Is Building Media Relationships through Alternate Channels of Obtaining Content*, eds. Manual Castells and Gustavo Cardoso (Los Angeles: USC Annenberg Press, 2013): x.

129. Wolfson, "The New Pirate Radio Crackdown."

130. Matthew Fuller, *Media Ecologies: Materialist Energies in Art and Technoculture* (Cambridge, Mass.: MIT Press, 2005), 15–16.

131. Ibid., 16.

2. Steel and Ink

1. Jacob August Riis, *How the Other Half Lives: Studies among the Tenements of New York* (New York: Charles Scribner's Sons, 1914), 100–101. See also Kate Eichhorn on the cultural politics of artists' and activists' use of photocopied

flyers and posters in North American towns and cities in the 1980s and '90s: "If borrowed time on copy machines and borrowed space on city walls once offered artists and activists a way to carve out a space for themselves in downtowns and actively participate in defining cities," they used the "city as a bulletin board. . . . By the late 1990s these practices were increasingly being constructed as antithetical to efforts to clean up, gentrify, and privatize the same public spaces." Kate Eichhorn, *Adjusted Margin: Xerography, Art, and Activism in the Late Twentieth Century* (Cambridge, Mass.: MIT Press, 2016), 94.

2. Christopher Moraff, "ShotSpotter Coming to a Streetlight Near You?" *Next City*, October 7, 2015, https://nextcity.org/daily/entry/shotspotter-installed -in-city-streetlights-ge.

3. Lisa Gitelman, "Holding Electronic Networks by the Wrong End," *Amodern* 2 (2013), http://amodern.net/article/holding-electronic-networks-by-the -wrong-end/.

4. See John Moreland, "Archaeology and Texts: Subservience or Enlightenment," *Annual Review of Anthropology* 35 (2006): 135–51; Leah Price, "From History of a Book to a 'History of the Book,'" *Representations* 108 (Fall 2009): 120–38; Christopher S. Wood, "Early Archaeology and the Book Trade: The Case of Peutinger's *Romanae vetustatis fragmenta (1505)*," *Journal of Medieval and Early Modern Studies* 28 (1998): 83–118.

5. Christopher Reed, "Gutenberg and Modern Chinese Print Culture: The State of the Discipline II," *Book History* 10 (2007): 291–315; Tsuen-Hsuin Tsien, *Paper and Printing*, vol. 5, part 1, *Science and Civilization in China*, ed. Joseph Needham (New York: Cambridge University Press, 1985).

6. Quoted in Pow-key Sohn, "Early Korean Printing," *Journal of the American Oriental Society* 79 (1959): 96–103. See also Hy Ok Park, "The History of Pre-Gutenberg Woodblock and Movable Type Printing in Korea," *International Journal of Humanities and Social Science* 4 (July 2014): 9–17 and Sohn Pow-kee, "Printing Since the 8th Century in Korea," *Koreana* 4 (Summer 1993), http:// koreana.kf.or.kr/pdf_file/1993/1993_SUMMER_E004.pdf.

7. Elizabeth Eisenstein, *The Printing Press as an Agent of Change* (New York: Cambridge University Press, 1979); Marshall McLuhan, *The Gutenberg Galaxy: The Making of Typographic Man* (Toronto: University of Toronto Press, 1962); Walter J. Ong, *Orality and Literacy: The Technologizing of the Word* (New York: Routledge, 1982).

8. Adrian Johns, *Piracy: The Intellectual Property Wars from Gutenberg to Gates* (Chicago: University of Chicago Press, 2010).

9. Armando Petrucci, *Public Lettering: Script, Power, and Culture*, trans. Linda Lappin (Chicago: University of Chicago Press, 1993), 18; Christine Sciacca, *Building the Medieval World* (Los Angeles: J. Paul Getty Museum, 2010), 68–86.

10. Frank Solomon and Mercedes Niño-Murcia, *The Lettered Mountain: A Peruvian Village's Way with Writing* (Durham, N.C.: Duke University Press, 2011), 235.

11. Petrucci, *Public Lettering*, 1.

12. Ibid.,17–18.

13. See Ella Chmielewska's long-running "Text and the City" course at the University of Edinburgh, http://text-and-city.blogspot.com/; David Frisby, "The Metropolis as Text: Otto Wagner and Vienna's 'Second Renaissance,'" in *The Hieroglyphics of Space: Reading and Experiencing the Modern Metropolis*, ed. Neil Leach (New York: Routledge, 2002), 15–30.

14. Victor Hugo, *The Hunchback of Notre Dame* [1831], http://www.online-literature.com/victor_hugo/hunchback_notre_dame/24/.

15. Lewis Mumford, *Sticks and Stones* (New York: Dover Publications, 1955), 6. Earlier, in *The Culture of Cities*, he proclaimed: "The invention of printing gave to the processes of standardization the authority of the printed word and the mechanically copied drawing and plan: book knowledge assumed greater authority than craft-experience, and literacy presently became an indispensable mark of good building. To know the classic forms described in the newly printed work of Vitruvius, to keep in touch with the printed prescriptions of an Alberti, a Vignola, a Palladio became more important than to understand the needs and the processes of life of one's contemporaries." Lewis Mumford, *The Culture of Cities* (New York: Harcourt Brace Jovanovich, 1938 [1966]), 129.

16. Mario Carpo, *Architecture in the Age of Printing: Orality, Writing, Typography, and Printed Images in the History of Architectural Theory* (Cambridge, Mass.: MIT Press, 2001), 34–35.

17. Carpo, *Architecture in the Age of Printing*, 6.

18. Hélène Lipstadt, "Architectural Publications, Competitions, and Exhibitions," in *Architecture and Its Image: Four Centuries of Architectural Representation; Works from the Collection of the Canadian Centre for Architecture*, eds. Eve Blau and Edward Kaufman (Montreal: Canadian Centre for Architecture, 1989), 113.

19. Christoph Thoenes and Hubert Günther note that "the canon of the five orders with defined rules" was an invention of the Italian Renaissance ["Gli ordini architettonici: rinacità o invenzione?" in *Roma e l'antico nell'arte e nella cultura del Cinquecento*, ed. Marcello Fagiolo (Rome: Istituto della Enciclopedia Italiana, 1985), 298–310; referenced in Michael J. Waters, "A Renaissance Without Order: Single-Sheet Engravings, and the Mutability of Architectural Prints," *Journal of the Society of Architectural Education* 71 (2012): 500].

20. Carpo, *Architecture in the Age of Printing*, 7, 51; see also Hanno-Walter Kruft, *A History of Architectural Theory from Vitruvius to the Present* (New York: Princeton Architectural Press, 1994), 73–78. Kruft states that the 1521 Cesariano edition of Vitruvius's *Ten Books on Architecture* was "the first time the Orders are brought together in one diagram" (68).

21. Carpo, *Architecture in the Age of Printing*, 46. There's also a great deal of scholarship on "architects as readers"—how architects collected, read, and annotated architectural treatises and other print material, and how those reading practices informed their architectural practice, which in turn shaped the built landscape. See Kenneth Hafertepe and James O'Gorman, eds., *American Architects and Their Books to 1848* (Amherst: University of Massachusetts

Press, 2001); Sarah McPhee, "The Architect as Reader," *Journal of the Society of Architectural Historians* 58 (1999/2000): 454–461; Linda Pellecchia, "Architects Read Vitruvius: Renaissance Interpretations of the Atrium of the Ancient House," *Journal of the Society of Architectural Historians* 51 (1992): 377–416; Jade Preddy, "The Influence of the Japanese Print on the Architecture of Frank Lloyd Wright," *Journal of Popular Culture* 23 (1990): 1–20.

22. Waters, "A Renaissance Without Order," 488–523.

23. Ibid., 489.

24. Ibid., 514.

25. Mumford, *The Culture of Cities*, 132.

26. Ibid., 131.

27. Nick Yablon, *Untimely Ruins: An Archaeology of American Urban Modernity, 1819–1919* (Chicago: University of Chicago Press, 2009), 69.

28. Thomas Low Nichols, *Forty Years of American Life*, vol. 1 (London: John Maxwell and Company, 1864), 168; referenced in Yablon, *Untimely Ruins*, 74.

29. Anthon Vidler, "Building the Urban Book: Nodier in the Library," in *The Scenes of the Street and Other Essays* (New York: Monacelli Press, 2011), 209.

30. Ibid., 210.

31. Siegfried Giedion, *Space, Time, and Architecture: The Growth of a New Tradition* (Cambridge, Mass.: Harvard University Press, 1967).

32. Neil Levine, "The Book and the Building: Hugo's Theory of Architecture and Labrouste's Bibliothèque Sainte-Geneviève," in *The Beaux Arts and Nineteenth-Century French Architecture*, ed. Robin Middleton (Cambridge, Mass.: MIT Press, 1982): 155.

33. Shannon Mattern, "Stack Aesthetics II: Labrouste's Bibliothèques," *Words in Space*, March 16, 2013, http://www.wordsinspace.net/wordpress/2013/03/16/stack-aesthetics-ii-labroustes-bibliotheques/.

34. Shannon Mattern, *The New Downtown Library: Designing with Communities* (Minneapolis: University of Minnesota Press, 2007); Shannon Mattern, "Library as Infrastructure," *Places*, June 2014, https://placesjournal.org/article/library-as-infrastructure/; Shannon Mattern, "Before BILLY: A Brief History of the Bookcase," *Harvard Design Magazine* 43, Fall 2016, http://www.harvarddesignmagazine.org/issues/43/before-billy-a-brief-history-of-the-bookcase.

35. See Rob Walker, "Implausible Futures for Unpopular Places," *Places*, July 2011, https://placesjournal.org/article/implausible-futures-for-unpopular-places/.

36. James Raven, *Bookscape: Geographies of Printing and Publishing in London before 1800* (London: British Library, 2014). Raven's previous studies on "lost libraries" incorporated archaeological research, and his work here draws on urban and book history, historical geography, and material culture studies. See also Kristen Doyle Highland on the physical and cultural geographies of New York City's mid-nineteenth-century bookstores, from which urban patrons navigated both literary culture and urban culture more generally: http://www.kristendoylehighland.com/.

37. John Hinks, "The Book Trade in Early Modern Britain: Centres, Peripheries, and Networks," in *Print Culture and Peripheries in Early Modern Europe: A Contribution to the History of Printing and the Book Trade in Small European and Spanish Cities*, ed. Benito Rial Costas (Leiden, The Netherlands: Brill, 2013), 101–26.

38. Jeremiah Dittmar, "Information Technology and Economic Change: The Impact of the Printing Press," *VoxEU*, February 11, 2011, http://www.voxeu .org/article/information-technology-and-economic-change-impact -printing-press.

39. Tobie Meyer-Fong, "The Printed World: Books, Publishing Culture, and Society in Late Imperial China," *Journal of Asian Studies* 66 (2007): 790.

40. Ibid., 802.

41. Majid Sheikh, "The Fabled Bazaar Where Epics and Legends Abounded," *Dawn*, August 12, 2013, http://www.dawn.com/news/1035399/the-fabled -bazaar-where-epics-and-legends-abounded.

42. Much of this discussion of Paju Bookcity is drawn from my "Paju Bookcity: The Next Chapter," *Places* (January 2013), https://placesjournal.org/article/ paju-bookcity-the-next-chapter/.

43. Paju Bookcity, "Asia Publication Culture and Information Center Introduction," https://web.archive.org/web/20160305201607/http://pajubookcity.org/ english/sub_02_01.asp.

44. Paju Bookcity, "Future of Bookcity," https://web.archive.org/web/ 20130223082413/http://www.pajubookcity.org/english/sub_03_02.asp; see also Planning Department of Bookcity Culture Foundation, *The Story of Paju Bookcity: Through Wind and Rain: Past and Present of the Book Village* (Paju, South Korea: Bookcity Culture Foundation, 2008), 91.

45. Yi Ki-Ung, "About Bookcity," *Paju Bookcity*, https://web.archive.org/web/ 20130223082413/http://www.pajubookcity.org/english/sub_03_02.asp.

46. Keller Easterling, "Zone: The Spatial Softwares of Extrastatecraft," *Places*, November 2014, https://placesjournal.org/article/zone-the-spatial -softwares-of-extrastatecraft/.

47. Ahn Chang-hyun, "Paju Set to Become Film Town, in Addition to Being Book Hub," *The Hankyoreh* (May 1, 2015), http://english.hani.co.kr/arti/ english_edition/e_entertainment/689408.html.

48. Mattern, "Paju Bookcity: The Next Chapter."

49. Petrucci, *Public Lettering* , 92.

50. Bronwen Wilson, *The World in Venice: Print, the City, and Early Modern Identity* (Buffalo: University of Toronto Press, 2005), 22.

51. Rose Marie San Juan, *Rome: A City Out of Print* (Minneapolis: University of Minnesota Press, 2001), 17.

52. Ibid., 10; Petrucci, *Public Lettering*, 36.

53. Wilson, *The World in Venice*, 3, 24, 30.

54. Ibid., 71–72.

55. San Juan, *Rome: A City Out of Print*, 92.

56. Joanna Rappaport and Tom Cummins, *Beyond the Lettered City: Indigenous Literacies in the Andes* (Durham, N.C.: Duke University Press, 2012), 12.

57. Ibid., 14.

58. Jürgen Habermas, *The Structural Transformation of the Public Sphere: An Inquiry into a Category of Bourgeois Society*, trans. Thomas Berger (Cambridge, Mass.: MIT Press, 1991), 34.

59. See Eichhorn, *Adjusted Margin*; Shannon Mattern, "Click/Scan/Bold: The New Materiality of Architectural Discourse and Its Counter-Publics," *Design and Culture* 3 (2011): 329–54; Michael Warner, *Publics and Counterpublics* (Cambridge, Mass.: Zone Books, 2002).

60. Sylvia Lavin, "Re-Reading the Encyclopedia: Architectural Theory and the Formation of the Public in Late-Eighteenth-Century France," *Journal of the Society of Architectural Historians* 53 (1994): 185.

61. Ibid., 191.

62. Ibid., 192.

63. See Richard Cheek, *Selling the Dwelling: The Books that Built America's Houses, 1775–2000* (New York: The Grolier Club, 2013); Hyungmin Pai, *The Portfolio and the Diagram: Architecture, Discourse, and Modernity in America* (Cambridge, Mass.: MIT Press, 2002); and Daniel D. Reiff, *Houses from Books: Treatises, Pattern Books, and Catalogs in American Architecture, 1738–1950* (University Park: Penn State University Press, 2001).

64. See Gwendolyn Wright, "Populist Visions," in *Moralism and the Model Home: Domestic Architecture and Cultural Conflict in Chicago, 1873–1913* (Chicago: University of Chicago Press, 2000), 9–45.

65. David Henkin, *City Reading: Written Words and Public Spaces in Antebellum New York* (New York: Columbia University Press, 1998), 3.

66. Another text that aided in urban navigation, worth a footnote, is *Tallis's London Street Views*, a directory of London merchants and landowners along with views of the streets where they were located. Published from 1830 to 1840, the complete set included 88 views, each individually wrapped in colored paper. As the Canadian Centre for Architecture explains, "the novelty of his publication lay in its illustrations that provide a visual frame of reference for the otherwise unremarkable address listings—some 200 years before the advent of Google Street View. . . . Tallis framed each of his views with a pictorial vignette and an accurate map of the vicinity of the featured street. The entire scheme seems to have no direct precedents among representations of the urban environment" ("Tallis's London Street Views," Canadian Centre for Architecture, https://web.archive.org/web/20140711020721/http://www.cca.qc.ca/en/collection/1028-talliss-london-street-views).

67. Henkin, *City Reading*, 3.

68. Peter Fritzsche, *Reading Berlin 1900* (Cambridge, Mass.: Harvard University Press, 1996), 149.

69. Quoted in Fritzsche, ibid., 150.

70. Henkin, *City Reading*, 12.

71. Ibid., 37; See also Hilary Ballon, ed., *The Greatest Grid: The Master Plan of Manhattan, 1811–2011* (New York: Columbia University Press, 2012).

72. Fritzsche, *Reading Berlin 1900*, 16.

73. Herbert George Wells, *In the Days of the Comet* (New York: The Century, 1906), 123–4.
74. Henkin, *City Reading*, 15, 104.
75. Ibid., 113.
76. Aurora Wallace, *Media Capital: Architecture and Communications in New York City* (Urbana: University of Illinois Press, 2012), 33.
77. Wallace, *Media Capital*, 2.
78. Ibid.
79. Anthony King, *Spaces of Global Cultures: Architecture, Urbanism, Identity* (New York: Routledge, 2004), 11. Much of this discussion on newspaper architecture is drawn from my "Edge Blending: Light, Crystalline Fluidity, and the Materiality of New Media at Gehry's IAC Headquarters," in *Media Houses: Architecture, Media, and the Production of Centrality*, eds. Kristina Riegert and Staffan Ericson (New York: Peter Lang, 2010), 137–61.
80. Kim Dovey, *Framing Places: Mediating Power in Built Form* (New York: Routledge, 2001), 107.
81. Mona Domosh, "The Symbolism of the Skyscraper: Case Studies of New York's First Tall Buildings," *Journal of Urban History* 14 (1998): 327. See also Katherine Solomonson, *The Chicago Tribune Tower Competition: Skyscraper Design and Cultural Change in the 1920s* (Chicago: University of Chicago Press, 2001).
82. Aurora Wallace, "A Height Deemed Appalling: Nineteenth-Century New York Newspaper Buildings," *Journalism History* 31 (2006): 184.
83. Wallace, *Media Capital*, 55.
84. Ibid., 58.
85. Decades after the newspaper residents of Printing House Square "published" breaking news on their buildings' facades, students plastered Paris's walls with text-heavy, silk-screened political posters; amid the uprisings of 1968 the "entire city became a huge mural newspaper" (R. Tiberi, quoted in Petrucci, *Public Lettering*, 119). Benedict Anderson, *Imagined Communities: Reflections on the Origin and Spread of Nationalism* (New York: Verso, 1991).
86. Mumford, *The Culture of Cities*, 256. Paperwork was critical to administration in colonial and postcolonial cities, too. See Matthew S. Hull, *Government of Paper: The Materiality of Bureaucracy in Urban Pakistan* (Berkeley, University of California Press, 2012); Akhil Gupta, *Red Tape: Bureaucracy, Structural Violence, and Poverty in India* (Durham, N.C.: Duke University Press, 2012).
87. James Donald, *Imagining the Modern City* (Minneapolis: University of Minnesota Press, 1999), 127.
88. See Jon Agar, *The Government Machine: A Revolutionary History of the Computer* (Cambridge, Mass.: MIT Press, 2003); JoAnne Yates, *Control through Communication: The Rise of System in American Management* (Baltimore, M.D.: Johns Hopkins University Press, 1999); and my "Indexing the World of Tomorrow," *Places*, February 2016, https://placesjournal.org/article/indexing-the-world-of-tomorrow-1939-worlds-fair/.
89. Paul Rabinow, *French Modern: Norms and Forms of the Social Environment* (Chicago: University of Chicago Press, 1989), 67.

90. "Not merely did the bureaucracy itself require office space and living space," Mumford writes, "but the by-products of its routine came to occupy an increasing share of the new quarters: files, vaults, places for live storage and dead storage, parade grounds and cemeteries of documents, where the records of business were alphabetically kept, with an eye to the possibility of future exploitation, future reference, future lawsuits, future contracts" (Mumford, *The Culture of Cities*, 227). See also my "Bureaucracy's Playthings," Reanimation Library's *Word Processor*, October 28, 2013, http://www.reanimationlibrary.org/pages/wpmattern, on the history of filing furniture and accouterments; and "Puffs of Air: Communicating by Vacuum," in *Air: Alphabet City 15*, ed. John Knechtel (Cambridge, Mass.: MIT Press, 2010), 42–56, on the history of pneumatic tubes as a conduit for communication, particularly for distributing paper-based records.

91. Alexandra Lange, "White Collar Corbusier: From the *Casier* to the *Cités d'affaires*," *Grey Room* 9 (2002): 58.

92. Ibid., 59.

93. C. Wright Mills, *White Collar: The American Middle Classes* (New York: Oxford University Press, 2002), 189.

94. Lange, "White Collar Corbusier," 65.

95. Ibid., 63.

96. Ibid., 59.

97. See Kate Eichhorn, *Adjusted Margin*, on various "marginal" print urban forms—flyers, posters, zines (photocopied, not printed)—and the "abject" zones of copy shops that lived on the periphery of many urban college campuses in the 1980s and '90s.

98. Muhsin Madhi, "From the Manuscript Age to the Age of Printed Books," in *The Book in the Islamic World: The Written Word and Communication in the Middle East*, ed. George Nicholas Atiyeh (Albany: State University of New York Press, 1995), 1–15.

99. Beau Beausoleil and Deema Shehabi, eds., *Al-Mutanabbi Street Starts Here: Poets and Writers Respond to the March 5th, 2007, Bombing of Baghdad's 'Street of the Booksellers'* (Oakland, Calif.: PM Press, 2012).

100. Aditi Sriram, "Resurrecting the Book Market of Baghdad," *Narratively*, December 30, 2013, http://narrative.ly/stories/resurrecting-the-book-market-of-baghdad/.

101. Borzou Daragahi, "The Baghdad Bookseller Who Trades in Big Answers as Well as Texts," *Financial Times*, March 13, 2015, http://www.ft.com/cms/s/0/0ba68bdc-c251–11e4-bd9f-00144feab7de.html#axzz3liK5UFTr.

102. Molly Hennessy-Fiske, "Iraq Book Market Comes Back to Life Seven Years after Bombing," *Los Angeles Times*, February 9, 2015, http://www.latimes.com/world/middleeast/la-fg-iraq-baghdad-books-20150209-story.html; Hussam al-Saray, "Book-Selling on Mutanabbi Street: Texts from Vital Sidewalks," *Alakhbar*, November 14, 2014, http://english.al-akhbar.com/content/book-selling-mutanabbi-street-texts-vital-sidewalks.

103. Alia Gilbert, "'Where Are the Libraries?' The Literary Radical Fighting Sudan's Crackdowns," *The Guardian*, February 12, 2015, http://www.theguardian.com/world/2015/feb/12/sudan-save-khartoum-literary-culture.

104. Marcia Lynx Qualey, "Shutting Down Writers in Sudan," *Al Jazeera*, February 1, 2015, http://www.aljazeera.com/indepth/opinion/2015/02/shutting-writers-sudan-books-censorship-150201053020090.html.

105. Isma'il Kushkush, "In a Faded Literary Capital, Efforts at a Revival," *New York Times*, September 17, 2013, http://www.nytimes.com/2013/09/18/world/africa/in-a-faded-literary-capital-efforts-at-a-revival.html.

106. Evan Osnos, "Arabs Close the Book on Reading," *Chicago Tribune*, November 12, 2003, http://articles.chicagotribune.com/2003–11–12/news/0311120148_1_arab-world-arab-human-development-report-arab-countries.

107. Sal Robinson, "The Booksellers of the Arab World," *Melville House*, September 16, 2013, http://www.mhpbooks.com/the-booksellers-of-the-arab-world/. Hong Kong's booksellers also risk censure and imprisonment for stocking titles that are critical of Chinese officials and are thus banned in mainland China. See, for instance, Isabelle Steger, "Hong Kong Bookseller Describes His Abduction, Detention in Mainland China," *Wall Street Journal*, June 16, 2016, http://www.wsj.com/articles/hong-kong-bookseller-describes-his-abduction-detention-in-mainland-china-1466095494.

108. Robinson, "The Booksellers of the Arab World." See also, again, Kristin Doyle Highland's work on physical and cultural geographies of New York City's mid-nineteenth-century bookstores: http://www.kristendoylehighland.com/.

109. Trevor Naylor, "Booksellers in Revolution," *OUP Blog*, September 11, 2013, http://blog.oup.com/2013/09/booksellers-in-revolution-egypt/.

110. Akshay Pathak, "Publishing in India Today: Growing Imports/Exports, Territoriality, Piracy, and Digital," *Publishing Perspectives*, July 7, 2011, http://publishingperspectives.com/2011/07/publishing-in-india-imports-exports-piracy-digital/; "The Book Deal: Territorial Rights," Andy Ross Agency, November 9, 2009, https://andyrossagency.wordpress.com/2009/11/09/the-book-deal-territorial-rights/.

111. Sonia Faleiro, "The Book Boys of Mumbai," *New York Times*, January 4, 2013, http://www.nytimes.com/2013/01/06/books/review/the-book-boys-of-mumbai.html?_r=1.

112. Dennis Abrams, "What City Has More Bookstores Per Capita than Any Other?" *Publishing Perspectives*, May 13, 2015, http://publishingperspectives.com/2015/05/what-city-has-more-bookstores-per-capita-than-any-other/.

113. Beatriz Sarlo, "Cultural Landscapes: Buenos Aires from Integration to Fracture," in *Other Cities, Other Worlds: Urban Imaginaries in a Globalizing Age*, ed. Andreas Huyssen (Durham, N.C.: Duke University Press, 2008), 32, 37.

114. Angel Rama, *The Lettered City*, ed. and trans. John Charles Chasteen (Durham, N.C.: Duke University Press, 1996), 70.

115. Rama, *The Lettered City*, 71.

116. As Argentine literary critic Beatriz Sarlo argues, several other cultural and media forms—soccer, radio, tabloids and magazines, and, of course, the tango—joined printed books in helping Argentines make sense of their new, modern urban identity (Sarlo, *Other Cities, Other Worlds*, 41).

117. Frank Solomon and Mercedes Niño-Murcia, *The Lettered Mountain: A Peruvian Village's Way with Writing* (Durham, N.C.: Duke University Press, 2011), 33.

118. Ibid., 40.

119. Ibid., 32.

120. Ibid., 46.

121. Ken Auletta, "Citizens Jain," *New Yorker*, August 10, 2012, http://www.newyorker.com/magazine/2012/10/08/citizens-jain.

122. Gabrielle Parussini, "India Ink: Newspapers Boom Where the Internet Doesn't Reach," *Wall Street Journal*, September 8, 2015, http://www.wsj.com/articles/india-ink-newspapers-boom-where-the-internet-doesnt-reach-1441740780.

123. Jen Kirby, "These Photos of '90s Newsstands Will Take You Back to a Grittier (and Cheaper) New York City," *Daily Intelligencer*, May 10, 2015, http://nymag.com/daily/intelligencer/2015/04/photos-of-90s-newsstands-capture-nyc-nostalgia.html; Gary M. Stern, "Are NYC Newsstands Nearing Oblivion?" *Observer*, September 3, 2014, http://observer.com/2014/09/are-nyc-newsstands-nearing-oblivion/.

124. "Moyra Davey: Newsstands, 1994," Murray Guy, http://murrayguy.com/moyra-davey/selected-works/#newsstands-1994.

125. Glenn Collins, "Newsstands of Tomorrow Get Mixed Reviews Today," *New York Times*, August 29, 2008, http://www.nytimes.com/2008/08/30/nyregion/30newsstand.html; Jeremiah Moss, "The End of the Classic Newsstand," *Forgotten New York*, September 2008, http://forgotten-ny.com/2008/09/end-of-the-classic-newsstand-guest-post-by-jeremiah-moss/; Giles Worsley, "Design of a New Eden," *The Telegraph*, March 15, 2001, http://www.telegraph.co.uk/culture/4722179/Designer-of-a-new-Eden.html.

126. Collins, "Newsstands of Tomorrow Get Mixed Reviews Today."

127. Erika Allen, "No Porn, Just Books and Zines," *New York Times*, July 2, 2013, http://www.nytimes.com/2013/07/03/books/no-porn-just-books-and-zines.html; "The Newsstand," http://www.alldayeveryday.com/the-newsstand.

128. Dan Hill, "The Papers," *City of Sound*, April 20, 2010, http://www.cityofsound.com/blog/2010/04/the-papers.html.

129. Matt Richtel, "E-Commerce: Convenience Built on a Mountain of Cardboard," *New York Times*, February 16, 2016, http://www.nytimes.com/2016/02/16/science/recycling-cardboard-online-shopping-environment.html.

130. See my "Click/Scan/Bold," 329–54; and "*Archizines*' Rustling Pages," *Arquine* 60 (2012): 16.

131. Much of this discussion of "little libraries" is drawn from my "Marginalia: Little Libraries on the Urban Margins," *Places*, May 2012, https://placesjournal.org/article/marginalia-little-libraries-in-the-urban-margins/.

3. Of Mud, Media, and the Metropolis

1. Jack Goody, *The Logic of Writing and the Organization of Society* (New York: Cambridge University Press, 1986); Stephen Houston, "The Archaeology of Communication Technologies," *Annual Review of Anthropology* 33 (2004): 223–50; Harold Innis, *Empire and Communications* (New York: Rowman & Littlefield, 1950 [2007]); Innis, *The Bias of Communication* (Toronto: University of Toronto Press, 1951); Lewis Mumford, *The City in History: Its Origins, Its Transformations, and Its Prospects* (New York: Harcourt, Brace & World, 1961); Denise Schmandt-Besserat, *How Writing Came About* (Austin: University of Texas Press, 1992); Christopher Woods, "The Earliest Mesopotamian Writing," in *Visible Language: Inventions of Writing in the Ancient Middle East and Beyond*, ed. Christopher Woods (Chicago: Oriental Institute of the University of Chicago, 2010), 33–34.

2. Innis, *Empire and Communications*, 46.

3. Ibid., 55.

4. Genevieve von Petzinger, "Geometric Signs: A New Understanding," Bradshaw Foundation, http://www.bradshawfoundation.com/geometric_signs/; Genevieve von Petzinger and April Nowell, "A Place in Time: Situated Chauvet within the Long Chronology of Symbolic Behavioral Development," *Journal of Symbolic Human Evolution* 74 (2014): 37–54.

5. Simon Holdaway and Susan A. Johnston, "Upper Paleolithic Notation Systems in Prehistoric Europe," *Expedition* 31 (1989), http://www.penn.museum/sites/expedition/upper-paleolithic-notation-systems-in-prehistoric-europe/; Alexander Marshack, "The Art and Symbols of Ice Age Man," *Human Nature* 1 (1987): 32–41.

6. Ira Spar, "The Origins of Writing," *Heilbrunn Timeline of Art History*, Metropolitan Museum of Art, October 2004, http://www.metmuseum.org/toah/hd/wrtg/hd_wrtg.htm; Marc Van De Mieroop, *A History of the Ancient New East, ca. 3000–323 BC*, 3rd ed. (West Sussex, U.K.: John Wiley & Sons, 2016).

7. A. Leo Oppenheim, *Ancient Mesopotamia: Portrait of a Dead Civilization*, rev. ed. (Chicago: University of Chicago Press, 1977), 325.

8. Schmandt-Besserat, *How Writing Came About*.

9. Dominique Collon, *First Impressions: Cylinder Seals in the Ancient Near East* (London: British Museum Press, 2005); Frederick G. Kilgour, *The Evolution of the Book* (New York: Oxford University Press, 1998), 16; Woods, "The Earliest Mesopotamian Writing."

10. David Wengrow, "'The Changing Face of Clay': Continuity and Change in the Transition from Village to Urban Life in the Near East," *Antiquity* 72 (1998): 783–95.

11. Olof Pedersén, Paul J. J. Sinclair, Irmgard Hein, and Jakob Andersson, "Cities and Urban Landscapes in the Ancient Near East and Egypt with Special Focus on the City of Babylon," in *The Urban Mind: Cultural and Environmental Dynamics*, ed. Paul J. J. Sinclair, Gullög Nordquist, Frands Herschend, and Christian Isendahl (Uppsala, Sweden: African and Comparative

Archaeology, Department of Archaeology and Ancient History, Uppsala University, 2010), 132.

12. The materiality of the historical record conditions the possibilities of historiography. As Innis noted, "The significance of a basic medium to its civilization is difficult to appraise since the means of appraisal are influenced by the media, and indeed the fact of appraisal appears to be peculiar to certain types of media. A change in the type of medium implies a change in the type of appraisal and hence makes it difficult for one civilization to understand another. The difficulty is enhanced by the character of the material, particularly its relative permanence. [Henri] Pirenne has commented on the irony of history in which as a result of the character of the material much is preserved when little is written and little is preserved when much is written. Papyrus has practically disappeared whereas clay and stone have remained largely intact, but clay and stone as permanent material are used for limited purposes and studies of the periods in which they predominate will be influenced by that fact" (Innis, *Empire and Communications*, 29).

13. In a 1975 report by the U.S. National Academy of Sciences, a group of materials scientists and engineers wondered about the cultural and methodological implications of materials development: how might the materials used to produce historical records inform the nature of writing, and thereby shape a culture's language and their "mode of thought." How did the angular script necessitated by the reed stylus and clay tablet shape Sumerian thought? "The differences between the cuneiform and hieroglyphic culture," which used a more flexible medium, papyrus, "were made dependent on the differences in materials available, quite as much as were the mud-brick and stone architecture of their respective regions" (National Academy of Sciences, *Materials and Man's Needs: Materials Science and Engineering*, Supplementary Report of the Committee on the Survey of Materials Science and Engineering, vol. 1, *The History, Scope, and Nature of Materials Science and Engineering* (Washington, D.C.: National Academy of Sciences, 1975), 1–14).

14. Quoted in Kilgour, *The Evolution of the Book*, 16.

15. Suzanne Staubach, *Clay: The History and Evolution of Humankind's Relationship with Earth's Most Primal Element* (New York: Berkeley Books, 2005), 114.

16. Woods, "The Earliest Mesopotamian Writing," 34.

17. Ann Olga Koloski-Ostrow, *The Archaeology of Sanitation in Roman Italy: Toilets, Sewers, and Water Systems* (Chapel Hill: University of North Carolina Press, 2015), 45; Carol Rawcliffe, *Urban Bodies: Communal Health in Late Medieval English Towns and Cities* (Woodbridge, U.K.: Boydell Press, 2013), 25.

18. See Koloski-Ostrow and Rawcliffe, ibid.; see also Duccio Balestracci, "Regulation of Public Health in Italian Medieval Towns," in *Di Vielfalt der Dinge; Neue Wege zur Analyse mittelalterlicher Sachkultur*, Proceedings of the International Kongress, October 4–7, 1994, Krems an der Donau, Austria (Vienna: Verlag der Österreichischen Akademia der Wissenschaften, 1998), available at https://www.academia.edu/10350663/the_regulation_of_public_health_in_italian_medieval_towns_ . In sharing earlier versions of this article I was

asked a few times why I chose to focus on mud and not its "technical" realization in the form of the brick (such queries came with an obvious nod to Gilbert Simondon). My response is that the brick is only one of the many productive forms that mud can take, and that it implies a fixed, normative (eventually, standardized) form. I wish to emphasize instead the continual re-forming of mud into writing substrates and building materials, just as Simondon prioritized the "form-taking activity," the process, whereby matter becomes form (Gilbert Simondon, "The Genesis of the Individual," in *Incorporations*, ed. Jonathan Crary and Sanford Kwinter, trans. Mark Cohen and Sanford Kwinter (New York: Zone Books, 1992). See also Tim Ingold, *Making Anthropology: Archaeology, Art, and Architecture* (New York: Routledge, 2013), 24–26).

19. Bernhard Siegert, *Cultural Techniques: Grids, Filter, Doors, and Other Articulations of the Real*, trans. Geoffrey Winthrop-Young (New York: Fordham University Press, 2015), 9.

20. Ibid., 11. As Siegert states, "cultural techniques are conceived of as operative chains that *precede the media concepts they generate*" (my emphasis).

21. Ibid., 10.

22. Geoffrey Winthrop-Young, "Cultural Techniques: Preliminary Remarks," *Theory, Culture & Society* 30 (2013): 5.

23. See Shannon Mattern, *Deep Time of the Media City* (Minneapolis: University of Minnesota Press, 2015).

24. Debates over attempts to recreate these artifacts using digital technology, and then to tour those 3D-printed recreations through various global cities, demonstrate how material composition and place are integral components of these artifacts' meaning and value (Claire Voon, "What's the Value of Recreating the Palmyra Arch with Digital Technology?" *Hyperallergic*, April 19, 2016, http://hyperallergic.com/292006/whats-the-value-of-recreating -the-palmyra-arch-with-digital-technology/). We'll revisit these concerns in the conclusion.

25. UNESCO, "Lines and Geoglyphs of Nasca and Pampas de Jumana," World Heritage Convention, http://whc.unesco.org/en/list/700. See also Paolo Tavares, "In the Forest Ruins," *e-flux*, December 6, 2016, http://www.e-flux .com/architecture/superhumanity/68688/in-the-forest-ruins/, on the large collection of pre-Columbian geoglyphs in Amazonia, created between 900 and 1500 CE for military, religious, or resource-management purposes. This Netherlands-sized patch of etched earth demonstrates that "before European colonialism, great territorial expanses of the Amazon basin were occupied by populous and complex societies that employed advanced spatial technologies to produce large-scale modifications in the layout of the land. Moreover, the evidence shows that indigenous modes of inhabitation, both in the pre-colonial past and in the modern present, not only leave profound marks in the landscape but also play an essential role in shaping the forest ecology."

26. Johanna Drucker says that inscriptions like these, as well as on the limestone

palace walls at Babylon and the tomb paintings of ancient Egyptian monarchs, constitute spaces in which "authority is constituted through spatial signs." She explains: "These monuments are frontal in their mode of address: flat surfaces large in scale and authoritative in intention and effect. They dwarf their viewers and often, as at Behistun, are placed in a position so difficult to access that they appear to have been produced by a superhuman force. . . . The speaking subject of monumental spaces entertains no dialogue with the spoken subject." Johanna Drucker, "Species of *Espaces* and Other Spurious Concepts Addressed to Reading the Invisible Features of Signs Within Systems of Relation," *Design and Culture* 2 (2010): 139.

27. Robert E. Harrist Jr., *The Landscape of Words: Stone Inscriptions from Early and Medieval China* (Seattle: University of Washington Press, 2008), 15.

28. Ibid., 23, 28, 32.

29. Henri Lefebvre, *The Production of Space*, trans. Donald Nicholson-Smith (Oxford: Wiley-Blackwell, 1992).

30. Malcolm McCullough, in his study of "ambient," or environmental communication, notes that "buildings were the first communication medium," and that "too few histories of information acknowledge this architectural power; too few histories of information are environmental." Malcolm McCullough, *Ambient Commons: Attention in the Age of Embodied Information* (Cambridge, Mass.: MIT Press, 2013), 140.

31. Stephen Houston and Simon Martin, "Through Seeing Stones: Maya Epigraphy as a Mature Discipline," *Antiquity* 90 (2016): 443–55.

32. Innis, *Empire and Communications*, 90.

33. Ibid.

34. Monica L. Smith, Thomas W. Gillespie, Scott Barron, and Kanika Kalra, "Finding History: The Locational Geography of Ashokan Inscriptions in the Indian Subcontinent," *Antiquity* 90 (2016): 376–92.

35. Ramsay MacMullen, "The Epigraphic Habit in the Roman Empire," *The American Journal of Philology* 103 (1982): 233–46. McCullough also acknowledges epigraphy as a form of environmental communication (*Ambient Commons*, 118–21). Much of this passage on epigraphy is drawn from Shannon Mattern, "Deep Time of Media Infrastructure," in *Signal Traffic: Critical Studies of Media Infrastructures*, ed. Lisa Parks and Nicole Starosielski (Champaign: University of Illinois Press, 2015), 94–112.

36. Christopher Johanson, interview with the author, Skype, February 26, 2013.

37. Armando Petrucci, *Public Lettering: Script, Power, and Culture* (Chicago: University of Chicago Press, 1993), 1. For more on the material properties of public lettering and their modes of address, see Drucker, "Species of *Espaces* and Other Spurious Concepts"; Johanna Drucker, "Language in the Landscape," in *Figuring the Word: Essays on Books, Writing, and Visual Poetics* (New York: Granary Books, 1998), 90–99.

38. Jane Webster concurs that "individuals at all levels of Roman society"—including slaves—made literary and (nonlinguistic) figural inscriptions, both *dipinti* (painted) and *graffiti* (carved). Jane Webster, "Less Beloved: Ro-

man Archaeology, Slavery, and the Failure to Compare," *Archaeological Dialogues* 15 (2008): 118. See also Peter Keegan, *Graffiti in Antiquity* (New York: Routledge, 2014) and Henry Mouritsen, *The Freedman in the Roman World* (New York: Cambridge University Press, 2011), 127–35.

39. Louise Revell, *Roman Imperialism and Local Identities* (New York: Cambridge University Press, 2009), 3–4.

40. Yasser Tabbaa, *The Transformation of Islamic Art During the Sunni Revival* (Seattle: University of Washington Press, 2001), 54. As Laura U. Marks notes, however, some Islamic art traditions, particularly Persian paintings and carpets, did allow for the representation of animals or human figures (Laura U. Marks, *Enfoldment and Infinity: An Islamic Genealogy of New Media Art.* (Cambridge, Mass.: MIT Press, 2010).

41. Irene A. Bierman, *Writing Signs: The Fatimid Public Text* (Los Angeles: University of California Press, 1998), 4.

42. Ibid. 20.

43. Yasser Tabbaa, "Review of *Islamic Inscriptions* by Sheila S. Blair; *Writing Signs: The Fatimid Public Text,* by Irene A. Bierman; *Islamic Ornament* by Eva Baer," *Ars Orientalis* 29 (1999): 182. See also Sheila S. Blair, *The Monumental Inscriptions from Early Islamic Iran and Transoxiana* (Leiden, The Netherlands: Brill, 1992); Sheila S. Blair, *Islamic Inscriptions* (New York: New York University Press, 1998).

44. John Charles Chasteen, introduction to *The Lettered City,* by Angel Rama, trans. John Charles Chasteen (Durham, N.C.: Duke University Press, 1996), vii.

45. Angel Rama, *The Lettered City,* trans. John Charles Chasteen (Durham, N.C.: Duke University Press, 1996), 19, 24.

46. See also Siegert's work on grids: "(Not) in Place: The Grid, or, Cultural Techniques of Ruling Spaces," in Siegert, *Cultural Techniques,* 97–120.

47. Eugenia María Azevedo-Salomao and Catherine R. Ettinger-McEnulty, "Indigenous Contributions to City Planning in New Spain," *Repenser les limites: l'architecture à travers l'espace, le temps et les disciplines* (2005), http://inha .revues.org/289; Setha Low, "Indigenous Architecture and the Spanish American Plaza in Mesoamerica and the Caribbean," *American Anthropologist* 97 (1995): 748–62. Archaeologist Timothy Pugh has recently discovered that the Maya site of Nixtun-Ch'ich' in Petén, Guatemala, inhabited from 600 to 300 BCE, was organized in accordance with a clear grid structure (Owen Jarus, "Early Urban Planning: Ancient Mayan City Built on Grid," *Live Science,* April 29, 2015, http://www.livescience.com/50659-early-mayan-city -mapped.html).

48. Frank Solomon and Mercedes Niño-Murcia, *The Lettered Mountain: A Peruvian Village's Way with Writing* (Durham, N.C.: Duke University Press, 2011), 120–21.

49. Rama also acknowledges that, during the nineteenth century, the graphic universe, the "universe of signs," expanded dramatically beyond the "mute text": Neo-Baroque discourse "bloomed with a profusion of emblems,

hieroglyphs, apologues, and ciphers, all commonly incorporated into theatrical displays along with painting, sculpture, music, dance, and decorate use of colors. . . . The best examples of this discourse are obviously not the mute texts that we have conserved but in these ephemeral festivals of the arts, best represented by the triumphal arches that commemorated great events" (Rama, *The Lettered City*, 24).

50. Joanna Rappaport and Tom Cummins, *Beyond the Lettered City: Indigenous Literacies in the Andes* (Durham, N.C.: Duke University Press, 2012), 232.

51. Low, "Indigenous Architecture and the Spanish American Plaza in Mesoamerica and the Caribbean."

52. Rama, *The Lettered City*, 9.

53. Ibid., 27.

54. Solomon and Niño-Murcia, *The Lettered Mountain*, 10, 33. Rappaport and Cummins note that these territorial claims were also *performed* by landholders, who "rolled on the ground, tearing up bits of turf to symbolize the act of claiming possession" (*Beyond the Lettered City*, 121).

55. Much of this passage on Islamic spiral texts and urban form is drawn from my "Deep Time of Media Infrastructure."

56. Brinkley Messick, *The Calligraphic State: Textual Domination and History in a Muslim Society* (Berkeley: University of California Press, 1993), 231.

57. Ibid., 246–47.

58. See, for instance, the work of the Instruments Project: http://www .theinstrumentsproject.org/.

59. Siegert, "White Spots and Hearts of Darkness: Drafting, Projecting, and Designing as Cultural Techniques," in Siegert, *Cultural Techniques*, 121–46.

60. Reyner Banham, "A Black Box: The Secret Profession of Architecture," *New Statesman and Society*, October 12, 1990; reprinted in *A Critic Writes: Essays by Reyner Banham*, ed. Mary Banham (Berkeley: University of California Press, 1996), 298.

61. Mario Carpo, *Architecture in the Age of Printing: Orality, Writing, Typography, and Printed Images in the History of Architectural Theory* (Cambridge, Mass.: MIT Press, 2001), 19.

62. Lothar Haselberger, "The Construction Plans for the Temple of Apollo at Didyma," *Scientific American* 253 (1985): 126–32; A. R. Millard, "Cartography in the Ancient Near East," in *Cartography in Prehistoric, Ancient, and Medieval Europe and the Mediterranean*, vol. 1, *The History of Cartography*, ed. J. B. Harley and David Woodward (Chicago: University of Chicago Press, 1987): 109–11.

63. Vitruvius, the first-century BCE architect and engineer, wrote his *De Architectura*, the only surviving architectural treatise from antiquity, on a scroll; and as Carpo explains, the materiality of his writing informed the advice he dispensed to fellow architects: "Vitruvian architectural theory did not escape either in its form or content from the conditions of use inherent in the manuscript medium" (Carpo, *Architecture in the Age of Printing*, 13). He

couldn't rely on the accurate reproduction of any illustrations he might choose to include in his text—and, furthermore, "there were in his day . . . so many ignorant architects that Vitruvius preferred to be obscure rather than teach 'to the multitudes of those who do not understand' " (ibid., 17).

64. Solomon and Niño-Murcia, *The Lettered Mountain*, 9.
65. See John Moreland, "Archaeology and Texts: Subservience or Enlightenment," *Annual Review of Anthropology* 35 (2006), 135–51.
66. Rappaport and Cummins, *Beyond the Lettered City*, 118.
67. Solomon and Niño-Murcia, *The Lettered Mountain*, 2, 24.
68. Ibid., 36.
69. Ibid., 25.
70. Peter Gwin, "The Telltale Scribes of Timbuktu," *National Geographic*, January 2011, http://ngm.nationalgeographic.com/2011/01/timbuktu/gwin-text/1; Peter Gwin, "Timbuktu's Vulnerable Manuscripts Are City's 'Gold,' " *National Geographic*, January 30, 2013, http://news.nationalgeographic.com/news/2013/13/130129-mali-timbuktu-manuscripts-islamists-fighting-geography-culture/; Joshua Hammer, "The Treasures of Timbuktu," *Smithsonian Magazine*, December 2006, http://www.smithsonianmag.com/making-a-difference/the-treasures-of-timbuktu-138566090/?no-ist; Joshua Hammer, "The Race to Save Mali's Priceless Artifacts," *Smithsonian Magazine*, January 2014, http://www.smithsonianmag.com/history/Race-Save-Mali-Artifacts-180947965/; Luke Harding, "Timbuktu Mayor: Mali Rebels Torched Library of Historic Manuscripts," *Guardian*, January 28, 2013, http://www.theguardian.com/world/2013/jan/28/mali-timbuktu-library-ancient-manuscripts. See also Joshua Hammer, *The Bad-Ass Librarians of Timbuktu: And Their Race to Save the World's Most Precious Manuscripts* (New York: Simon and Schuster, 2016), which was published after I completed this chapter. I must also acknowledge my former student Christopher Bentley's excellent ethnographic research project on the Malian manuscripts, which he completed for my 2011 "Archives, Libraries, and Databases" seminar at The New School.
71. Joshua Hammer, "The Treasures of Timbuktu."
72. Consider also various cultural organizations' use of 3D modeling and image databases to "preserve" those heritage sites destroyed or threatened by ISIS; we'll explore one such project in the concluding chapter. See Stephen Farrell, "Using Lasers to Preserve Antiquities Threatened by ISIS," *New York Times*, December 27, 2015, http://www.nytimes.com/2015/12/28/arts/design/using-laser-scanners-to-preserve-antiquities-in-isiss-cross-hairs.html.
73. Hammer, "The Race to Save Mali's Priceless Artifacts."
74. Quoted in Gwin, "Timbuktu's Vulnerable Manuscripts Are City's 'Gold.' "
75. Much of this section is informed by Hammer, "The Race to Save Mali's Priceless Artifacts," and Colin Schultz, "Timbuktu's Priceless Manuscripts Are Safe After All," *Smithsonian Magazine*, February 4, 2013, http://www.smithsonianmag.com/smart-news/timbuktus-priceless-manuscripts-are-safe-after-all-10800004/

76. See, for instance, Matthew Battles, *Library: An Unquiet History* (New York: W. W. Norton, 2004), and Pamela Karimi and Nasser Rabbat's "The Destruction of Cultural Heritage: From Napoléon to ISIS," a special themed "dossier" of *Aggregate*, December 12, 2016, http://we-aggregate.org/project/the-destruction-of-cultural-heritage-from-napoleon-to-isis.

77. UNESCO, "Timbuktu: The Mythical Site," October 25, 2007, https://web.archive.org/web/20071025024232/http://whc.unesco.org/whreview/article7.html.

78. Jean-Pierre Adam, *Roman Building: Materials and Techniques* (Hoboken, N.J.: Taylor & Francis, 1999); James C. Anderson Jr., *Roman Architecture and Society* (Baltimore, M.D.: Johns Hopkins University Press, 1997); John P. Bodel, *Roman Brick Stamps in the Kelsey Museum* (Ann Arbor: University of Michigan Press, 1983), 1.

79. Adam, *Roman Building*, 293.

80. Quoted in Nader Vossoughian, "Standardization Reconsidered: *Normierung* in and after Ernst Neufert's *Bauentwurfslehre* (1936)," *Grey Room* 54 (2014), 39.

81. Notably, Peruvian villagers, by the late nineteenth century, came to a similar conclusion regarding paper's transformative potential: their customary uses of paper—particularly, their recording of information in tabular formats, and their maintenance of separate, consistent books for different topics (labor records, marriages, census, etc.)—ultimately demonstrated that paper matched, if not surpassed, the strengths of their khipus, which had long served as a tactile form of proto-infographics (Solomon and Niño-Murcia, *The Lettered Mountain*, 83–97).

82. Vossoughian, "Standardization Reconsidered ," 46.

83. Ibid., 47; see also Nader Vossoughian, "From A4 Paper to the Octametric Brick: Ernst Neufert and the Geopolitics of Standardization in Nazi Germany," *Journal of Architecture* 20 (2015): 675–98.

84. Vossoughian, "Standardization Reconsidered," 49.

85. Francesca Hughes, *The Architecture of Error: Matter, Measure, and the Misadventures of Precision* (Cambridge, Mass.: MIT Press, 2014), 119.

86. Ibid., 126. "That an epistemological trend—such as increasing precision, quantification, or standardization—might be directly accelerated by the physical characteristic of certain materials is telling. It reveals the possibility that such a trend might directly stem from a deep-seated fear of instability of form and matter relations, an instability most embodied in a material that has both liquid and chemically active properties" (126).

87. Ibid., 119.

88. Ibid., 127.

89. Adrian Forty, *Concrete and Culture: A Material History* (London: Reaktion Books, 2012), 16.

90. Antonio Sant'Elia, "Manifesto of Futurist Architecture" (1914), http://www.unknown.nu/futurism/architecture.html ; Jean-Louis Cohen and G. Merlin Moeller, Introduction to *Liquid Stone: New Architecture in Concrete*, ed. by Cohen and Moeller (New York: Princeton Architectural Press, 2006), 6.

91. Forty, *Concrete and Culture*, 32–33, 34.

92. Quoted in ibid., 23.

93. Ibid., 69–70; Portland Cement Association, "How Cement Is Made," http://www.cement.org/cement-concrete-basics/how-cement-is-made.

94. Forty, *Concrete and Culture*, 70–71, 73.

95. Sand is a particularly valuable commodity in the global concrete trade and thus in urban development. Extractions of ocean and river sand in the coastal regions around Singapore and Nigeria, for instance, present grave threats to those ecosystems and have sparked heated geopolitical debate. See Joshua Comaroff, "Built on Sand: Singapore and the New State of Risk," *Harvard Design Magazine* 39 (2014), http://www.harvarddesignmagazine.org/issues/39/built-on-sand-singapore-and-the-new-state-of-risk, and the research of Benjamin Mendelsohn, a doctoral student at New York University who is studying "earthmaking"—resource extraction, dredging, etc.—in African coastal cities.

96. Forty, *Concrete and Culture*, 101; HeidelbergCement, *Global Local: Annual Report 2014*, http://www.heidelbergcement.com/en/system/files_force/assets/document/hc_annual_report_2014.pdf?download=1.

97. Forty, *Concrete and Culture*, 40.

98. Cohen and Moeller, Introduction to *Liquid Stone*, 6–7. On *architecture parlante*, see Adrian Forty, *Words and Buildings: A Vocabulary of Modern Architecture* (New York: Thames & Hudson, 2000); Karsten Harries, *The Ethical Function of Architecture* (Cambridge, Mass.: MIT Press, 1998), 70–72. For an example of concrete inscription, see the architectural work of Wiel Arets, http://www.wielaretsarchitects.com/en/projects/utrecht_university_library/.

99. Julie Peteet, "The Writing on the Walls: The Graffiti of the Intifada," *Cultural Anthropology* 11 (1996): 140–41. I transformed the verbs in this passage from past to present tense. For more on the wall as a writing substrate, see Jussi Parikka, "McLuhan at Taksim Square," *Journal of Visual Culture* 13 (2014): 91–93.

100. Peteet, "The Writing on the Walls," 139, 145.

101. Ibid., 148.

102. Swati Chattopadhyay, *Unlearning the City: Infrastructure in a New Optical Field* (Minneapolis: University of Minnesota Press, 2012), 139. See also Stuart Tappin, "The Early Use of Reinforced Concrete in India," *Construction History* 18 (2002): 79–98.

103. Chattopadhyay, *Unlearning the City*, 139, 141.

104. Ibid., 151.

105. In another challenge to state and corporate infrastructures, in other parts of the world, various artists and designers and advocacy groups have sought to interpret official markers of infrastructure's presence and thereby "make visible the invisible" conduits of power. Of particular interest—as evidenced by decades'-old Flickr communities, guidebooks, and walking tours—are those spray-painted inscriptions on the streets and sidewalks that identify the location of electric wiring, communications and gas lines,

and sewers. That marking system emerged when, in June 1976, a Los Angeles construction crew working on a road-widening project cut through an oil pipeline that was much nearer the surface than they had anticipated. The resulting explosion caused much destruction and resulted in nine deaths. In response, California instituted its DigAlert spray-paint utility marking system, with electric lines identified in red, sewers in green, communication lines in orange, and gas lines in yellow. See American National Standard, *Safety Color Code* (Washington, D.C.: National Electronic Manufacturers Association, 1991), http://www.scribd.com/doc/59771358/ANSI-Z535–1991-Safety-Color-Code; DigAlert, http://www.digalert.org/cybd.html; Scott Harrison, "1976 Palms-Culver City Gasoline Pipeline Explosion," *Los Angeles Times*, June 14, 2014, http://framework.latimes.com/2014/06/14/1976-palms-culver-city-gasoline-pipeline-explosion/#/0; L.A. One Call, APWA Color Codes, http://www.laonecall.com/apwa_color_codes.htm; Jimmy Stamp, "Decoding the City: The Road Graffiti Placed by Utility Workers," *Smithsonian Magazine*, April 26, 2013, http://www.smithsonianmag.com/arts-culture/decoding-the-city-the-road-graffiti-placed-by-utility-workers-42822014/?no-ist; Nicola Twilley, "Finding Tarzan at the Sanitation Department," *Good*, April 12, 2011, http://magazine.good.is/articles/finding-tarzan-at-the-sanitation-department.
106. Chattopadhyay, *Unlearning the City*, 152, 155, 158, 161.
107. Ibid., 162.

4. Speaking Stones

1. World Monuments Fund, "Shukhov Tower," https://www.wmf.org/project/shukhov-tower. This passage re the Shabolovka tower and the *Lenin Tribune* is drawn from my "Sounding Towers," which I wrote as part of a visiting scholarship at the Canadian Centre for Architecture in 2012: http://www.cca.qc.ca/en/collection/1776-sounding-towers.
2. Letter from Vladimir Lenin to N. P. Gorbunov, January 26, 1921, *Lenin Collected Works*, vol. 35 (Moscow: Progress Publishers, 1976), 473; reprinted on Marxists Internet Archive, https://www.marxists.org/archive/lenin/works/1921/jan/26npg.htm.
3. Susan Buck-Morss, *Dreamworld and Catastrophe: The Passing of Mass Utopia in East and West* (Cambridge, Mass.: MIT Press, 2000), 137.
4. Susan Buck-Morss, "The Masses," http://falcon.arts.cornell.edu/sbm5/Documents/Masses.pdf.
5. Quoted in Margarita Tupitsyn, *El Lissitzky: Beyond the Abstract Cabinet* (New Haven, Conn.: Yale University Press, 1999), 32.
6. Victoria E. Bonnell, *Iconography of Power: Soviet Political Posters under Lenin and Stalin* (Berkeley: University of California Press, 1997), 143–44.
7. Quoted in Tupitsyn, *El Lissitzky*, 20.
8. Jean-Luc Nancy, *Listening*, trans. Charlotte Mandell (New York: Fordham University Press, 2007).

9. Friedrich A. Kittler, "The City Is a Medium," *New Literary History* 27 (1996): 724.

10. I choose the term vocality over orality because, as Adriana Cavarero and Paul Zumthor acknowledge, "orality" tends to regard "the functioning of the voice as the bearer of language," whereas vocality acknowledges "the whole of the activities and values that belong to the voice as such, independently of language" (Paul Zumthor, preface to *Flatus vocis: Metafisica e antropologia della voce*, by Corrodo Bologna (Bologna: Mulino, 2000), vii; quoted in Adriana Cavarero, "Multiple Voices," in *The Sound Studies Reader*, ed. Jonathan Sterne (New York: Routledge 2012), 528. The function of the voice in urban space is not merely to deliver speech. The cry, the laugh, the shriek, for instance: all are vocalizations that reverberate through city streets and carry meaning. See also Andrea Cavarero, *For More Than One Voice: Toward a Philosophy of Vocal Expression*, trans. Paul A. Kottman (Stanford: Stanford University Press, 2005). I'm grateful to Jonathan Sterne for recommending this particular conceptual framework.

11. Lewis Mumford, *The City in History: Its Origins, Its Transformations, and Its Prospects* (New York: Harcourt, Brace & World, 1961), 63.

12. See, for instance, Barry Blesser and Linda-Ruth Salter, *Spaces Speak, Are You Listening?: Experiencing Aural Architecture* (Cambridge, Mass.: MIT Press, 2007), 67–97; Ian Sample, "Stonehenge Was Based on a 'Magical' Auditory Illusion, Says Scientist," *The Guardian*, February 16, 2012, http://www .guardian.co.uk/science/2012/feb/16/stonehenge-based-magical-auditory -illusion?newsfeed=true; Aaron Watson and David Keating, "Architecture and Sound: An Acoustic Analysis of Megalithic Monuments in Prehistoric Britain," *Antiquity* 73 (1999): 325–36. Anthropologists, too, have studied how sound functions within particular cultures' environments. See, for instance, Steven Feld's work with the Kaluli of Papua New Guinea and Jerome Lewis's work with the Mbendjele Yaka in the Congo basin; and, for a review of sonic considerations within anthropology, as well as a proposed framework for studying prehistoric sonic environments, see Elizabeth C. Blake and Ian Cross, "The Acoustics and Auditory Contexts of Human Behavior," *Current Anthropology* 56 (2015): 81–103.

13. Nadia Drake, "Archaeoacoustics: Tantalizing, but Fantastical," *Science News*, February 17, 2012, http://www.sciencenews.org/view/generic/id/338543/ description/Archaeoacoustics_Tantalizing_but_fantastical. See also Chris Scarre and Graeme Lawson, eds., *Archaeoacoustics* (Cambridge, U.K.: McDonald Institute for Archaeological Research, 2006). Sensory history has addressed similar epistemological and methodological concerns; see Mark M. Smith, "Producing Sense, Consuming Sense, Making Sense: Perils and Prospects for Sensory History," *Journal of Social History* 40 (2007): 841–58.

14. Iegor Reznikoff, "On the Sound Related to Painted Caves and Rocks," in *Sounds Like Theory* XII, Nordic Theoretical Archaeology Group Meeting, Oulu, April 25–28, 2012, Monographs of the Archaeological Society of Finland 2, eds. Janne Ikäheimo, Anna-Kaisa Salmi, and Tiina Äikäs, http://

www.sarks.fi/masf/masf_2/SLT_07_Reznikoff.pdf. Riaan Rifkin has noted similar acoustic anomalies at the site of 26,000-year-old rock art engravings in Klipbak, South Africa (Riaan F. Rifkin, "Engraved Art and Acoustic Resonance: Exploring Ritual and Sound in North-Western South Africa," *Antiquity* 83 (2009): 585–601.

15. Blesser and Salter, *Spaces Speak, Are You Listening?* 85–86. See also David Lubman, "Acoustics of the Great Ball Court at Chichen Itza, Mexico," *Journal of the Acoustical Society of America* 120 (2006): n.p.

16. Julian Smith, "Listening to the Gods of Ancient Peru," *Archaeology Magazine* 64 (2011), http://archive.archaeology.org/1107/trenches/chavin_de_huantar_caves_acoustics.html.

17. Matthew Helmer and David Chicione, "Soundscapes and Community Organization in Ancient Peru: Plaza Architecture at the Early Horizon Centre of Caylán," *Antiquity* 87 (2013): 92–107.

18. Katya Stroud, "Hal Saflieni Hypogeum—Acoustic Myths and Science," in *Archaeoacoustics: The Archaeology of Sound*, Proceedings of the Archaeoacoustics Conference, Malta, 2014, ed. Linda C. Einix (Myakka City, FLOTS Foundation, 2014), 37–43.

19. Wouter F. M. Henkelman and Sepideh Khaksar, "Elam's Dormant Sound: Landscape, Music, and the Divine in Ancient Iran," in *Archaeoacoustics: The Archaeology of Sound*, Proceedings of the Archaeoacoustics Conference, Malta, 2014, ed. Linda C. Einix (Myakka City, FLOTS Foundation, 2014): 211–31.

20. Blesser and Salter, *Spaces Speak, Are You Listening?* 77–89.

21. Ibid., 94.

22. Philip Ball, "Why the Greeks Could Hear Plays from the Back Row," *Nature*, March 23, 2007, http://www.nature.com/news/2007/070319/full/news070319–16.html.

23. Anthony Vidler, "How to Invent Utopia: The Fortunes and Misfortunes of Plato's Polis," (presentation, Mellon Lecture, Canadian Centre for Architecture, Montreal, Canada, May 17, 2005).

24. "For who can be the general of such a vast multitude, or who the herald, unless he have the voice of a Stentor?" Aristotle, "Politics," in *Complete Works of Aristotle*, revised Oxford translation, ed. Jonathan Barnes (New York: Princeton University Press, 1998), 1326b5–7.

25. Mladen Dolar, *A Voice and Nothing More* (Cambridge, Mass.: MIT Press 2006), 105. Only *some* voices were able to exercise their political function. Planner and urbanist Peter Hall notes that, at the beginning of the Peloponnesian War, Athens' population was between 215,000 and 300,000, with 35,000 to 45,000 citizens—"dangerously large" by our philosopher's standards. Greek democracy thus "worked only because some 6,000 citizens, one in five, regularly turned up for the assembly and the People's Courts. . . . So what Athens demanded of the average citizen was passive democracy: listening and voting." Peter Hall, *Cities in Civilization* (New York: Pantheon, 1998), 37.

26. Christopher Lyle Johnstone, "Greek Oratorical Settings and the Problem of the Pnyx," in *Theory, Text, Context: Issues in Greek Rhetoric and Oratory*,

ed. Chris Johnstone (Albany: State University of New York Press, 1997), 99; Christopher Lyle Johnstone, "Communicating in Classical Contexts: The Centrality of Delivery," *Quarterly Journal of Speech* 87 (2001): 121–43. Indra Kagis McEwen also reminds us that "Greek political communities first took shape around a sacred fire, which burned in a public hearth set up in the agora: the place where people assembled to *agoreuein*—to speak to one another." Indra Kagis McEwen, *Socrates' Ancestor: An Essay on Architectural Beginnings* (Cambridge, Mass.: MIT Press, 1993), 113.

27. Johnstone, "Communicating in Classical Contexts," 137–38.

28. Johnstone, "Greek Oratorical Settings and the Problem of the Pnyx," 103; Johnstone, "Communicating in Classical Contexts," 138.

29. Johnstone, "Greek Oratorical Settings and the Problem of the Pnyx," 106. See also Richard Sennett, *Flesh and Stone: The Body and the City in Western Civilization* (New York: W. W. Norton, 1994), 56–57.

30. Sennett, *Flesh and Stone*, 60, 66.

31. James Fredal, *Rhetorical Action in Ancient Athens: Persuasive Artistry from Solon to Demosthenes* (Carbondale: Southern Illinois University Press, 2006), 4.

32. Blesser and Salter, *Spaces Speak, Are You Listening?* 95. Some archaeologists have suggested that forms of proto-democracy may have flourished in early-sixth-century Indian republics or in the complex political system of Sparta. We might wonder if geography and built space contributed to the rise of such governing forms here, too.

33. Quintilian, *Institutio Oratoria* (ca. 95 CE), 2.16.9, http://perseus.uchicago. edu/perseus-cgi/citequery3.pl?dbname=LatinAugust2012&getid=1&query =Quint.%202.16.15; See also Indra Kagis McEwen, "Hadrian's Rhetoric I: The Parthenon," *RES: Anthropology and Aesthetics* 24 (1993): 55–66.

34. Catharine Edwards, *Writing Rome: Textual Approaches to the City* (New York: Cambridge University Press, 1996), 20–21.

35. Vitruvius, *The Ten Books on Architecture* (Cambridge, Mass.: Harvard University Press, 1914), 139.

36. Peter Hall, *Cities in Civilization* (New York: Pantheon, 1998), 623, 633.

37. David Hendy, "Babble," *Noise: A Human History*, BBC [radio], March 27, 2013. Art historian Niall Atkinson writes about how the philosopher Seneca chose to deal with the din: he presumed that those city noises "had every right to participate in shaping the soundscape," and that it was his duty to "remain engaged with that world," to shape his own mental disposition regarding how to hear those noises and "orient himself spatially and socially within his neighborhood" and within his society. Niall Atkinson, "Thinking through Noise, Building toward Silence: Creating a Sound Mind and Sound Architecture in the Premodern City," *Grey Room* 60 (2015): 14–5, 18.

38. Diane Favro and Christopher Johanson, "Death in Motion: Funeral Processions in the Roman Forum," *Journal of the Society of Architectural Historians* 69 (2010): 15.

39. Favro and Johanson, "Death in Motion," 31. Favro identifies several other studies examining how rituals and processions shaped the forum of ancient

Rome, focusing in particular on "the close connections among events, meaning, and the physical locale." A continuing blind spot, or silence, in such work, Favro argues, is the perspective of non-elite participants (Diane Favro, "Meaning and Experience: Urban History from Antiquity to the Early Modern Period," *Journal of the Society of Architectural Historians* 58 (1999): 369).

40. Christopher Johanson, interview with the author, February 26, 2013.

41. For more on modeling sensory history, see my *Deep Mapping the Media City* (Minneapolis: University of Minnesota Press, 2015), 30–31, as well as the work of Richard Beacham at King's College London, who aims to model ancient theaters; and the work of the LCSE-MSI Visualization Laboratory at the University of Minnesota (in collaboration with Christopher Johnstone, whom we encountered earlier), which aims to model the acoustics of ancient Greek theaters and auditoriums, particularly "how variables of architecture design affected the sound, sight lines, and behaviors of speakers and listeners" ("Ancient Greek Rhetoric in Immersive Virtual Reality," University of Minnesota, https://www.msi.umn.edu/content/ancient-greek-rhetoric-immersive-virtual-reality); Richard Beacham, "THEATRON—Theatre History in Europe: Architectural and Textual Resources Online," http://www.didaskalia.net/issues/vol6no2/beacham.htm; Susan Schreibman, Ray Siemens, and John Unsworth, eds., *A Companion to Digital Humanities* (Malden, Mass.: Blackwell, 2004): 123–25. Finally, see also the work of classicist Anna Foka and information scientist Viktor Arvidsson, who employ a method they call "sonic *ekphrasis*" (description) to digitally model multisensory experience in Roman amphitheaters (Anna Foka and Viktor Arvidsson, "Experiential Analogies: A Sonic Digital *Ekphrasis* as a Digital Humanities Project," *Digital Humanities Quarterly* 10 (2016), http://www.digitalhumanities.org/dhq/vol/10/2/000246/000246.html).

42. Gregory S. Aldrete, *Gestures and Acclamations in Ancient Rome* (Baltimore, M.D.: Johns Hopkins University Press, 1999), 103–7; Megan Garber, "A Brief History of Applause, the 'Big Data' of the Ancient World," the *Atlantic*, March 15, 2013, http://www.theatlantic.com/technology/archive/2013/03/a-brief-history-of-applause-the-big-data-of-the-ancient-world/274014/.

43. Suetonius, *De Vita Caesarum*, trans. J. C. Rolfe, http://legacy.fordham.edu/halsall/ancient/suet-nero-rolfe.asp.

44. Garber, "A Brief History of Applause." In contrast, Mladen Dolar says that Stalinist rulers made public speeches not to garner an immediate reaction from a live audience, but for the purposes of recording their words for posterity. "Stalinist rulers—starting with Stalin himself—were never good public speakers. The voice of the Stalinist ruler is the very opposite of the Fuhrer's voice and its spectacular efficacy. When the Stalinist ruler makes a public speech, he reads in a monotonous voice, without proper intonation and rhetorical effects, as if he himself doesn't understand what he is saying. . . . The speech will be published anyway the next day in densely covered pages of the official newspaper, so nobody listens. . . . Yet the performance is essen-

tial and indispensable—not because of the delegates in the hall, nor of the people supposedly gathered in crowds around radios and loudspeakers, but as a scene staged for the benefit of the big Other. The performance is meant for the ears of the big Other of history, and after all, Stalinist measures were also justified in terms of the realization of the real historical laws, in view of a future which would supposedly validate them" (Dolar, *A Voice and Nothing More*, 117).

45. Carolyn Birdsall, *Nazi Soundscapes: Sound, Technology and Urban Space in Germany, 1933–1945* (Amsterdam: Amsterdam University Press, 2012).

46. Lewis Mumford, *The Culture of Cities* (New York: Harcourt Brace Jovanovich, 1938 [1966]), 141.

47. Ibid., 483. See also Frank M. Bryan, *Real Democracy: The New England Town Meeting and How It Works* (Chicago: University of Chicago Press, 2004).

48. Joseph Jackson, *American Colonial Architecture: Its Origin and Development* (Philadelphia: David McKay Co., 1924); Anne C. Loveland and Otis B. Wheeler, *From Meetinghouse to Megachurch: A Material and Cultural History* (Columbia: University of Missouri Press, 2003); Richard Cullen Rath, *How Early America Sounded* (Ithaca, N.Y.: Cornell University Press, 2003), 107–113.

49. Dolar, *A Voice and Nothing More*, 108–9. Dolar notes that the living voice is also central to legislature: "'Parliament,' after all, stems from *parlare*, it is a place reserved for speech" (110–11).

50. Mumford, *The Culture of Cities*, 182.

51. Hillel Schwartz, *Making Noise: From Babel to the Big Bang and Beyond* (New York: Zone Books, 2011), 288. Dell Upton also explains that, "in antebellum America, particularly in the second quarter of the nineteenth century, new popularly based politics and elaborate public ceremonies of all sorts during the early republic provided opportunities for lengthy, forcefully delivered oratory of a new sort" (Dell Upton, "Sound as Landscape," *Landscape Journal* 26 (2007): 30–31). This era, which "enshrined the art of oratory," heard the fiery rhetoric of politicians and reformers, the impassioned speech of participants at public meetings, public addresses at building openings and public holidays, new forms of popular theater, and the sermons of evangelical preachers.

52. Wendy Brown, *Undoing the Demos: Neoliberalism's Stealth Revolution* (New York: Zone Books, 2015). Brown asks: "What happens to rule by and for the people when neoliberal reason reconfigures both soul and city as contemporary firms, rather than polities?" (27).

53. Eric Wilson, "Plagues, Fairs, and Street Cries: Sounding Out Society and Space in Early Modern London," *Modern Language Studies* 25 (1995): 7.

54. Schwartz, *Making Noise*, 42.

55. Bruce R. Smith, *The Acoustics World of Early Modern England: Attending to the O-Factor* (Chicago: University of Chicago Press, 1999), 64. See also Andrew Jacobs, "In China's Alleys, Shouting Vendors Sow Echoes of the Past," *New York Times*, September 12, 2009, http://www.nytimes.com/2009/09/13/world/asia/13beijing.html.

56. Smith, *The Acoustics World of Early Modern England*, 58–60.

57. Mario Carpo, *Architecture in the Age of Printing: Orality, Writing, Typography, and Printed Images in the History of Architectural Theory* (Cambridge, Mass.: MIT Press, 2001), 24, 36. See also David Turnbull, "The Ad Hoc Collective Work of Building Gothic Cathedrals with Templates, String, and Geometry," *Science, Technology & Human Values* 18 (Summer 1993): 315–40.

58. Anthony Vidler, *The Scenes of the Street and Other Essays* (New York: Monacelli Press, 2011), 20, 30.

59. See also seventeenth-century Jesuit scholar Athanasius Kircher's *Phonurgia Nova*, which explored various techniques and architectural technologies for sound propagation within enclosed spaces: http://monoskop.org/File: Kircher_Athanasius_Phonurgia_nova.pdf.

60. Schwartz, *Making Noise*, 62.

61. Leon Battista Alberti, *On the Art of Building in Ten Books*, trans. Joseph Rykwert, Neil Leach, and Robert Tavernor (Cambridge, Mass.: MIT Press, 1988), 149.

62. Schwartz, *Making Noise*, 64. Atkinson argues that the "Renaissance palace was emerging as a distinct architectural genre in which auditory relationships could be intentionally structured"; "site and design could be integrated to mediate between noise and silence, revelry and thinking. . . . Sound was fully integrated into the design process and became a medium through which domestic relations were expressed." Certain members of the household were or were not permitted to make—to voice—particular sounds. "The result was that architecture played a more formal role in organizing social life," including relations between class and gender, labor and leisure (Atkinson, "Thinking through Noise, Building toward Silence," 22, 24, 26–27, 30). Ideally, this is how it would work.

63. Report of Harrison et al. vs. St. Marks' Church, Philadelphia: A Bill to Restrain the Ringing of Bells so as to Cause a Nuisance to the Occupants of the Dwellings in the Immediate Vicinity of the Church, Court of Common Pleas, No. 2, Philadelphia, February 1877 (Philadelphia: Allen, Lane & Scott, 1877), https://archive.org/stream/cu31924031028438#page/n37/mode/2up/ search/%22ordinary+and+usual%22, 19; referenced in Schwartz, *Making Noise*, 311.

64. Alain Corbin, *Village Bells: Sound and Meaning in the Nineteenth-Century French Countryside*, trans. Martin Thom (New York: Columbia University Press, 1998), 97.

65. Joanna Rappaport and Tom Cummins, *Beyond the Lettered City: Indigenous Literacies in the Andes* (Durham, N.C.: Duke University Press, 2012), 226.

66. Schwartz, *Making Noise*, 309.

67. Rappaport and Cummins, *Beyond the Lettered City*, 227.

68. Ana Maria Ochoa Gautier, *Aurality: Listening and Knowledge in Nineteenth-Century Colombia* (Durham, N.C.: Duke University Press, 2014), 7. Latin America, Gautier argues, "was simultaneously and just as importantly constituted by audile techniques cultivated by both the lettered elite and peoples

historically considered 'nonliterate.' . . . Lettered elites constantly encountered sounding and listening practices that differed from their own: vocalities that seemed out of tune, difficult to classify as either language or song, improper Spanish accents that did not confirm to a supposed norm, sounds of indigenous languages for which there were no signs in the Spanish alphabet, an abundance of noises or 'voices' coming from natural entities that seemed to overwhelm the senses" (4).

69. Jonathan Sterne, *The Audible Past: Cultural Origins of Sound Reproduction* (Durham, N.C.: Duke University Press, 2003).

70. Schwartz, *Making Noise*, 309, 314.

71. Mark D. Meyerson, *The Muslims of Valencia in the Age of Fernando and Isabel: Between Coexistence and Crusade* (Berkeley: University of California Press, 1991), 43.

72. Olivia Remie Constable, "Regulating Religious Noise: The Council of Vienne, the Mosque Call, and Muslim Pilgrimage in the Late Medieval Mediterranean World," *Medieval Encounters* 16 (2010): 69.

73. Ibid., 78–80.

74. Oleg Grabar, "Symbols and Signs in Islamic Architecture," *Architecture and Community: Building in the Islamic World Today*, ed. Renata Holod (Millerton, N.Y.: Aperture, 1983), 29.

75. Ergin explains that sixteenth-century architect Sinan carefully tuned his buildings—using abutting domes, muqarnas (ornamental vaulting), windows, columns, plaster, and Helmholtz resonators, among other tools and techniques—to "create an acoustic space appropriate for Qur'an recitation and other worship activities" (Nina Ergin, "The Soundscape of Sixteenth-Century Istanbul Mosques: Architecture and Qur'an Recital," *Journal of the Society of Architectural Historians* 67 (2008): 214). Many art historians and archaeologists studying historical Christian religious spaces have examined the acoustic signature, or the "voice," of particular churches, and how those spaces accommodated and amplified the voices of the clergy and the choir. Some of this work, regarding the "angel wing"–like acoustical flutter in Byzantine churches, has attracted popular attention (see Adrienne Le France, "Hearing the Lost Sounds of Antiquity," the *Atlantic*, February 19, 2016, http://www.theatlantic.com/technology/archive/2016/02/byzantine-angel-wings/470076/; and Allison Meier, "An Acoustic Museum of Byzantine Sound," *Hyperallergic*, March 3, 2016, http://hyperallergic.com/279695/an-acoustic-museum-of-byzantine-sound/.

76. Ergin, "The Soundscape of Sixteenth-Century Istanbul Mosques," 213.

77. Charles Hirschkind, *The Ethical Soundscape: Cassette Sermons and Islamic Counterpublics* (New York: Columbia University Press, 2006), 22. See also Jon W. Anderson's work on newer forms of mediating Islamic discourse, and their creation of new religious publics.

78. Brian Larkin, "Techniques of Inattention: The Mediality of Loudspeakers in Nigeria," *Anthropological Quarterly* 8 (2014): 991. Larkin shared this work in a lecture series that I organized at The New School in Spring 2015.

79. Ibid., 992.

80. Lawrence Abu Hamdan, *The All-Hearing*, 2014, http://lawrenceabuhamdan
.com/blog/2014/7/3/the-all-hearing; Keynote Address, *What Now? The
Politics of Listening*, The New School, New York, April 2015, http://
lawrenceabuhamdan.com/blog/2015/6/12/video-of-my-keynote-lecture
-what-now-the-politics-of-listening. In the spirit of full disclosure, I should
note that I played a small role in organizing this event; and Hamdan presented a slightly modified version of this same talk in a separate Spring 2015
lecture series that I organized at The New School. See also Hamdan on the
conversion of Syria's Druze population, which had not traditionally used
communal prayer, to Wahhabi Islam: "By teaching one of the Druze to become a Muezzin he constructs the loud audio infrastructure of Islam into
villages which have only heard the hushed and private voice of religious belief before. As a remnant of his visit [Saudi Sheikh] Al-Ghamidi intends the
Azan to be bellowed from the top of these mountains as a form of sonic territoriality." Lawrence Abu Hamdan, "Contra-diction," *Trans-figurations:
Curatorial and Artistic Research in an Age of Migration*, eds. Victoria Walsh,
Paul Goodwin, Pamela Sepúlveda (London: Royal College of Art, 2014), 119.
See also Emily Apter, "Shibboleth: Policing by Ear and Forensic Listening in
Projects by Lawrence Abu Hamdan," *October* 156 (2016): 100–115.

81. See also Richard Gale, "Representing the City: Mosques and the Planning
Process in Birmingham," *Journal of Ethnic and Migration Studies* 31 (2005):
1161–79, for a discussion of how daily patterns of Islamic religious practice, particularly its sonic dimensions, might impact urban planning; and
Isaac A. Weiner, "Calling Everyone to Pray: Pluralism, Secularism, and the
Adhān in Hamtramck, Michigan," *Anthropological Quarterly* 87:4 (Fall 2014):
1049–77.

82. Tong Soon Lee, "Technology and the Production of Islamic Space: The Call
to Prayer in Singapore," *Ethnomusicology* 43 (1999): 92.

83. Larkin, "Techniques of Inattention," 1007.

84. Galen Cranz, *The Politics of Park Design: A History of Urban Parks in America*
(Cambridge, Mass.: MIT Press, 1982); Roy Rosenzweig and Elizabeth Black-
mar, *The Park and the People: A History of Central Park* (Ithaca, N.Y.: Cornell
University Press, 1992); David Schuyler, "Parks in Urban America," *Oxford
Research Encyclopedia of American History*, November 2015, http://
americanhistory.oxfordre.com/view/10.1093/acrefore/9780199329175.001
.0001/acrefore-9780199329175-e-58.

85. Schwartz, *Making Noise*, 309.

86. Ibid., 274.

87. David Henkin, *City Reading: Written Words and Public Spaces in Antebellum
New York* (New York: Columbia University Press, 1998).

88. Joanna Merwood-Salisbury, "Patriotism and Protest: Union Square as Public
Space, 1832–1932," *Journal of the Society of Architectural Historians* 68 (2009):
543.

89. Ibid., 551.

90. Schwartz, *Making Noise*, 629.

91. Israel Rodríguez-Giralt, Daniel López Gómez, and Noel García López, "Conviction and Commotion: On Soundspheres, Technopolitics, and Urban Spaces," in *Urban Assemblages: How Actor-Network Theory Changes Urban Studies*, ed. Ignacio Farías and Thomas Bender (New York: Routledge, 2010), 179–95.

92. Chris Buckley and Adam Wu, "In China, the 'Noisiest Park in the World' Tries to Tone Down Rowdy Retirees," *New York Times*, July 3, 2016, http://www.nytimes.com/2016/07/04/world/asia/china-chengdu-park-noise.html. See also *People's Park*, directed by Libbie D. Cohn and J. P. Sniadecki (Cambridge, Mass.: Sensory Ethnography Lab, 2012), https://peoplesparkfilm.wordpress.com/.

93. See Paolo Patelli and Giuditta Vendrame, "Choreographies of Everyday Fiction," *continent* 4 (2015), http://www.continentcontinent.cc/index.php/continent/article/view/207. The authors describe a public art project in which they make explicit the often implicit regulations defining use of public space—e.g., how many can gather without a permit—and choreograph "new forms of civic and aesthetic engagement with hidden or abstract layers of the city."

94. Asef Bayat, *Life as Politics: How Ordinary People Change the Middle East* (Stanford, Calif.: Stanford University Press, 2010), 162.

95. Azam Khatam, "The Space Reloaded: Publics and Politics on Enqelab Street in Tehran," in *Beyond the Square: Urbanism and the Arab Uprisings*, eds. Deen Sharp and Claire Panetta (New York: Terraform, 2016), 84–102.

96. See Sharp and Panetta, *Beyond the Square*.

97. Nasser Rabbat, "Circling the Square: Architecture and Revolution in Cairo," *Artforum* 49, no. 8 (April 2011), 182–188, 190–191.

98. Ibid, 191.

99. Jussi Parikka notes that, during Turkey's coup in July 2016, amid the cacophony of helicopters, explosions, and gunfire, the calls from Istanbul's dense network of mosques served to "amplify the political leadership's social media call" for order (Jussi Parikka, "Earwitness of a Coup Night," *Machinology*, August 4, 2016, https://jussiparikka.net/2016/08/04/ear-witnesses-of-a-coup-night/). Egyptian artist Lara Baladi addresses the various material forms of protest—banners, projected films, graffiti, cell-phone videos, etc.—present at Tahrir Square (Lara Baladi, "Archiving a Revolution in the Digital Age, Archiving as an Act of Resistance," *Ibrazz*, July 28, 2016, http://www.ibraaz.org/essays/163). And Kate Eichhorn discusses the prevalent presence of print at the various Occupy rallies in 2012: "Though most of the protesters were posting updates on Facebook and Twitter, Occupy sites were littered with photocopied posters and flyers"—perhaps because, she suggests, "xerography is readily recognized by people across generations as a medium through which regular folks historically have successfully occupied public spaces." Print also became a more *secure* medium for proclamations and instruction, as protesters discovered that law enforcement was tracking their social

media posts (Kate Eichhorn, *Adjusted Margin: Xerography, Art, and Activism in the Late Twentieth Century* (Cambridge, Mass.: MIT Press, 2016), 104, 162). It's also worth noting that in many other uprisings throughout history, bricks and stones, the subjects of our last chapter, have been transformed into symbolically charged projectiles; bricks, we might say, become an extension of the voice.

100. See Susana Galán, "From the Square to the Streets: Sexual Harassment and Assault in Cairo after the 2011 Egyptian Revolution," in *Beyond the Square: Urbanism and the Arab Uprisings*, eds. Deen Sharp and Claire Panetta (New York: Terraform, 2016), 208–28.

101. Vishaan Chakrabarti, "Liberation Squares," *Urban Omnibus*, February 16, 2001, http://urbanomnibus.net/2011/02/liberation-squares/; David Lepeska, "Fight over Istanbul Park Is Also a Fight for Freedom of Speech," *NextCity*, January 13, 2015, https://nextcity.org/daily/entry/gezi-park-protests-istanbul -development-plans.

102. Liat Clark, "Architecture Firm Creates Blog to Document Gezi Park's Temporary Structures," *Wired UK*, June 26, 2013, http://www.wired.co.uk/ news/archive/2013–06/26/turkey-activists-temporary-architecture; Anna Feigenbaum, "Occupy Architecture," *Icon*, February 4, 2015, http://www .iconeye.com/architecture/features/item/11741-occupy-architecture; Pelin Tan, "A Report from Gezi Park," *Domus*, June 1, 2013, http://www.domusweb .it/en/architecture/2013/06/1/gezi_park_occupation.html.

103. Jennifer Kabat, "Turkish Protesters' War on Bad Architecture" [interview with Gökhan Karakuş], *Salon*, June 15, 2013, http://www.salon.com/2013/ 06/15/taksim_protesters_wage_war_on_government_shopping_malls_ partner/. See also the excellent syllabus for Ipek Türeli's New Architectures of Spatial Justice course at the McGill School of Architecture: https:// architecturesofspatialjustice.wordpress.com/instructor/.

104. Saskia Sassen, "Does the City Have Speech?" *Public Culture* 25 (2013): 209–21. Galán argues that "the escalation of sexual violence" in Cairo, rather than driving women from the streets, has instead galvanized mixed-gender groups to patrol the city's public spaces and streets, partner with anti-harassment organizations, and contribute to the flourishing of anti-harassment street art and graffiti (a form of urban inscription intended to claim terrains where women's bodies can safely be present and their voices can be heard). These activists' efforts have "encouraged women to maintain their presence and visibility"—and, I'd add, audibility—"in public space" (Galán, "From the Square to the Streets," 210).

105. John Markoff, "No Privacy in Your Cubicle? Try an Electronic Silencer," *New York Times*, May 30, 2005, http://www.nytimes.com/2005/05/30/technology/ no-privacy-in-your-cubicle-try-an-electronic-silencer.html; "Sonare Technologies / A Herman Miller Company Introduces Babble, Voice Privacy Without Walls" *PR Leap*, press release, September 30, 2005, http:// www.prleap.com/pr/16005/sonare-technologies-a-herman-miller

-company. See also Herman Miller's demo video: https://www.youtube
.com/watch?v=F48Q3EKgASA.

106. Much of the following material about Arup Acoustics was derived from a personal conversation with Arup's Global Leader of Acoustics, Raj Patel, on February 26, 2013, and from Patel's visit to my City and Sound course at The New School in Fall 2009.

107. Arup SoundLab, http://www.arup.com/Soundlab.aspx. Listen also to George Bodarky, Cityscape: Arup Sound Lab. Interview with Raj Patel of Arup Sound Lab," wfuv.org, September 29, 2012, http://www.wfuv.org/content/cityscape-arup-sound-lab.

108. "Audio Architecture," *Dwell*, June 2008, 62.

109. Ibid.

110. Doris Kleilein and Anne Kockelkorn, "Disconnection," in *Tuned City: Between Sound and Space Speculation*, eds. Doris Kleilein, Anne Kockelkorn, Gesine Pagels, and Carsten Stabenow (Idstein: Kookbooks, 2008), 105. For more on sonic branding, see Jonathan Sterne, "Sounds Like the Mall of America: Programmed Music and the Architectonics of Commercial Space," *Ethnomusicology* 41 (1997): 22–50; Devon Powers, "Strange Powers: The Branded Sensorium and the Intrigue of Musical Sound," in *Blowing Up the Brand: Critical Perspectives on Promotional Culture*, ed. Melissa Aronczyk and Devon Powers (New York: Peter Lang, 2010), 285–306.

111. See also Daniel Pope, Adam Lawrence, and Inan Ekici, "The Future Sound of Cities," Proceedings for Invisible Places Conference, Viseu, Portugal, July 18–20, 2014, 279–92, http://invisibleplaces.org/pdf/ip2014-pope.pdf.

112. Olivier Balaÿ, *L'espace sonore de la ville au XIXe siècle* (Isère, France: Bernin, 2003); CRESSON: http://www.cresson.archi.fr/ACCUEILeng.htm. See also Matt Bevilacque, "Shaping the Sounds of the City," *Next City*, April 15, 2012, https://nextcity.org/daily/entry/the-city-is-my-audio-booth.

113. See Sandy Isenstadt, Margaret Maile Petty, and Deitrich Neumann, eds., *Cities of Light: Two Centuries of Urban Illumination* (New York: Routledge, 2015); Nathalie Rozot, "Architectural Lighting Design," *PBS POV*, http://www.pbs.org/pov/citydark/architectural-lighting-design/; and the lighting design work of Linnea Tillett, who is strongly informed by environmental psychology: http://www.tillettlighting.com/.

114. Desmond Fennell, *Investigation into the King's Cross Underground Fire* (London: Department of Transport / Her Majesty's Stationery Office, 1988), http://www.railwaysarchive.co.uk/documents/DoT_KX1987.pdf.

115. Christopher Maag, "Silencing the Subway," *Narratively*, January 31, 2013, http://narrative.ly/stories/silencing-the-subway/; Yanni Alexander Loukissas, *Co-Designers: Cultures of Computer Simulation in Architecture* (New York: Routledge, 2012), 102; Sam Lubell, "Step into the Comfiness of NYC's 2nd Ave. Subway (Yes, Comfiness)," Wired, January 11, 2017, https://www.wired.com/2017/01/new-york-second-avenue-subway/.

116. Emily Thompson, *The Soundscape of Modernity: Architectural Acoustics and*

the *Culture of Listening in America, 1900–1933* (Cambridge, Mass.: MIT Press, 2002), 324.

117. This passage is drawn from my "Deep Time of Media Infrastructure," in *Signal Traffic: Critical Studies of Media Infrastructures*, eds. Lisa Parks and Nicole Starosielski (Champaign: University of Illinois Press, 2015), 94–112.

118. See London School of Economics, *Electric City* (London: LSE, December 2012), http://lsecities.net/publications/conference-newspapers/the-electric -city, which includes work by several key "smart city" critics, including Orit Halpern, Dan Hill, Saskia Sassen, and Richard Sennett. See also *Volume* 34, "City in a Box" special issue (December 2012); Adam Greenfield's *The City Is Here for You to Use* series of e-books; and Shannon Mattern, "Methodolatry and the Art of Measure," *Places*, November 5, 2014, https://placesjournal.org/ article/methodolatry-and-the-art-of-measure.

119. Richard Sennett, "No One Likes a City That's Too Smart," *Guardian*, December 4, 2012, https://www.theguardian.com/commentisfree/2012/dec/04/ smart-city-rio-songdo-masdar.

120. R. Murray Schafer, *The Soundscape: Our Sonic Environment and the Tuning of the World* (Rochester, Vt.: Destiny Books, 1994 [1977]).

121. Birdsall, *Nazi Soundscapes*, 28.

Conclusion

1. Stephen Farrell, "Using Lasers to Preserve Antiquities Threatened by ISIS," *New York Times*, December 27, 2015, http://www.nytimes.com/2015/12/28/ arts/design/using-laser-scanners-to-preserve-antiquities-in-isiss-cross -hairs.html.

2. The Million Image Database: http://www.millionimage.org.uk/.

3. Institute for Digital Archaeology, "Million Image Database," http:// digitalarchaeology.org.uk/projects.

4. Institute for Digital Archaeology, "Our Purpose," http://digitalarchaeology .org.uk/our-purpose.

5. CyArk: http://www.cyark.org/; New Palmyra: http://www.newpalmyra.org/; Rekrei: https://rekrei.org/. See also the 3D reconstruction efforts by the privately funded Cultural Capital Group of Nimrod, and the Hermitage Museum's pledge to restore Palmyra's temples, as well as Project Agama's documentation of Central Asian tile patterns so that they can be "translated into something completely modern and malleable" (http://www.projectagama. com/). And several universities, like Michigan State and the University of California at Berkeley, as well as nonprofits like Open Context and the Center for Digital Archaeology, are advancing work in digital archaeology (https://opencontext.org/; https://codifi.org/about/).

6. For more in IDA politics, see Nigel Richardson, "The Arch of Triumph of Palmyra Is Recreated in London—1,800 Years after It Was Built," *Telegraph*, April 18, 2016, http://www.telegraph.co.uk/news/2016/04/08/why-the-arch -of-triumph-of-palmyra-is-being-recreated-in-london/.

7. Museum of the Future: http://motf.ae/. His High Highness Sheikh Mohammed bin Rashid Al Maktoum explains the museum's aspirations: "While
others try to predict the future, we create it. . . . Museum of the Future will
be an integrated environment empowering creative minds to test, fund, and
market ideas for futuristic prototypes and services." The institution's own
3D-printed facilities "will change over time to test and reflect the latest ad-
vancements in various fields."

8. See, for instance, Timothy Clark and Marcus Brittain, eds., *Archaeology
and the Media* (Walnut Creek, Calif.: Left Coast Press, 2007); Adrienne La-
france, "Archaeology's Information Revolution," *The Atlantic*, March 3, 2016,
http://www.theatlantic.com/technology/archive/2016/03/digital-material
-worlds/471858/; Colleen Morgan, "Archaeology and the Moving Image,"
Public Archaeology 13 (2014): 323–44; and the work of Michael Ashley, Angela
Piccini, and Ruth Tringham.

9. James Harkin, "The Race to Save Syria's Archaeological Treasures," *Smithsonian Magazine*, March 2016, http://www.smithsonianmag.com/history/race
-save-syrias-archaeological-treasures-180958097/?no-ist. See also Pamela
Karimi and Nasser Rabbat, "The Demise and Afterlife of Artifacts," *Aggregate*, December 12, 2016, http://we-aggregate.org/piece/the-demise-and
-afterlife-of-artifacts; and Deborah Amos, "Palmyra's Ancient Arch, Destroyed by ISIS, to Rise Again in London," *NPR*, April 18, 2016, http://www
.npr.org/sections/parallels/2016/04/18/474686269/palmyras-ancient-arch
-destroyed-by-isis-to-rise-again-in-london.

10. Harkin, "The Race to Save Syria's Archaeological Treasures." Some critics
have lamented the disproportionate outcry over these treasures of *global* cultural heritage, versus the international audience's relative silence in response to the destruction of local resources, including towns' and cities' libraries and universities, and the threat posed to local residents. It is worth
noting, too, that the Syrian army itself caused significant damage to Palmyra before ISIS's arrival. See Hugh Eakin, "Ancient Syrian Sites: A Different Story of Destruction," *The New York Review of Books*, September 29, 2016,
http://www.nybooks.com/articles/2016/09/29/ancient-syrian-sites-palmyra
-destruction/.

11. Chiara De Cesari, "Post-Colonial Ruins: Archaeologies of Political Violence
and IS," *Archaeology Today* 31, December 2015, 22–26.

12. "Director-General Irina Bokova Firmly Condemns the Destruction of Palmyra's Ancient Temple of Baalshamin, Syria," *UNESCO*, http://en.unesco
.org/news/director-general-irina-bokova-firmly-condemns-destruction
-palmyra-s-ancient-temple-baalshamin. The FBI warned that looted Near
Eastern antiquities were appearing in the United States and that buyers
could be prosecuted for providing financial support to a terrorist organization ("ISIL and Antiquities Trafficking," Federal Bureau of Investigation,
August 26, 2015, https://www.fbi.gov/news/stories/2015/august/isil-and
-antiquities-trafficking. For more on the destruction of cultural artifacts as
an instrument of war, see Eakin, "Ancient Syrian Sites."

13. See Sarah Almukhtar, "The Strategy behind the Islamic State's Destruction of Ancient Sites," *New York Times*, March 28, 2016, http://www.nytimes.com/interactive/2015/06/29/world/middleeast/isis-historic-sites-control.html?_r=0. Yet there is much debate over how profitable the antiquities trade has been for Islamic State (see Eakin, "Ancient Syrian Sites").

14. Even IS acknowledges this nationalist heritage in *Dabiq*, its online propaganda magazine: in an article titled "Erasing the Legacy of a Ruined Nation," an author argues that celebrating ruins "as a part of cultural heritage and identity" "only serve(s) a nationalist agenda" and dilutes Muslims' loyalty toward Allah (De Cesari, "Post-Colonial Ruins," 24). See also Maira al-Manzali "Palmyra and the Political History of Archaeology in Syria: From Colonialists to Nationalists," *Mangal Media*, October 2, 2016, http://www.mangalmedia.net/english//palmyra?rq=palmyra.

15. De Cesari, "Post-Colonial Ruins," 25. For more on the history of archaeological interest in Palmyra, see Ingrid D. Rowland, "Breakfast in the Ruins," *New York Review of Books*, September 17, 2016, http://www.nybooks.com/daily/2016/09/17/breakfast-in-the-ruins-palmyra-photographs/.

16. De Cesari, "Post-Colonial Ruins," 25–26. Karimi and Rabbat ("The Demise and Afterlife of Artifacts") also acknowledge colonialism's legacies in the Middle East—in urban renewal, in the damage inflicted by earlier wars with Western forces, in Western institutions' determination of what sites, artifacts, and historic periods are deserving of memorialization, and so forth.

17. For more on Islamic State's use of media, see Thomas Stubblefield, "Iconoclasm beyond Negation: Globalization and Image Production in Mosul," *Aggregate*, December 12, 2016, http://we-aggregate.org/piece/iconoclasm-beyond-negation-globalization-and-image-production-in-mosul.

18. For more on local officials', curators', activists', and archaeologists' preservation efforts, see Eakin, "Ancient Syrian Sites."

19. Quoted in Farrell, "Using Lasers to Preserve Antiquities Threatened by ISIS."

20. Tim Abrahams, "Palmyra Arch Lives Again (Again), *RIBA Journal*, May 26, 2016, https://www.ribaj.com/culture/palmyra-arch-venice.

21. Quoted in "IDA Palmyra Arch Copy," *Factum Foundation*, http://www.factumfoundation.org/pag/236/.

22. Landing Page, Institute for Digital Archaeology, http://digitalarchaeology.org.uk/.

23. See Peter Der Manuelian, *Digital Giza: Visualizing the Pyramids* (Cambridge, Mass.: Harvard University Press, 2016), for a discussion of similar issues in regard to the pyramids of Giza.

24. Andrew Smith argues that because Palmyra was a central market for manufactured goods, a wealthy city whose elites funded the monuments, it likely attracted skilled labor to build those monuments: Andrew W. Smith III, *Roman Palmyra: Identity, Community, and State Formation* (New York: Oxford University Press, 2013), 69. See also Ben Russell, "Gazetteer of Stone Quarries in the Roman World," Version 1.0 (Oxford Roman Economy Project, 2013), http://oxrep.classics.ox.ac.uk/docs/Stone_Quarries_Database.pdf.

25. Artist Ryan Woodring asks such questions about the quality and quantity of information in a visual archive. In his Decimate Mesh project, Woodring extracts data about destroyed antiquities from ISIS videos, then translates that limited information into (necessarily partial) 3D prints. By removing human actors from ISIS's footage, Woodring asserts "the object's agency in being remembered" (Jessica Breedlove Latham, "In the Studio—Ryan Woodring," *Duplex Gallery*, July 28, 2015, http://www.duplexgallery.com/in-the-studio-ryan-woodring/.

26. Of course New York's first builders wiped away much of the terrain that was home to the Lenape tribe.

27. Thomas Ricker, "First Click: This $1 Chip Will Connect Your Things to the City for Free," *The Verge*, February 17, 2016, http://www.theverge.com/2016/2/17/11030692/Lorawan-internet-of-things-network-amsterdam; Thomas Ricker, "Samsung's Building the First National Network Dedicated to Smart Cities," *The Verge*, May 24, 2016, http://www.theverge.com/2016/5/24/11759272/Samsung-commercial-smart-city-network.

Index

Page reference in italics refer to illustrations.

Abbey of St. Mary (Leicester), scriptorium of, 56–57
Abbott, Berenice, 71, 80, *81*
acoustics: of ancient spaces, xxxix, 120–24; Christian, 133, 134, 207n75; earbud, 156; Greek appreciation of, 121–23; political use of, 126–27; spatial archaeology of, 120–24; territorial, 131, 208n80. *See also* architecture, sonic; sound
Adam, Jean-Pierre, 106
adhān (call to prayer), 132; in diverse communities, 134; mediation through loudspeakers, 133–35; over radio, 134–35
administration, colonial: scripts of, 95–101
administration, urban: architecture in, 73–74; print and, 49, 72–74
advertising: by developers, 56; on informal posters, 113; kiosks, 66, 67; in New York City, 30, 31; oral, 129; Renaissance, 60; transit, 80–81; on utility poles, 20, 44
agora, Athenian: public hearth of, 203n26; sonic architecture of, 122–23; transit, 80–81
Ahmed Baba Institute, 103
Alamogordo (New Mexico), landfill items, *xix*
Alberti, Leon Battista: *On the Art of Building*, 130

Aldrete, Gregory, 126
Alexandria, urban sound of, 126
Allahyari, Morehshin: "Marten," xxx
All Souls Church (London), 13, *14*
Alphabet (company), 31; Sidewalk Labs, 30, 35
al-Qaeda, destruction in Timbuktu, 104–5
Al-Qasr (Egypt), mud structures of, *87*Amazon: distribution by, 83; effect on print industry, 60; Web Services data center, *xi*
amphitheaters, New York, 72
amphitheaters, Roman: civic identity in, 126; digital modeling of, *125*; multisensory experience of, 121, 123, 204n41
Andeans, literacy of, 79, 101–2
Anderson, Jon W., 207n77
anthropocentrism, xvi, xxi, xxii
antiquity: local stakeholders in, 153; mediated cities of, xv; Mesopotamian, 85–88, *150*, *151*; Million Image Database of, 147–48; sonic architecture of, 120–24, *126*. *See also* architecture, ancient; cities, ancient; Mesopotamia
Arab Spring, 140
archaeoacoustics, xxxix, 120–22, 144; modeling in, *124*, *125*, *126*, *141*
archaeology: agency in, xxi–xxii; colonialism in, 150–53; Foucauldian,

xxii–xxiii, 169n69; gaps in record, xxiv–xxvi, 119, 148; heritage industry and, xxii; intellectual histories of, 167n46; masculinism in, xxii, xxiii; politics of, xxi–xxii, xxvi, xxxi, 149–54; processualist, xxxiii; of product distribution, 83; Romanticism in, xxiii, 168n50; stratification in, xxvii; technical media of, xxiv, xxxiv, 147–49; temporal aspects of, xxvii–xxviii; of textual materials, 45; timelessness/timeliness of, xxvii. *See also* media archaeology

Archaeology: The Discipline of Things (Olsen, Shanks, Webmoor, and Witmore), xxxiv

architecture, ancient: acoustic properties of, 121–24, 126; designs for, 101; digital modeling of, 147–53; remediation of, 153; Vitruvian, 196n63

architecture, indigenous: colonial refashioning of, 96, 98

architecture, medieval, 50; domestic, 130; oral transmission of, 129. *See also* cities, medieval

architecture, Renaissance, 9, 51–53; auditory relationships in, 206n62; new forms of, 50; proportions of, 106

architecture, sonic, 12–16; of antiquity, 120–24, 126; of Athenian agora, 122–23; of BBC Broadcasting House, 12–13; of radio, 5–11, 14–15, 70, 115, 117; telegraphic, 25–26; of telephone exchanges, 19, 22, 23, 24, 31; wired, 19, 20–22, 24–25, 37. *See also* Rockefeller Center

Architecture of Radio (iOS app), 1, 2

archives: cities as, 93, 111, 114; cuneiform tablet, 86; destruction of, 149; digital, 4, 147–48; gaps in, xviii–xix, xxiv, 4, 102, 119; manuscript, 95, 102–5; print, 45, 49; technical nature of, xviii–xx, xxiv

Arch of Triumph (Palmyra). *See* Palmyra Arch

Argentina: literary culture of, 78; urban identity in, 190n116

Aristotle: ideal city of, 121–22, 127; on voice of populace, 202n24

artifacts: destruction in warfare, 104–5, 149–51, 213n12; digital recreation of, *xxx*, 147–49, 153, 193n24; trafficking in, 214nn12–14; of urban sound, 40–41. *See also* monuments

Arup Acoustics, 211n106; artistic endeavors of, 143; SoundLab of, 141

Arvidsson, Viktor, 204n41

Atget, Eugène, 80

Athens, ancient: agora, 122–23, 203n26; population of, 202n25; stoa, 122

Atkinson, Niall, 203n37, 206n62

AT&T: Long Distance Building (New York), 22, 31; Long Lines Building (New York), 24

Baath Party, Project for the Rewriting of History, 150

Babble (Applied Minds' sound processor), 141, 175n58

Babylon, palace inscriptions of, 194n26

Baghdad, literary culture of, 76, 77, 78

Baladi, Lara, 209n99

Balaÿ, Olivier, 142

Banco Santander call center (Querétaro, Mexico), 32

bandos (street posters), Roman, 61, 62

Bandung (West Java), telephone service of, 28–29

Banham, Reyner, 101

al-Bashir, Omar, 76, 77

Bauentwurfslehre (architectural standards), 106

Bauordnungslehre, "Oktametersteine und Normalformat," *108*

Bayat, Asef, 137

BBC Broadcasting House, *13*, 174n47;
    architecture of, 12–13
Beacham, Richard, 204n41
behaviorism, x
Beigel, Florian, 59
Beijing, urban sound of, 129
Beirut (Lebanon), literary culture of,
    78
bells, in communities, 130–31
Bell Telephone Company, *Planning for
    Home Telephone Conveniences*, 24–25
Benjamin, Walter, xiv; *Arcades Project*,
    xxxiv; on cities, xxxvi; radio talks
    of, 12
Bennett Coleman & Co. (publisher),
    79–80
Berg research and design group, Im-
    materials project of, 1
Bibliothèque nationale de France,
    55–56
Bibliothèque Sainte-Geneviève (Paris),
    54–55, *55*, 69
Bierman, Irene, 93
Bills, Emily, 28
Birdsall, Carolyn, 126
Blesser, Barry, 121
Bokova, Irina, 149, 152
Bookcity (South Korea), 58–60
book trade: boutique, 60; contempo-
    rary, 58–60, 76–80, 83; early Mod-
    ern, 56–58; of Hong Kong, 189n107;
    independent, 83; Middle Eastern,
    57, 76–78; mid-nineteenth-
    century, 184n36, 189n108; South
    Asian, 57; Venetian, 60
Boyd, Brian, 167n45
Bratton, Benjamin, 164n29
Brazil, pichação script of, 156
breakdancing, sound systems for,
    xxxii
bricks: ancient, 105–6; contribution to
    local culture, 114; as media, 106–7;
    as projectiles, 210n99; standardiza-
    tion of, 106–7
Buck-Morss, Susan, 115, 117

Buenos Aires, radio in, 18
buildings: as communication media,
    194n30; mud, *104*, *105*

cable, buried, 21
Cairo (Egypt), Tahrir Square demon-
    strations, 138, *139*, *140*, 209n99
Cairo (Illinois): architectural plan for,
    53–54; patrolling of public space,
    210n104
Calcutta, graffiti of, 111, *112*, 113
Cambridge (U.K.), muddy environ-
    ment of, 88
Canadian Centre for Architecture, 115,
    186n66
Caracas, colonial map of, *98*
Carey, James, 2–3
Carpo, Mario, 50–51, 53; on ancient
    architecture, 101; on Vitruvius,
    196n63
Çatalhöyük, clay tablets of, xiv
cathedrals, as books of stone, 50
Cavarero, Adriana, 201n10
Caylán (Peru), sonic activities of, 121
cell networks: antennae for, 32, *33*, 34,
    35, *36*; base stations for, 34–35, *36*;
    wired infrastructure for, 37. *See also*
    telecommunication, digital
cell-phone infrastructure, xxxvi, 32,
    33, 34–37, 155, 171n5
Center for Digital Archaeology, 212n5
Center for Urban Science and Progress
    (CUSP, New York University), viii
Centro Financiero Confinanzas
    (Caracas, Venezuela), *108*
Chakrabarti, Vishaan, 140
Chashnik, Ilia, 117
Chasteen, Charles, 95
Chattopadhyay, Swati, 113
Chavín (Peru), sound transmission
    tubes of, 120
Chen, Michael, 34, 35
Chengdu, People's Park, 137
Child, Lydia Maria Francis: home
    management writings of, 65

coffeehouses, European: printed materials of, 64

Cohen, Jean-Louis, 111

colonialism, Iberian: literary legacy of, 78–79; printing in, 62, 64; urban sound of, 130–31; urban writing of, 95–96, 101–2

colonialism, in Middle Eastern archaeology, 150–51

communication: artifacts of, xxvi; centralized networks for, 26–27; on doors, 44–45; in Greek antiquity, 121; hyper-local, 44; mud as media of, xxxix, 113–14; networks of, 119; of niche ideas, 83; prehistoric, 86; protocological surrounds for, 37; role in urban form, xxv. See also infrastructure, communication; printing; voice; writing

communication, digital: material record for, 4; topologies of, 34–35, 37–41

communities: bells in, 130; delimiting by wiring, 20, 176n71; imagined, 77, 135; manuscript texts of, 102; notices on utility poles, 43–44, 44

communities, marginalized: print media of, 64; sonic resistance by, 37–38, 40

computation, xxvii; networks of, 119; spatialized, 164n29

concrete: embodiment of modernism, xxxvii–xxxviii; global trade in, 199n95; graffiti on, 111; material properties of, 107, 109–10; modernity of, 109–10; standardization of, 110

constructivism, Russian, 115

Corbin, Alain, 130

Council of Vienne, on *adhān*, 132

CRESSON research center, 142

Crossland, Zoe, 167n45

Cultural Capital Group of Nimrod, 212n5

Cummins, Tom, 196n54

cuneiform script, 86, *87*; of Darius the Great, 90; effect on Sumerian thought, 192n13; in spaces of authority, 193n26. See also clay; writing

CyArk (documentation project), 148

Dabiq (IS propaganda magazine), 214n14

Daragahi, Borzou, 76

Darius the Great, cuneiform inscriptions of, 90

data: actionable, ix; Big, x; centers for, 31–32; politics of, x; for surveillance, ix–x, 37

data centers, *x*, xiv, xxvi, 13, 29, 31, 115, 156

data collection, ideologies of, x

Davey, Moyra: "Newsstand #19, 1994," 82

Davis, Mike, 28

decentralization, urban, 179n96; in Los Angeles, 27–28

de Cesari, Chiara, 150

deep time, xvii–xviii, xxv–xxvi, 144, 152, 165n32; of urban mediation, xxv, xxvi. See also temporality

de Forest, Lee, 6, 8, 70

Delhi: literary culture of, 78; overhead wiring in, 20

demonstrations, 155–56; at Tahrir Square (Cairo), 138, *139*, 140, 209n99; at Union Square, 136; voices of, 135–38

design: as cultural technique, 100; and graph paper, 100; print-schooled, 129–30; sound, 140–45

Deskey, Donald, 14

Dhaka (Bangladesh), buried cable of, 21

Diabaté, Toumani, 103

DigAlert (utility marking system), 200n105

digital modeling, xiv–xv, 147–48; of sound, 124, *125*, 141

digital modeling, 3D: of heritage sites,

147–53; ontological implications of, 153; at Pergamon Museum, 151; politics of, 152–54. *See also* Palmyra Arch

digitization: of inscriptions, 148; of manuscripts, 103; past/present mediation by, 149

Dittmar, Jeremiah, 57

Djingareyber Mosque (Timbuktu), restoration of, 105

DJs, at Notting Hill Carnival, *38*

DMB (Digital Multimedia Broadcasting), 7

Doctoroff, Daniel, 35

Dolar, Mladen, 128, 204n44, 205n49

Domosh, Mona, 70

Dongtan (China), eco-city project of, 141

dot-com boom, first, xii

drawing, historical practice of, 100–101

Drucker, Johanna, 193n26

Dumbo neighborhood (Brooklyn), olfactory elements of, xxxii

Durban (South Africa), radio in, 18

Easterling, Keller, 59

Edwards, Catharine, 123

Eichhorn, Kate, 181n1, 209n99

Eiffel Tower, radio mast on, 6

Eisenschmidt, Alexander, 12

Eisenstein, Elizabeth, 46

electromagnetic signals: in ether, 2–3; extraterrestrial, 171n5; health effects of, 1, 155; in media architecture, 11, 19

Elsaesser, Thomas, xvi

Empedocles, xviii

environments, urban: as information machine, xvii; material, 129, 156; muddy, 88–89; multisensory, xxxi–xxxv, 133; newspapers' shaping of, xxxviii, 70; olfactory, xxxii; radio-listening and, 172n18; radiophonic, 12–16; regulation via signal space, 35, 37; residual media of, 156; responsive, 144, 162n11; textural, xxxii. *See also* cities; infrastructure; sound, urban

Epic of Gilgamesh, 85

epigraphy, 48, 88, 92–95, *94*, 148; as environmental communication, 194n35; Islamic, 93, *94*, 95. *See also* inscriptions

Ergin, Nina, 133, 207n75

Ernst, Wolfgang, xvii, xxxviii, 148; on media materiality, 165n32; on signal processing, xviii–xix, xxiii; on sonic architecture, 15; on technical media, xxiv

eruvin, demarcation by wiring, 20, 176n71

ether: as communication media, xxxii; as mediating substance, xxxviii; Michelson-Morley experiment on, 2; in radiophonic cities, xxxviii; recycling of ore for, 37; in urban form, 7

e-waste, xvi, xxvi

Experiential Technologies Center (UCLA), 124

Faleiro, Sonia, 78

Fatimids, epigraphy of, 93

Favro, Diane, xxxiii, 142–43; digital models of, 124; on non-elites, 126; on Roman ritual, 203n39

Federal Communication Commission, noncommercial licenses from, 38–39

Feld, Stephen, 201n12

Ferriss, Hugh: *Metropolis of Tomorrow*, 7, *8*

file cabinets, xxxviii, 49, 73–74, 75

film: city in, xiv; mediating space of, xvii

Fischer, Claude, 27

flyers, 43, 44, 60–62; cultural politics of, 181n1

Ford, Paul, 22, 27

Hicks, John, 56
Highland, Kristen Doyle, 184n36, 189n108
High Line Park (Manhattan), vii
Hilgert, Markus, 151
Hill, Dan, 83
Hilmes, Michelle, 2
Hirschkind, Charles, 133
historiography: backward reading of, xxxvi–xxxvii; materiality and, 192nn12–13; sensory, 120, 124, 131, 201n13, 204n41. *See also* media history
history, anonymous, xxxvii
Hitler, Adolf: acoustic engineers of, 145; oratory of, 204n44
Hong Kong, booksellers of, 189n107
Hood, Raymond, 14
Horfei, Luca, 62
Hudson Yards (Manhattan), *viii*, xvii, 154–55; construction of, vii–x; embedded technology of, viii–ix; as "Quantified Community," viii, ix; techno-solutionism of, xxxi; urban imaginary of, viii–x, 155
Hughes, Francesca, 107, 109
Hugo, Victor, 14; *The Hunchback of Notre Dame*, 50
Huhtamo, Erkki, xix, 165n30; on media archaeology, xx–xxi; on mediated spaces, xvii
humanities, cycles of evolution in, 168n51
Hussein, Saddam, 150
Hutton, James, xvii–xviii
Hyŏn, Sŏng, 46

Ibb (Yemen): satellite view of, *99*; urban script of, 99, 100
Iguala (Mexico), kidnapping at, 156
India, local-language newspapers of, 79–80
information, embodiment in landscape, xii
information management, urban, xvii

infrastructure: critical studies in, xxv-xxviii, 169n59; official markers of, 199n105, 200n105; smart city, viii–ix; sonic, xxvi, 22, 117, 120–24
infrastructure, communication, xxv–xxvi, 168n59; of Internet, xxi; layering of, 144; manifestation of past, xxxiv; of radio, 115; repurposing from old infrastructure, 3; for telecommunication, xxix; telegraph, 25–26. *See also* communication; palimpsests
infrastructure, media, xxvi, xxxvi, 168n53; adaptation to fiber optics, 29–32; critical sensibility about, xxvi; distribution, 79; expansion of, 25; residual, xxxvi; and urban form, 29, 100
infrastructure, pneumatic, ix, xxvi, xxxvi, 4, 21, 22, 24, 30, 161n3
Innis, Harold, xiii, 192n12; on stelae, 92; on writing, 85–86
inscriptions: architectural, 88, 90–95; Chinese, 90, *91*, 92, 114; digitization of, 148; geoglyphs, 193n25; of Indian subcontinent, 92; Islamic, 93–95, 100; Mesoamerican, 92; new forms of, 156; Roman, 92–93, 194n38; spray-painted, 199n105. *See also* epigraphy; graffiti; writing
Institute for Digital Archaeology (IDA): Palmyra Arch reconstruction, 147, 151–52, 153; politics of, 212n6
intelligence, urban, x; ambient, xi
Internet: media architecture for, 31–32; submarine infrastructure of, xxi; of Things, 35, 156
Intersection (company), "Links" of, 30–31
Iraq, radio stations of, 19
iron, in urban construction, 54–56
Islam: epigraphy of, 93, 94, 95; imagined communities of, 77, 135; material culture of, 150; print culture

of, 76–78; voice in, 132–35. *See also* mosques

Islamic State: cultural cleansing by, 150–51, 152, 155; destruction of monuments, 85, 149–52, 154, 197n72; media use by, 135, 150–51, 214n17; "Ministry of Antiquities," 149; nationalist agenda of, 214n14; Palmyra Arch destruction, 147; trafficking in antiquities, 214nn13–14

Jacob, Sam, 8

Jacobs, Jane, 44

Japan, free radio movement, 181n124

Johanson, Christopher, xxxiii, 126, 142–43; digital models of, 124

John, Richard, xxix

John II (king of Castile), 133; on minarets, 132

Johns, Adrian, 46

Johnstone, Christopher Lyle, 122

Jos (Nigeria), loudspeakers of, 134

kabupaten (Indonesia), telephone service of, 29

Kafka, Franz: on wiring, 20, 176n71

Kahn, Douglas, 21

Kahn, Louis, 110

Kaluli (Papua New Guinea), sonic culture of, 201n12

Karakuş, Gökhan, 140

KAR Bosscha plantation, telephone company of, 29

Kashmiri Bazaar, book trade of, 58

Khartoum (Sudan): literary culture of, 76–77, 78; self-image of, 77

Khatam, Azam, 138

khipu (Peruvian knot-cord record), 96

King, Anthony, 70

King's Cross fire (London, 1987), 143

Kircher, Athanasius, xviii; *Phonurgia Nova*, 206n59

Kittler, Friedrich, xvi–xvii, 164n29; on information processing, 86, 144;

on sonic architecture, 15; on urban computation, xxvii; on urban media, 119

Klee, Paul: *A Leaf from the Book of Cities*, 59

Kleilein, Doris, 142

Knight, Gary: *Palmyra Arch of Triumph Unveiling*, 148

Kockelkorn, Anne, 142

Kogawa, Tetsuo, 181n124

Kontokosta, Constantine, ix, x

Koolhaas, Ram, 14

Korea, typography of, 46

Kropotkin, Peter, 179n96

Kubisch, Christina: Electric Walks of, 1

Kuhn, Hans Peter, 143

Kūl-e Farah sanctuary, acoustic properties of, 121

Kulturtechniken: destructive, 150; lineages of cultivation, 114; of masonry and building, 98; in media theory, 89; radical forms of, 114

Kunreuther, Laura, 18–19

kurakas (Andean nobles), prose of, 101

Kushkush, Isma'il, 77

Labrouste, Henri, 65; Bibliothèque nationale de France, 55–56; Bibliothèque Sainte-Geneviève, 54–55, 55, 69

La Guardia, Fiorello, 11

Lahore (Pakistan), book trade of, 57

landscapes: and architectural inscription, 90–95; cell technology in, 34–35; effect of ethereal technology on, 3; information embodied in, xii; material, 3, 19, 29, 35, 49, 65; material from, 88; palimpsests in, 30; old technology in, 31, 40; pre-colonial habitation of, 193n25; printed matter in, 60; radio's influence in, 9; scripts of, 59; temporal/spatial relations of, xxxi. *See also* soundscapes

Lane, Asa H.: German meeting house, 127

Miller, Herman, 141, 175n58
Million Image Database, 153; antiquities in, 147–48
Mills, C. Wright, 73–74
Milutis, Joe, xxxviii; on ether, 2–3
minarets, 132; loudspeakers on, 19, 133–35
Ming dynasty (China), publishing centers of, 57
Moeller, G. Merlin, 111
Montseny, Federica: public address of, 137
monuments: destruction of, 85, 90, 149–53, 154, 197n72. *See also* artifacts
Morgan, Collen, 167n45
mosques: acoustic concerns of, 132–33; minarets of, 19, 132, 133–35; as social media, 209n99; of Timbuktu, 102, 105
Mosul Museum, destruction of, 151
moya (cliff carvings), 92, 93
mud: as communication medium, xxxix, 113–14; as destructive force, 88–89; in development of writing, 86; in history of civilization, 88; material analogs of, 113; messages carried by, 90; productive forms of, 193n18; protocological surrounds for, 37; translation into form, 101; writing substrates of, 193n18
muezzin: calls to prayer, 132; Druze, 208n80. See also *adhān*
Mumbai, book market of, 78
Mumford, Lewis, xxv, 87; on cities, xxxi; on neotechnics, 27; on offices, 188n90; on paper, 73; on political auditoriums, 128; on printing, 50, 183n15; on urban communication, 119, 127; on urban decentralization, 179n96; on urban development, 212n120
Museum of the Future (Dubai), 147, 213n7

Mutanabbi book market (Baghdad), 76, 77
MVRDV Teletech center (Dijon, France), 32
Myanmar, phone rental shops, 32

Nancy, Jean-Luc, 119
Nash, John, 14
National Academy of Science, U.S., 192n13
National Radio Quiet Zone (West Virginia), 171n5
Navy, U.S.: telecommunication networks of, 171n5
Naylor, Trevor, 78
Nazca Lines (Peru), 90, 91, 114
Negro Motorist Green Book, The (1947), 63
neotechnics, 27
Nepal, radio in, 18–19
Nero (emperor of Rome), 126
Neufert, Ernst: Octametric System of, 106
New Palmyra Project, 149
newspapers: aid to immigrants, 67; alternatives to, 80; architecture of, 70–72, 71, 186n79; broadcasting of announcements, 72; digital alternatives to, 82; format of, 69; front pages, 68; infrastructure of, 69; and material city, 65–72; move from cities, 76; in urban landscape, xxxviii, 49, 70; urban legacy of, 72; urban sound of, 69; and urban typography, 69
"Newsstand, 32nd Street and Third Avenue, Manhattan" (1935), 81
newsstands, 80–83, 81, 82; as art installations, 82; ephemerality of, 81; replacement of, 80–81
New York: Book Row, 78; Civic Center, 155; data centers of, 31–32; emergency services of, 32; newsstands of, 80–81, 81, 82; Noise Abatement Commission, 11; overhead wiring in, 20; Park Row, 70–72; phone in-

201n12; bodily, 119, 126; as disciplinary tool, 142; economic activity and, 128–29; Jamaican systems of, 38; on pirate radio, 40; propagation techniques, 206n59; territorial, 131, 208n80. *See also* architecture, sonic

sound, urban, 9, 11; in age of print capitalism, 129; Alexandrians', 126; amplified, 132–38, 140; of ancient Rome, 123–24, 126; containment of, 10–11, 12, 141–43; in democratic processes, 119–24, 126–28; dissent in, 135–38; effective range of, 120; electronically amplified, 117; of elites, 206n68; infrastructural, xxvi, 22, 120–24; Islamic, 132–35, 208nn80–81; loss to history, xxxiii; masking technologies for, 144; measurement of, 11, 134, 173n30, 174n32; Nazi, 126; of newspapers, 69; nineteenth-century, 136; of non-elites, 126, 207n68; in place-making projects, 142; of prayer, 132; regulation of, 9; resistance to containment, 145; of telegraph, 26; in transit systems, 143; vocal intelligibility of, 143. *See also* acoustics; architecture, sonic; media, sonic

soundscapes, urban, 133, 141; noise in, 41; qualities of, 144

space: acoustic, xviii, 135, 207n75; communicative, 6, 9, 141; monumental, 194n26; production of, 92; of proto-democracies, 203n32; quantitative conceptions of, xxxv

space, urban: civic/aesthetic engagement in, 209n93; design of, 142; diminished sound in, 135–36; dissent in, 136–38, 139, 140; gatherings at, 135–38; inscriptions articulating, 100; maps of, 62; material properties of, 135–38; multisensory, xxxiii, 69; occupation of, 209n99; privatization of, 84; representational strategies for, xxxiv; social

difference in, 69; sound design for, 140–45; telephony in, 32; unplanned encounters in, 140–41; for vocality, 141; of vocality, 120; women in, 210n104. *See also* environments, urban; landscapes

spaces, ancient: acoustic conditions of, xxxix, 120–24

speakers' podiums, 117

Spigel, Lynn, xiv

spiral texts, Arabic, 100, 196n55; of Ibb (Yemen), 99

Stalin, Josef: public speaking by, 204n44

standardization: of architecture, 53, 106–7, 109–10; of bricks, 106–7; of concrete, 107, 109, 110; material instability and, 198n86; of paper, 106–7

Starosielski, Nicole, xxi

steel: for office furniture, 74, 75; in architecture, vii, x, 5, 9, 14, 16, 49, 56, 59, 70–72, 74; in printing, 49

Steelcase office furniture company, 74, 75

stelae, Greek: public writing of, 92

Sterne, Jonathan, 131–32

stoa, Athenian: reverberation effect of, 122

structuralism, deep structures of, 165n32

Sudanese Writers Union, 76, 77

Sunset Telephone (Los Angeles), 28

surveillance: data for, ix–x, 37; global, 73; role of sound in, 142

Sybaris (Greek colony), noise abatement in, 173n30

Tabbaa, Yasser, 93–94

Tahrir Square (Cairo), protesters at, 138, 139, 140, 209n99

Taksim Gezi Park (Istanbul), dissent at, 140

Tallis's London Street Views (1830–1840), 186n66

Tarr, Joel A.: "The City and the Telegraph," 25–26
Tawil-Souri, Helga, 168n53
technologies: acoustical, 126; communication, 28; cultural/political functions of, 131; embedded, viii–ix, xii, 89; ethereal, xxxviii, 2–3; global, 3, 31; integration with nature, 58; linear progress in, xv; locative, 136; microchip, 80; mixed materialities of, xl; and nationalism, 115; networked, xi; police, 37; of poverty, 110; radio, 117; subterranean, 165n32; telegraphy, 25; telephone, 24, 26; temporality of, xvi; 3D printing, 49, 67; transportation, 27, 65; Western timeline for, 19. See also digital modeling
Tehran, gathering spaces of, 137–38
telecommunication: archaeology of, 3–5; cables, 14, 19, 21, 24, 30; cellular, 24–25, 27–41; centripetal/centrifugal, 25–29; in commercial imagery, 6; development costs of, 179n101; effect on urban form, xiii, 25–29; lines of sight for, 41; physical infrastructure of, xxix; in urban environment, xxxviii; wired, 19, 20, 20–22, 24–25, 37. See also radio; telegraph; telephone
telecommunication, digital: adaptation from precedent infrastructure, 29–32; signal space in, 35, 37; topologies of, 34–35, 37–41. See also cell networks
telecommunication, electromagnetic: as ether, 2–3
telegraph: centripetal/centrifugal influences of, 29; within cities, 19, 25–26; development of, 25–26, 177n86; effect on transportation, 2–3; financial information via, 26; infrastructure of, 4, 22; printing, 26
telephone, 3; call centers, 32;

centripetal/centrifugal influences of, 26–27, 29; effect on urbanization, 27; effect on urbanization in Los Angeles, 28–29; European development of, 178n89; infrastructure of, 4, 19–21, 22–25; networks, 26; payphones, 177n85; signal-processing machines for, 24; as symbol of progress, 27; urban evolution of, 178n88
telephone booths, 25, 30, 255, 279n103
telephone exchanges: amateur histories of, 177n80; architecture of, 19, 22, 23, 24, 31; automatic, 22; labor for, 24
telephone kiosks, British: archaeological examination of, 172n14; media archaeology of, 172n14
telephone poles. See utility poles
Telx company, data center of, 32
temporality, 2; of archaeology, xxvii–xxviii; of cities, xxxi–xxxii, 154; community, 131; of media archaeology, xix, xxvii–xxxi; of media infrastructure, 79; media/spatial entanglements of, xxx; of palimpsests, xxvii; urban, 67
Tenochtitlán, Great Temple of: remaking of, 96
texts: archaeology of, 45; circulating, 101–5; colonial, 101; display, 60; hierarchical authority of, 102; production sites of, 56–60. See also advertising; graffiti; inscriptions; print; writing
texts, urban, xxxii, 50, 65–72; aesthetic properties of, 93; aid to navigation, 65, 186n66; building materials of, 114; cities as, 49–50, 88
Thibaud, Jean-Paul, 172n18
Thoenes, Christoph, 183n19
Thomas, Julian, 168n49
Thompson, Emily, 143; The Soundscape of Modernity, xxxiii
Thoreau, Henry: on wiring, 21

warfare, sonic, 37–38
Waters, Michael J., 51–52
Webster, Jane, 194n38
Web 2.0, material network of, 1
Wells, H. G.: *Days of the Comet*, 69
West Bank (Israel), graffiti of, 111, *112*
WGN (Chicago), transmitter of, 6
White, Stanford, 72
Whitney Museum, Diller + Scofidio exhibition, xiii
WiFi signals, in public sculpture, 1
Wigley, Mark, 8
Williams, Raymond, xxviii
Williams, Rosalind, 165n32
Wilson, Bronwen, 60, 62
Wilson, Eric, 128–29
Winthrop-Young, Geoffrey, 89
wireless media: in design projects, 1; rise of, 2
wiring: delimiting of communities, 20; overhead, 20, 21–22; planning for, 24–25; in subway tubes, 21; threatening aspects of, 176n76; underground, 21; use as sensing array, 21. *See also* architecture, sonic; eruvin
Witmore, Christopher, xxvii–xxviii
WMAQ (Chicago), transmitter of, 5
Wölfflin, Heinrich, xxxvii
Wolfson, Sam, 40
Woodger, Neill, 141–42
Woodring, Ryan: Decimate Mesh project of, 215n25

Work Culture Group (Khartoum), 77
World of Fragile Parts exhibition (Venice, 2016), 152
Wright, Frank Lloyd: on urban form, 7–8
writing: of colonial subjects, 101–2; curvilinear, *99, 100*; development of, 85–86; effect of materials on, 192n13; formal properties of, 88; Peruvian, 101, 198n81; Sumerian, 85, *86*; of urban cultures, 101–5; and urban development, 86, 95–101, 114. *See also* cuneiform script; epigraphy; inscriptions; texts
writing, indigenous: marking of territory, 99
writing, public: building materials and, 90; competition with sound, 124; in Greek antiquity, 92; on walls, 111, *112, 113*, 114, 199n99. *See also* epigraphy
Wythoff, Grant, xxix, 167n45

Yi Ki-ung, 58–59
Yusaf, Shundana, 12, 13

Zielinski, Siegfried, xvii, xxix; on anarchaeology, xviii; on media archaeology, xxvi
zoning, acoustic, 9
Zuccotti Park (New York), public assembly at, 140
Zumthor, Paul, 201n10

Shannon Mattern is associate professor of media studies at The New School in New York. She is the author of *The New Downtown Library: Designing with Communities* and *Deep Mapping the Media City*, both published by the University of Minnesota Press.